*ESSAYS*

*DIPLOMATIC AND UNDIPLOMATIC*

*of*

*THOMAS A. BAILEY*

Thomas A. Bailey

# ESSAYS
# DIPLOMATIC AND UNDIPLOMATIC
## of
# THOMAS A. BAILEY

*Edited with a Preface
and Introduction by*

## ALEXANDER DECONDE
*and*
## ARMIN RAPPAPORT

APPLETON-CENTURY-CROFTS

Educational Division

New York    MEREDITH CORPORATION

# PREFACE

As former doctoral candidates of Thomas A. Bailey, we conceived the idea of assembling in book form a dozen or so of his more noteworthy essays on American diplomatic history. Our plan was to present the volume to him during his sixty-fifth year, on the occasion of his retirement from formal classroom lecturing after thirty-eight consecutive years of service in the History Department of Stanford University.

We chose the essays for this volume, but also asked the author himself to judge which of his articles have best stood the test of time, and gave him an opportunity to suggest such changes as he found desirable. He has made a number of relatively minor alterations, although the substance of each article remains as originally published. He also participated in the preparation of the epigraphs, prologues, and postscripts, whenever the latter seemed necessary. Additionally, we asked him to check our Biographical Introduction for factual accuracy. His sense of modesty caused him to protest that we had praised him beyond his desserts, but we overruled him and take full responsibility for our judgments. We also suggested a few minor changes, which the author found acceptable.

The publishers of Professor Bailey's *A Diplomatic History of the American People* were pleased, even honored, to sponsor this volume. We are indebted to Mr. Walter J. Green, editor of Appleton-Century-Crofts, for his invaluable encouragement and help, and to the editors of the relevant journals who graciously granted permission to republish individual articles. Appropriate acknowledgement appears in a footnote on the first page of each essay.

A. D.

A. R.

# BIOGRAPHICAL INTRODUCTION

Professor Thomas A. Bailey, distinguished historian and teacher, has cherished a deep interest in American history almost as long as he can remember. A native Californian, he was born near the city of San Jose on December 14, 1902, the son of James Andrew Bailey and Annie Nelson Bailey, a former grade-school teacher. His mother endowed him with an enduring appreciation of books and of America's past. He once wrote that one of his earliest recollections was hearing her read to the children from a volume entitled *Lives of Our Presidents*. With such a background, he was fortunate in entering school well prepared to benefit from instruction. He applied himself seriously and graduated from both elementary school and the Santa Clara High School with excellent grades.

Aiming at a career in law (subsequently the ministry), he entered Stanford University in 1920, majoring in Greek and history. Elected to Phi Beta Kappa in his junior year, he was graduated in 1924 "with great distinction," after having served for two years on the varsity debating team. He then embarked upon graduate work in history at Stanford, earning the Master of Arts degree in 1925 and the Ph.D. in 1927. During these graduate years his long and productive teaching career began. While securing his doctorate, he served as a teaching assistant for one year at the University of California at Berkeley, under Herbert E. Bolton, and the next year held a one-year appointment at Stanford as an Instructor in Citizenship. He completed his work for the doctorate at Stanford in American political history, writing on party irregularity in the Senate under the direction of Edgar E. Robinson, a disciple of Frederick Jackson Turner.

Ph.D. in hand, the fledgling Bailey obtained his first full-time teaching position in 1927 as Instructor in History and Political Science at the University of Hawaii, advancing to Assistant Professor the following year. He found life in the islands pleasant, but his high academic aspirations would not permit him to succumb to the languorous delights of this Pacific paradise. He turned his surplus energies to writing and to research in the Archives of Hawaii, and in 1930 produced the first of many articles and subsequent books. He also conscientiously improved his teaching skills, and many former students, including United States Senator Hiram Fong, recall his vigorous speaking style and his merciless exposure of historical myths.

Academic occupations did not keep him from other important pursuits. While at Hawaii he courted and won Sylvia Dean, the attractive daughter of the University's former president, Arthur L. Dean. They were married in August, 1928. One son, now an electrical engineer, was born in 1932.

In 1930 Bailey was invited to return to Stanford as an Acting Assistant Professor of History, to take over some of the work of the fatally ill diplomatic historian, E. D. Adams. When Adams died before the year was out, Bailey was invited to stay, and there he remained. Although his training had been primarily in American political history, he accepted the challenge to expand into the diplomatic field. Research on Hawaii's relations with the United States had prepared him for such a transition, and he now immersed himself in the subject. From his typewriter came a series of articles and books that within a few years earned him recognition as one of the nation's leading young diplomatic historians. In 1935 he was promoted to Associate Professor, obtaining tenure and a permanent place at Stanford. He became a Professor in 1940, Margaret Byrne Professor of American History in 1952, and served for a total of five years in the 1950's as Executive Head of the Department of History.

His contribution to the academic community has extended far beyond Stanford. He has served as a visiting lecturer at various universities in the United States, among them Harvard and Cornell. He has been a Fellow of the Rockefeller Foundation in International Relations; a member of the Institute for Advanced Study at Princeton, New Jersey; the Albert Shaw lecturer in diplomatic history at The Johns Hopkins University; and an observer in Europe and civilian staff member of the National War College. In recognition of his scholarly achievements, he was elected president of the Pacific Coast Branch of the American Historical Association in 1959–60, and of the Organization of American Historians in 1967–68. In 1967–68 he was chosen the first president of the newly formed Society for the Historians of American Foreign Relations.

He once said in jest that he liked teaching too well to spend his life on research. Several generations of Stanford students can testify to the excellence of his instruction. Thousands of undergraduates have relished his lectures as among the most stimulating and penetrating that they have heard during their college years. His presentations are

noted for witticisms, artfully turned phrases, and illustrative anecdotes, as well as for their careful organization
and substantive content. He has also proved to be a dedicated graduate teacher. Although his time is precious, his
door has always been open to students of all levels, but
especially to his graduate students. Nor has his concern
ended with the granting of the Ph.D. degree. He has actively encouraged these young scholars in their research
and writing, and has always been ready to offer helpful
criticism of their work. He has made a point of keeping in
touch with his former students and doing all he can to
advance their academic careers.

Yet Bailey's reputation as a scholar far exceeds that
as a teacher. It is as scholar and writer that countless thousands of Americans know him. Many of the qualities that
make his lectures memorable also contribute to the popularity of his writing. His love for America, his fair-minded-
ness, his sympathy for the underdog, his impatience with
ineptitude, and his keen sense of humor are all there. His
works reflect opinions strongly held, but judiciously presented in a balanced historical context. They are distinguished by a vivid, colorful, and epigrammatic style,
marked by clarity of expression and simplicity of structure.
His graceful writing, as well as his erudition, helped to
make *A Diplomatic History of the American People,* published in 1940 and since issued in seven editions (the eighth
now in press), one of the great successes in American textbook publishing.

In his writing, Bailey matches grace of style with thor-
oughness of scholarship. All his essays and monographs
show evidence of painstaking investigation. So sound is his
research that his first two book-length monographs, *Theo-*

*dore Roosevelt and the Japanese–American Crises* and *The Policy of the United States Toward the Neutrals, 1917–1918*, endure as basic works. His next two books, entitled *Woodrow Wilson and the Lost Peace* and *Woodrow Wilson and the Great Betrayal*, brought him wide recognition. In them he offered a rare blending of careful inquiry and challenging insights with lively prose. These volumes still stand as landmarks in interpretive historical scholarship.

In Bailey's books on Wilson and in his masterful *Diplomatic History* can be found evidence of his most significant contribution to American historiography—his almost unique emphasis on the role of public opinion in shaping foreign policy. This is the cardinal contribution that many scholars and teachers associate with him. He felt that popular pressures have an important and often overlooked influence in forming foreign policy in a democracy. As a consequence he introduced careful analyses of public opinion and its influence whenever relevant. With whatever tools were available he measured, weighed, and assessed this elusive phenomenon as diplomatic historians had not previously done.

Bailey's *The Man in the Street: The Impact of American Public Opinion on Foreign Policy*, filled with provocative insights and written in his usual clear and sparkling style, is one of the first extensive historical studies of its kind. This pathbreaking work, though computerized research by behavioral scientists has now gone beyond his investigations, retains much of the freshness that distinguished it when first published. His *America Faces Russia* is a historical overview likewise oriented toward public opinion, and his *Presidential Greatness* and *The Art of*

*Diplomacy* offer many mature insights based on a lifetime of research and reflection.

With his concern for public opinion and the role of the people in the shaping of foreign policy, Bailey has taken diplomatic history out of the stifling embrace of the "he said, she said" of official dispatches and other government documents. He has shown that what the masses think, feel, and sometimes do in groups, no matter how difficult to appraise, has influenced and continues to influence the shaping of foreign policy. Today little is written on the diplomatic history of the United States that does not take into account public attitudes and pressures. No one has done more to pioneer this approach than Thomas A. Bailey.

Aside from stressing public sentiment, he has had an abiding interest in demolishing false historical beliefs, although he does not regard himself as essentially a debunker. In his deep concern for the American people—for both their past and their future—he has particularly attacked those myths that provide false guidelines. This concern for the so-called lessons of history is evident in his writings, especially *The Art of Diplomacy*.

Bailey has consistently tried to make history meaningful and to bring it close not only to students but to general readers. Few historians possess his ability to reach the public with his writing; he is a student's historian as well as a scholar's historian, a generalist as well as a specialist. When people read his *The American Pageant: A History of the Republic,* the past seems to involve them and to come alive in a way that it seldom does in other college textbooks. He consciously strove to achieve this involvement through his pungent prose and carefully chosen illustrative materials, and his keen sense of humor has in itself helped to add a new and refreshing dimension to historical writing.

This concern for his readers—the people—has helped make his *The American Pageant* for many years a leading one-volume textbook in its field. He has used a substantial portion of the royalties from it to endow the Thomas A. Bailey Book Fund at the Stanford Library for the purchase of books on history in memory of his mother.

While the essays in this volume do not include samples from Bailey's outstanding textbooks and more popular writings, they do exemplify his prose style, depth of research, breadth of scholarship, and revisionist thinking. His long preoccupation with various aspects of American diplomatic history provides the unifying theme. For those readers interested in the development of scholarship in this area during the past four decades, these essays offer a rich feast.

A. D.

A. R.

# CONTENTS

*This first essay, sweeping in scope, reflects the author's lifelong interest in rooting out historical fabrications. It also reveals his conviction that the past is fruitful in lessons that can help guide the present, if we will only take heed of them, with due regard for changed conditions. The paper was first presented as his presidential address to the Organization of American Historians, at Dallas, Texas, on April 18, 1968.*

# 1.

## THE MYTHMAKERS
## OF AMERICAN HISTORY

"Historians relate, not so much what is done, as
what they would have believed."
—Benjamin Franklin, 1739

I

Flse historical beliefs are so essential to our culture that,
like Voltaire's God, if they did not exist, they would
have to be invented. In this uncertain world we crave cer-
tainties, and if an iconoclast were suddenly to shatter all
myths, our social structure would suffer a traumatic shock.
We need only imagine how different our national history
would be if countless millions of our citizens had not been
brought up to believe in the manifestly destined superiority of the American people, in the supremacy of the white
race, in the primacy of the Nordics within the white race,
in the safety-valve "free" land in the West, in completely

*The Journal of American History*, LV (June, 1968), 5–21. Reprinted
by permission.

rugged individualism, and in the rags-to-riches dream of a millionaire's blank check in every workingman's lunch box.[1]

Historical myths and legends are needful in establishing national identity and stimulating patriotic pride.[2] If Switzerland has its William Tell and the arrowed apple, and if Scotland has its Robert Bruce and the persevering spider, the United States has its George Washington and the chopped cherry tree. The American colonials, having jettisoned George III, were under compulsion to fabricate homegrown tales of their own in a hurry; and this perhaps explains why so many of our heroic legends are associated with the "glorious" War of Independence.[3]

II

American children are indoctrinated with nonhistorical myths before they are hardly out of the bassinet. Santa Claus keeps small fry better behaved before Christmas, while the stork keeps them—or used to keep them—from asking embarrassing questions between Christmases. The youngster also hears hero tales about Washington kneeling in the snow at Valley Forge and Abraham Lincoln reading by the light of a flickering fireplace. Yet there is no credible evidence that either did either.

Many elementary teachers of history and literature are not well enough informed to separate the legend from the

[1] A historical myth is here defined as an account or belief that is demonstrably untrue, in whole or substantial part. I here exclude fantasies, like Coronado's Seven Cities of Cíbola, or the fabrications of hoaxers and charlatans.

[2] See Henry Steele Commager, *The Search for a Usable Past and Other Essays in Historiography* (New York, 1967), pp. 3–27.

[3] The numerous immigrants also needed the cohesion of legends; many newcomers had little in common except a miserable crossing of the Atlantic Ocean.

truth. They are only too happy to keep the children entertained. Others, I find, know the facts but continue to tell the time-tested stories, including the Parson Weems tale about the cherry tree. Many teachers have discovered that the pupil does not remember the stories anyhow, so the end result does not make much difference. If the children are taught the debunked account, they might become unsettled. They might even repeat it in garbled form in a superpatriotic home, thereby stirring up trouble with the school authorities and jeopardizing their jobs. The safest course for the instructor is to perpetuate the hallowed myths and not rock the boat.[4]

The poets studied in school have also done their part in creating historical mythology. John Keats had poetic license on his side when he had Cortés rather than Balboa discover the Pacific, but this was carrying his license a bit too far. The stirring tale of Paul Revere's ride was a legend in search of a poet, and it found Henry Wadsworth Longfellow, who put the resolute rider on the wrong side of the river and had him thunder into Concord, which he failed to reach.[5] The playwrights, as cousins of the poets, have likewise sinned. Robert E. Sherwood's *Abe Lincoln in Illinois* (1938), whether on the stage or on the screen, has probably done more than any other single medium to implant the maudlin legend of Lincoln's grief-stricken love affair with Ann Rutledge.

<hr/>

4 I am indebted to Dr. Norman E. Tutorow for a number of personal interviews with teachers at various levels in the San Jose area of California.

5 Esther Forbes, *Paul Revere & the World He Lived In* (Boston, 1942), pp. 461, 472. Henry Wadsworth Longfellow also popularized the legends of Miles Standish, Evangeline, and Hiawatha, as John Greenleaf Whittier did the legend of Barbara Fritchie. Ballads have also played an important role in mythmaking. The popular song "The Hunters of Kentucky," for example, left the impression that the riflemen rather than the cannoneers inflicted the heaviest losses at the battle of New Orleans.

Historical novels are among our most effective teachers, but they are naturally more concerned with dramatic effect than undramatic truth. Nathaniel Hawthorne's harsh image of the blue-nosed Puritan, as portrayed in *The Scarlet Letter,* persists in the face of recent scholarship. The fading picture that many high school graduates retain of the Civil War and Reconstruction from their desiccated textbooks is probably overshadowed by Margaret Mitchell's *Gone with the Wind,* which presents the story with a southern exposure and a rebel yell. Literature, including historical novels and novelized history, is often the continuation of war by other means.

Star-spangled history textbooks still dish up much mythology, shaped as they are in part by patriotic pressure groups. In our dealings with foreign countries, especially Britain, we are not only about one hundred percent right but one hundred percent righteous. (It is only fair to add that British versions of the two Anglo-American wars generally reverse the process.[6]) Professional patriots, like the Sons of the American Revolution and Texans for America, are still demanding that we teach patriotism above all. They would exalt the "Spirit of '76," restore Nathan Hale and his undying dying regret, and combat socialism or any other "ism" that foreshadows social change. The United Daughters of the Confederacy are by no means mute more than a hundred years after the guns fell silent at Appomattox. The hyphenates are still vocal, especially the Italian-Americans, who insist on having Columbus, rather than the Norsemen, discover America.[7] The Italians are generally

[6] See Ray Allen Billington and others, *The Historian's Contribution to Anglo-American Misunderstanding* (New York, 1966); Arthur Walworth, *School Histories at War* (Cambridge, Mass., 1938).

[7] The publication by the Yale University Press in 1965 of a book containing a pre-Columbian map of America stirred up the Italians. See R. A. Skelton and others, *The Vinland Map and the Tartar Relation* (New Haven, 1965).

successful, except in Minnesota, where the Scandinavians, clinging to their questionable Kensington Stone, have more votes.

### III

A newly formed hyphenate group, but not a new element, consists of African-Americans. Seeking a quasi-national identity, much as white America did after 1776, they are now understandably clamoring for historical recognition. For many generations they were the "invisible men" of American history—the dusky hoers of weeds and pluckers of cotton. Now, with black balloting power and portentous rioting power, they are insisting on visibility, if not over-visibility, in the textbooks. In at least two of our great cities —New York and Detroit—the school authorities have issued separate booklets, a hundred or so pages in length, detailing the contributions of the Negro.[8]

This belated recognition, though praiseworthy in many respects, is fraught with danger. Most nonmilitant Negroes would probably like to think of themselves as dark-skinned Americans, and this self-imposed Jim Crow-ism can be self-defeating. Pressure-group history of any kind is deplorable, especially when significant white men are bumped out to make room for much less significant black men in the interests of social harmony.[9] If this kind of distortion gets completely out of hand, we can visualize what will happen when the Negroes become the dominant group in all our largest cities, as they already are in Wash-

[8] Board of Education, City of New York, *The Negro in American History* (New York, 1964); The Board of Education, City of Detroit, *The Struggle for Freedom and Rights: Basic Facts about the Negro in American History* (Detroit, 1964).

[9] See Kenneth M. Stampp and others, "The Negro in American History Textbooks," *Integrated Education,* II (October–November, 1964), 9–13; Howard N. Meyer, "Overcoming the White Man's History," *Massachusetts Review,* VII (Summer, 1966), 569–78.

ington, D.C. Coexistence may end, and we may even have hardbacked Negro histories of the United States, with the white man's achievements relegated to a subsidiary treatment.

The apotheosis of Crispus Attucks is illuminating. He was a runaway Negro slave, we are told, whose blood was the first to be shed in the American struggle for independence. We have long known that he was fatally shot in the so-called Boston Massacre of March 5, 1770. But we do not know for a certainty whether he was a Negro or an Indian or even a runaway. He and his fellows were guilty of hooliganism that night; several other people had earlier lost their lives in the struggle against British authority since 1763; and the armed outburst at Lexington and Concord was a full five years in the offing.[10]

This determination to stand American history on its head, so characteristic of minority groups, may stimulate pride among Negroes, but it can win little support from true scholarship. The luckless African-Americans while in slavery were essentially in jail; and we certainly would not write the story of a nation in terms of its prison population. Yet the pressure is on to overstress Negro initiative in organizing revolts, in escaping from bondage, and in securing emancipation. President Andrew Johnson, who was once downgraded by James Ford Rhodes and John W. Burgess because he messed up Reconstruction for the southern whites, is again being downgraded, this time because he messed it up for the unfortunate blacks.[11]

10 E. K. Alden, "Crispus Attucks," Allen Johnson and Dumas Malone, eds., *Dictionary of American Biography* (20 vols.; New York, 1928–37), 1, 415. A recent pro-Attucks version is an editorial, "The Boston Massacre and the Martyrdom of Crispus Attucks," *Negro History Bulletin*, XXX (March, 1967), 4.

11 See Albert Castel, "Andrew Johnson: His Historiographical Rise and Fall," *Mid-America*, XLV (July, 1963), 175–84.

## IV

Once the pupil, white or black, has escaped the tyranny of the timid teacher and timeserving textbook, he is at the mercy of the journalists. He scans the columns of his daily newspaper, probably unaware that dramatic historical tales are the stock-in-trade of the newsman, and that a good reporter never exaggerates unless he improves the story.[12] Mr. Drew Pearson, for example, has continued to give currency to the fabrication that the official purchase price of Alaska contained a secret payment for the costs of bringing the two Russian fleets to American waters during the Civil War.[13] Mr. Walter Lippmann, in a hands-across-the-seas book published during the war year 1943, falsely but patriotically described the Monroe Doctrine as a quasi-alliance with Britain.[14]

Pictorial history, including cartoons and faked photographs, also presents numerous pitfalls.[15] The artist, like the poet, is entitled to draw on his imagination for details, as did John Trumbull, the painter of the American Revolution. But Benjamin West's famous painting of Penn's Treaty with the Indians depicts a colorful scene which

---

[12] This category includes radio and television commentators. Mankind evidently has a natural affinity for both exaggeration and error. Contrary to legend, the Salem witches were hanged (not burned); little George Washington (in the Weems version) only *barked* the tree; and the Liberty Bell was fatally cracked in 1846 (not while proclaiming independence).

[13] Drew Pearson and Jack Anderson, *U.S.A.—Second-Class Power?* (New York, 1958), p. 303.

[14] Walter Lippmann, *U.S. Foreign Policy: Shield of the Republic* (Boston, 1943), p. 17. I was informed by a Harvard historian in 1943 that he had prepared a lengthy critique of the Lippmann manuscript for the publishers, but evidently little heed was taken of his list of errors.

[15] Homer Davenport's cartoons of little "Willie" McKinley as a puppet of blowsy Mark Hanna implanted the picture of a wishy-washy President which to this day has not been fully corrected.

cannot be documented. The celebration which accompanied the dramatic "wedding of the rails," near Ogden, Utah, in 1869, was fortunately photographed. Yet the pasteurized painting of the scene, as later authorized by former Governor Leland Stanford of California, neatly eliminated the liquor bottles, included prominent men who had not been there, and excluded the numerous ladies of negotiable virtue who definitely were there.[16]

The television tube, in more ways than one, has helped to get the picture out of focus. We now discover Daniel Boone operating near West Point to rescue that key fortress from the treachery of Benedict Arnold. Television has turned murderous "hoods," like Jesse James and Billy the Kid, into veritable Robin Hoods. It has also contributed an additional encrustation of legend to such dubious frontier characters as Wyatt Earp and "Wild Bill" Hickok.[17]

Much of our historical mythology is created by the motion picture industry, which often spends enormous sums to get the facts straight and then proceeds to make them crooked. The pioneer cinema classic, *The Birth of a Nation* (1915), set back Reconstruction history by a generation or so by glorifying the hooded hoodlums of the old Ku Klux Klan and stimulating the besheeted bigots of the new.

The politician must also take high rank among the most prolific of mythmakers. His primary objective is to get into office and stay there, and his so-called history is apt to be hand-tooled for these ends. I invariably cringe

[16] Lucius Beebe, "Pandemonium at Promontory," *American Heritage*, IX (February, 1958), 21.

[17] R. F. Adams, *Burrs under the Saddle: A Second Look at Books and Histories of the West* (Norman, Okla., 1964); Kent Ladd Steckmesser, *The Western Hero in History and Legend* (Norman, Okla., 1965).

when a politician voices the sonorous "History teaches," because I know that he is going to make it teach whatever he wants it to teach.[18] Thomas Jefferson set an unfortunate example in the Declaration of Independence when he accused George III of many sins that the ill-starred monarch never dreamed of committing.

The worst history teachers of all in some respects are the Presidents of the United States, one of whose many roles is "Teacher-in-Chief." Only three of them could claim fairly solid credentials as historians—Theodore Roosevelt, Woodrow Wilson, and John F. Kennedy—and of these only Wilson had graduate training.[19] With tens of millions of listeners now in the living-room classroom, the President is keenly aware that he is making history, rather than writing it. A "credibility gap"—the phrase employed by journalists whose own credibility is often suspect—has existed since the days of George Washington, but the present gap is Texas-sized. President Lyndon B. Johnson's real problem is not so much misusing history as making statements that are obviously false. Perhaps he does not know enough about it to misuse it skillfully. The historian is a little disturbed to find him referring to the late President Diem (not Ho Chi Minh) as the Winston Churchill of Vietnam, to the Dominican intervention as "just like the Alamo," and to

---

18 A related expression is "The verdict of history will be. . . ." History is dead and speechless. Interpreters of history, including historians, return the verdicts.

19 The discredited legend that Marcus Whitman saved Oregon from the British by a hurry-up trip on horseback (or foot) to Washington appealed to President Warren G. Harding as a stirring hero tale, and he preferred to cherish it on the grounds that "it ought to be true." He also endorsed the poetical version of Paul Revere and Barbara Fritchie. *Speeches and Addresses of Warren G. Harding, President of the United States: Delivered During the Course of His Tour from Washington, D.C., to Alaska and Return to San Francisco, June 20 to August 2, 1923* (Washington, D.C., 1923), pp. 256–57.

the Vietnam War as a hunt which must end, in Davy Crockett fashion, "with that coonskin on the wall." [20] The historical Big Lie is just as much a lie when it comes from the banks of the Potomac as from the beer halls of Munich.

v

It is easy enough for historians to pillory the politicians and the press while overlooking their own faults. Samuel Butler, the English essayist, is quoted as saying that since God himself cannot change the past, he is obliged to tolerate the existence of historians. Other cynics have wondered why history is so dull when so much of it is obviously fiction. The ugly fact is that the professional keeper of the record does not have a good public "image": Clio, wrote Arthur Schopenhauer, "is as permeated with lies as a street-whore with syphilis." [21]

Too many so-called historians are really "hysterians"; their thinking is often more visceral than cerebral. When their duties as citizens clash with their responsibilities as scholars, Clio frequently takes a back seat. How many of us can march in Mississippi one week and teach Negro history with reasonable objectivity the next? How many of us can be shining eggheads for Adlai Stevenson in the evening and sober spokesmen for scholarship the next

[20] New York *Times,* May 13, 1961; Philip Geyelin, *Lyndon B. Johnson and the World* (New York, 1966), p. 237; Arthur M. Schlesinger, Jr., *The Bitter Heritage* (Boston, 1967), p. 32n. President Franklin D. Roosevelt was a frequent user of "managed history." In urging a repeal of the arms embargo upon Congress in 1939, he alleged that Thomas Jefferson's embargo, followed by limited sanctions, had been "the major cause" of the War of 1812. The evidence is strong that such economic pressures came within a few weeks of averting it. See *Department of State Bulletin,* I (September 23, 1939), 277.

[21] Quoted in Egon Friedell, *A Cultural History of the Modern Age* (3 vols.; New York, 1932), III, 7.

morning? How many of us who are professional southerners or New Englanders can deal fairly with other sections?[22] How many of us can forget that we are white or black when writing about whites or blacks? How many of us can avoid the academic homosexuality of falling in love with our own hero? We recall with scholarly shame that for some twenty-five years the only reasonably respectable one-volume biography of Woodrow Wilson was written with sticky adulation by an eminent American historian.[23]

How many of us can forget that we are Americans, presumably loyal Americans? To be sure, we have ample, if not admirable precedent, in the patriotic effusions of George Bancroft, whose every page seemingly voted for Andrew Jackson or American democracy or both. We remember without pride how certain prominent historians sprang to the colors in 1917 and prostituted their art in an effort to hamstring the Hun and make the world safe for normalcy.[24] The conduct of scholars during World War II was more commendable. Both they and the American people were more sophisticated, and, with Hitler on the loose, the issues were clearer cut. But even today our history texts suffer from being too America-centered, as though we were

[22] The New Englander Edward Channing made bare mention of Captain John Smith of Virginia in his six-volume history of the United States. Perhaps he was unduly influenced by Henry Adams' famous attack, which is a classic example of a young historian striving for quick fame by attacking a big name. See Henry Adams, *Historical Essays* (New York, 1891), pp. 42–79. In the light of recent evidence Smith seems somewhat more trustworthy than scholars previously assumed. Consult Philip L. Barbour, *The Three Worlds of Captain John Smith* (Boston, 1964).

[23] William E. Dodd, *Woodrow Wilson and His Work* (Garden City, N.Y., 1920).

[24] James R. Mock and Cedric Larson, *Words That Won The War: The Story of the Committee on Public Information, 1917–1919* (Princeton, 1939) pp. 158–86. I knew several of these scholars who, during the 1930's and 1940's, seemed to have a defensive guilt complex regarding their participation.

the hub of the universe and all other nations were bar-
barians dwelling in outer darkness.[25]

How many of us, seeking an instant reputation at the
expense of some towering figure, have embarked upon
dubious revisionism for the sake of sensationalism or in
response to faddism? No one will deny that fresh interpre-
tations are desirable, or that history becomes more meaningful when rewritten by succeeding generations in the
light of their own experience, as it invariably is. But much
of our revisionism comes about as a result of a flair for
novelty or a reaction against the monotony of repeating the
eternal verities year after year. And let us not forget that
revisionists, like evangelists, universally overstate their case
in their effort to get a hearing.

Sometimes revisionism comes from a conspiratorial
complex, for which mankind has a natural affinity, as recently demonstrated anew by the Kennedy assassination
case. The eminent historian who warned us most emphatically against the Devil Theory of history, ironically enough,
stumbled into his own well-described trap. Near the end
of a memorable career, he published two books that portrayed Franklin D. Roosevelt as a veritable Mephistopheles,
bent on having war at almost any price, including the destruction of our Pacific fleet.[26]

---

[25] The efforts of the United Nations Educational, Scientific and Cultural Organization (UNESCO) to rewrite national history from the viewpoint of the man on Mars has evoked violent outcries from right-wing
patriotic groups in the United States. On the other hand, there is the self-
flagellation school of historical writers which evidently takes pleasure in
finding the United States preponderantly in the wrong in its international
dealings. An example is D. F. Fleming, *The Cold War and Its Origins,
1917–1960* (2 vols.; Garden City, N.Y., 1961).

[26] Charles A. Beard, *American Foreign Policy in the Making, 1932–
1940: A Study in Responsibilities* (New Haven, 1946); Charles A. Beard,
*President Roosevelt and the Coming of the War, 1941: A Study in Ap-
pearances and Realities* (New Haven, 1948).

VI

The scholar often falls into the error of failing to understand the mentality of the masses, who obviously are not all fellow historians. Ensconced in his book-lined study, a century or two after the event, he betrays a species of arrogance when he assumes that men living in a bygone era did not have the fuzziest idea of what was going on about them or what they wanted. This assumption has led to what may be called "the flight from the obvious." We should take heed of Ralph Waldo Emerson's warning in 1836: "In analysing history do not be too profound, for often the causes are quite superficial." [27]

Let us look at America's wars. The men of 1776 thought they were fighting for liberty; the revisionists of the twentieth century played up economic motivations. Now, in something of a back-to-Bancroft movement, we are again stressing liberty. The men of 1812 believed they were fighting for a free sea; the revisionists of the 1920's had them fighting for Canada. Now we have left Tippecanoe Creek and are back again on the bounding main. The men of 1861, including Lincoln, assumed that slavery was the principal villain in the coming of the war. In the 1920's Beard and others shifted emphasis to the North's alleged industrial imperialism—a thesis which the southerners happily embraced as taking a load off their consciences. Now we think that slavery, directly or indirectly, had much to do with the guns of April. The men of 1917 concluded that the submarine plunged us into hostilities with imperial Germany. The revisionists of the 1930's

[27] Edward Waldo Emerson and Waldo Emerson Forbes, eds., *Journals of Ralph Waldo Emerson, with Annotations, 1820–1872* (10 vols.; Boston, 1909–14), IV, 160.

blamed the financiers, the "munitioneers," the "propa-
gandeers," and the "sloganeers." [28] Now, scores of volumes
and millions of casualties later, we are back, at the risk of
some oversimplification, with the submarine.

Much of our revisionism has come from premature
and half-baked hypotheses, launched, in Carl Becker's immortal phrase, "without fear and without research." New
hypotheses should certainly be encouraged, but if the evidence is lacking or scanty, they should be advanced with
the utmost tentativeness. Charles A. Beard, in his pathbreaking study of the Constitution, modestly acknowledged
in his preface that his research was "frankly fragmentary,"
and he implied that he was advancing views which would
be more firmly established by later evidence. His modesty
was fully justified by the revelations of subsequent hatchet-
wielders.

## VII

Sometimes historians degenerate into polemicists, as
did Harry Elmer Barnes, with an inevitable distortion of
the record. Their diatribes can become so shrill that they
cannot secure reputable publishers, whereupon they raise
pained cries of "Court History" or "historical blackout." [29]
David Starr Jordan once observed that no man can shout
and at the same time tell the truth.

Some scholars run to the other extreme. They are so
afraid of being labeled debunkers that they cling like bar-

[28] Slogans have contributed richly to the mythology of American
history. "He Kept Us Out of War" is often cited as a pledge by Wilson
in 1916. He did not devise it, did not use it, and did not really approve
of its use as a tacit promise.

[29] See Harry Elmer Barnes, ed., *Perpetual War for Perpetual Peace: A
Critical Examination of the Foreign Policy of Franklin Delano Roosevelt and Its Aftermath* (Caldwell, Idaho, 1953), pp. 1–78.

nacles to the tried and true bunk. Anatole France, in a classic passage in the preface of *Penguin Island,* points out that people do not like to be jolted but prefer the comfort of the old sillinesses *(les sottises).* The mythmaker simplifies and soothes; the critic complicates and agitates. The word "debunker," evidently coined by W. E. Woodward in 1923, has unfortunate overtones.[30] We certainly cannot get at the solid timber of truth unless we first clear away the underbrush of myth and legend. But the historian who spends his life hacking at underbrush in search of shockers is misapplying his talents. This Weemsianism-in-reverse runs the risk of "rebunking"—that is, substituting new bunk for old. And if the debunker manages to dig up dirt about our national heroes, say Lincoln, he is not likely to get a Book-of-the-Month Club adoption or even a *Reader's Digest* abridgment.[31] He who strikes at patriotic myths strikes at the foundations of our society; he is deemed guilty of sacrilege, at least by the antirevolutionary Daughters of the American Revolution.

Too many historical writers are the votaries of cults, which, by definition, are dedicated to whitewashing warts and hanging halos. Many of us have developed a warping bias for or against Jefferson, Andrew Jackson, Lincoln, Wilson, or the Roosevelts. The overnight birth in this city of a Kennedy cult, complete with an eternal flame, should provide a poignant reminder of the pitfalls of apotheosis.

30 W. E. Woodward and Rupert Hughes (the novelist) were in the forefront of a move to debunk Washington. Hughes's unfinished work stopped with volume three (1930), and reveals the conversion of a man who came to scoff and remained to worship.

31 Edgar Lee Masters, the poet, wrote a debunking life of Abraham Lincoln, *Lincoln, the Man* (New York, 1931); but it fell flat. For evidence that the editors of the *Encyclopaedia Britannica* softened an exposure of the Weemsian cherry tree myth, presumably in response to patriotic pressure, see Harvey Einbinder, *The Myth of the Britannica* (New York, 1964), pp. 173–74.

We recall that Kennedy's Secretary of the Navy, Fred Korth, was accused of involvement in a conflict-of-interest scandal, which led to his hush-hush resignation. By a tasteful coincidence this episode is not even mentioned in either of the lengthy books by Sorensen and Schlesinger, two of the President's close associates and admirers.[32]

Presidents of the American Historical Association, no less than those of the United States, are exposed to cultism, as evidenced by the embarrassing adoration of impressionable disciples. Frederick Jackson Turner, Beard, and Herbert Eugene Bolton were among those historians so honored. Their devotees have not only defended the mistakes of the master but have sometimes carried his theories beyond all reasonable bounds.

Special dangers lurk in a vested interest in a given interpretation, whether by the master or his students. The temptation is almost overpowering to ignore negative evidence or to manipulate positive evidence, in the Procrustean-bed fashion of an Arnold Toynbee. A case in point came to my attention some twenty-five years ago. A well-known defender of southern slavery urged a colleague to be on the alert, in his related researches, for as many instances as he could find of northern husbands beating their wives.

### VIII

A close cousin of cultism is monocausationism. Turner was by no means a monocausationist, but many of his fol-

---

[32] Arthur M. Schlesinger, Jr., in his prepublication series in *Life*, gives an account of John F. Kennedy's tearful breakdown after the Bay of Pigs botch; more tastefully, it does not appear in his later book. *Life*, 59 (July 23, 1965), 75; Arthur M. Schlesinger, Jr., *A Thousand Days* (Boston, 1965). For a revelation of some of the pressures brought to bear on William Manchester—*The Death of a President* (New York, 1967)—to put the Kennedys in a better light, see John Corry, *The Manchester Affair* (New York, 1967).

lowers tended to view the entire spectrum through the chinks of a log cabin. Karl Marx's lucubrations have led to an overemphasis on economic factors, as presently exemplified by some younger writers of the so-called New Left.[33] Beard's block-busting book on the Constitution was an attempt to deal with one set of causes—the economic. Narrowing the problem in this way is a perfectly legitimate historical exercise, given one's interest and available time. But such an approach invariably leads to distortion, no matter how emphatically the author sets forth his intentions in the preface, which all too often is skipped.[34]

Monocausation has also led the unwary to confuse causes with objectives. The major military goal of the Americans in the War of 1812 was Canada, because that was the only place where Britain was getatable. But the battle cry "On to Canada" has deceived shortsighted observers, then as now, into concluding that we went to war primarily because we lusted after the timbered lands of our semi-defenseless northern neighbor, rather than the right to sail the high seas unhindered.

Dexter Perkins has spoken eloquently of the scholarly joy of revising one's conclusions in the light of more information or reflection. Not all historians experience this praiseworthy thrill. Loyalty to one's errors is one of the lowest forms of loyalty, and repetition in the classroom for thirty-five years does not make truths of untruths or half-truths. Rigidity is a major vice in the historian, be he teacher, writer, or editor. Some twenty years ago I was

[33] See Irwin Unger, "The 'New Left' and American History: Some Recent Trends in United States Historiography," *American Historical Review*, LXXII (July, 1967), 1237–63.

[34] Julius W. Pratt's *Expansionists of 1812* (New York, 1925) quite legitimately focused on the West, but Marxists have out-Pratted Pratt in their emphasis on economic determinism.

puzzled by an eminent Lincoln scholar who flatly refused to accept new evidence that reflected unfavorably on Wilson. I began to wonder what he did with new evidence that reflected unfavorably on Lincoln. I later found the answer —he suppressed it.

The historian, despite his training in historical method and his presumed objectivity, is often unjustifiably emotional or gullible.[35] The diary of William E. Dodd, published under dubious auspices, is still too highly respected as a primary source.[36] After some humbling experience, I have concluded that most, if not all, of the pretty little stories of history are in some degree false, if pursued to their smallest details. In the absence of expert shorthand or mechanical recording, I would question all or most of the stirring utterances that have come down to us from John Paul Jones to Ronald Reagan. The text of Patrick Henry's famous "liberty-or-death" speech, for example, was pieced together some forty years after the event with the help of old men who contributed their motheaten recollections.[37] I now have less confidence than I had forty-five years ago in the memories of elderly men.

[35] After observing the conduct of trained historians in two world wars, I fear that they do not keep their heads much better than other scholars in times of great emotional stress.

[36] William E. Dodd, Jr., and Martha Dodd, eds., *Ambassador Dodd's Diary, 1933–1938* (New York, 1941). Internal and circumstantial evidence suggests that the Dodd diary was largely put together in some fashion by Dodd's son and daughter, the joint editors. Charles A. Beard was asked to write the introduction, and Martha Dodd inserted some hyperbole on her own. When Beard saw the galley proofs, he insisted on restoring his own prose, and demanded not only the page proofs but also the plate proofs. Declaring that he had seen only a typescript copy of what purported to be the original diary, he insisted that, in view of this experience, he would not believe a word of it. From the author's notes of a conversation with Beard at The Johns Hopkins University in the spring of 1941.

[37] Bernard Mayo, *Myths and Men: Patrick Henry, George Washington, Thomas Jefferson* (Athens, Ga., 1959), p. 4.

"Presentitis" is another cardinal sin of the mythmaking writer of history. Coupling historical events with current events can be most useful in stimulating classroom discussion and clarifying thought, but this practice may be carried to extremes, especially in strained analogies. The historian who attempts to interpret the past to the present in terms of present-day values often undertakes the almost impossible task of serving two masters—of trying to be both a chronicler and a chameleon. Surely we misuse the evidence when we read back into the Jackson era the beginnings of the New Deal, or when we apply to the so-called Robber Barons of the nineteenth century the same ethical standards that were finally sanctified in 1914 by the Federal Trade Commission Act. Recent scholarship tends to regard the Robber Barons as industrial statesmen, more baronial than piratical.[38]

IX

Textbook writers, from McGuffey on up, have been among the most active preservers of hoary myths. If they do not know any better, they are in beyond their depth. But if they deliberately falsify the record to secure lucrative state adoptions, they are prostitutes. Publishers have perhaps been more guilty than authors, for they have different ethical standards. But we can only look with shame upon the numerous textbooks dealing with the Negro and the Civil War that have been published in two editions, one for the North and one for the South, as though there could

---

[38] Thomas C. Cochran, "The Legend of the Robber Barons," *Pennsylvania Magazine of History and Biography*, LXXIV (July, 1950), 307–21; Edward C. Kirkland, "The Robber Barons Revisited," *American Historical Review*, LXVI (October, 1960), 68–73.

be a northern truth and a southern truth, on a take-your-pick basis.[39]

Perhaps the most fruitful contributor to historical mythology is sheer ignorance. Woodrow Wilson wondered how the conscientious scholar could sleep nights. The historian should be more than cautious in using such treacherous words as "the only," "always," "the first," and "never before"; and especially the superlatives "oldest," "best," "richest," and "greatest." For many years I told my students that Eli Whitney invented the cotton gin in 1793, and then I discovered that a successful gin was employed on a considerable scale by the French in San Domingo as early as the 1740's.[40] For many years I assured my classes that the American Civil War was the bloodiest thus far in history, with a loss of some 600,000 lives. I changed my tune somewhat when I finally learned that the contemporaneous Taiping Rebellion in China (circa 1850–64) lasted about fourteen years and cost some 20,000,000 lives.

The rising flood of books and articles is such a mighty torrent that there is an acute "Digestion Gap." The teacher of history simply cannot keep on top of all this material. Those of us who write books do not have time to read books—or at least not all the books and journals we should. In 1939 I published a lengthy article in the *American Historical Review* based on manuscript materials from the archives of three nations. It demonstrated that the British did *not* save George Dewey's fleet from the German fleet at Manila Bay in August, 1898. Yet the myth lives merrily

[39] Following the desegregation decision of the Supreme Court in 1954, some publishers brought out editions of books with integrated or non-integrated pictures, in an effort to cater to local prejudices.

[40] Daniel H. Thomas, "Pre-Whitney Cotton Gins in French Louisiana," *Journal of Southern History,* XXXI (May, 1965), 135–48.

on in works by distinguished scholars, including a brilliant survey by a onetime president of the American Historical Association who has shown unusual interest in ship movements. Aside from the "Digestion Gap," this particular tale endures, like other myths that endure, largely because it serves or has served a useful purpose: hands-across-the-sea for the British and fists-across-the-Rhine for the Germans.[41] One is tempted to say that old myths never die; they just become embedded in the textbooks.

Every year dozens of articles of a myth-shattering nature appear in the two hundred or so American magazines, often in journals so obscure that the overburdened teacher never heard of them. I herewith propose, in all earnestness, that the Organization of American Historians and the American Historical Association jointly set up in an appropriate place a centralized Myth Registry, for both articles and books. Abstracts of discredited myths can be recorded, much as dissertation titles are registered, either by the author or by an appropriate abstracting agency.[42] Then, with the marvelous data-recovery processes now being perfected, the requisite information can be made speedily available on request. Such an agency should be a gold mine for teachers, researchers, and especially textbooks writers, who have a heavy obligation to keep abreast of this verbal Niagara.

[41] Thomas A. Bailey, "Dewey and the Germans at Manila Bay," *American Historical Review*, XLV (October, 1939), 59–81. The Russian fleet myth of 1863 has also been useful during those periods when Americans were interested in promoting a hands-across-the-Volga policy. See Thomas A. Bailey, "The Russian Fleet Myth Re-Examined," *Mississippi Valley Historical Review*, XXXVIII (June, 1951), 81–90.

[42] A promising beginning in abstracting has been made by the American Bibliographical Center, Santa Barbara, California, in its quarterly publication, launched in 1964, and entitled *America, History and Life: A Guide to Periodical Literature.*

X

Most historical myths, I suppose, are not dangerous. The cherry tree yarn does no real harm, except perhaps to make young George an insufferable prig. It may even do some good in building youthful character by telling a lie to discourage lie telling. But a little history, to paraphrase Alexander Pope, can be a dangerous thing, and certain historical myths are infinitely mischievous, especially in the area of foreign relations.[43] As John F. Kennedy remarked in 1961, "Domestic policy can only defeat us, but foreign policy can kill us." [44]

The *Herrenvolk* myth, American style, has been with us since the early days of Massachusetts Bay. The conviction that we were God's chosen people, and that we had a divine mandate to spread our ennobling democratic institutions over the rest of the benighted globe, encouraged us to shoulder the White Man's Burden in the Philippines and elsewhere at the turn of the century. We Americans continue to believe that we are a mighty nation, not primarily because we were endowed with magnificent natural resources, but because there was something inherent in our

[43] In addition to those hereinafter discussed, one may mention the Lafayette myth (that nations help others primarily for sentimental reasons); the immutability myth (that a policy enunciated by Washington is good for all circumstances and ages); the Yalta myth (we cannot negotiate with the Russians); and the Marshall Plan myth (what will work industrially in sophisticated Europe will work in backward Latin America or Vietnam). For the dangers inherent in myths like the Jewish stab in the back, see Dietrich Orlow, "The Conversion of Myths into Political Power: The Case of the Nazi Party," *American Historical Review*, LXXII (April, 1967), 906–24.

[44] Robert D. Heinl, Jr., comp., *Dictionary of Military and Naval Quotations* (Annapolis, Md., 1966), p. 240.

genes that enabled us to become great. This superiority complex has strengthened the conviction that we can impose our democracy on illiterate peasants in faraway rice paddies, including those of Vietnam.

The myth of American omnipotence has led us into some strange and steamy jungles. We find in our America-centered textbooks that we won all our wars, although we certainly did not win the War of 1812 or the Korean War, second phase; neither did we lose them. The pride of unbroken victory—a false pride—pushed us ever deeper into the vortex of Vietnam at a time when face-saving negotiations held some promise of success. President Johnson, with his Alamo complex, has been charged with not wanting to be known as the first President of the United States who failed to win a war for which he was responsible.[45]

The myth that we won all our wars, in spite of being unready for them, has repeatedly caused us to skate to the brink of disaster. This was painfully true in 1916–17 and later in the pre-Pearl Harbor years, when we clung to the minuteman policy of not preparing until we saw the whites of the enemy's eyes. The myth of unlimited American might has also seduced our policy makers into assuming that we can halt Communist aggression all over the world,

---

[45] Mr. James Reston reported this statement on the basis of hearsay testimony, but it is in character. New York *Times,* October 1, 1967. Related to the myth of invincibility is that of "free security," which allegedly was provided in the nineteenth century by the oceans and defense in depth. "Free security" is like free love, which can be extremely costly in the end. This concept proved to be expensive in wars that we might have avoided with adequate preparedness, and in wasteful expenditures involved in trying to prepare after war was declared. Moreover, many Americans felt quite insecure during much of the nineteenth century, especially during the recurrent Anglo-American crises, which posed the threat of the British navy. For a contrary view, see C. Vann Woodward, "The Age of Reinterpretation," *American Historical Review,* LXVI (October, 1960), 1–19.

including Vietnam.[46] Many hawkish Americans still feel
that we could have saved China with American troops in
the mid-1940's. The recent costly experience in relatively
tiny Vietnam should silence some of the criticism in that
quarter.

The myth of permanent victory, fortified by the illusion of invariable "unconditional surrender," has resulted
in some expensive but ill-learned lessons. We Americans
seem not to realize that impermanence is one of the most
permanent features of history, and that victory does not
keep. We whipped the Kaiser in 1918 and then brought the
doughboys home before the fire was out. We repeated the
same process in 1945, when the "I Wanna Go Home" movement reached mutinous proportions. Some wag has said
that history repeats itself because no one was listening the
first time.

XI

The myth of American righteousness has resulted in
some glaring inconsistencies. Our nationalistic textbooks
tend to stress the view that there are two sides to every international dispute: our side and the wrong side. We excuse our sins, if excuse them we must, by pointing the
accusing finger at other nations, as was notably true of our
countercharges when the U-2 spy plane went down in
1960, along with America's holier-than-thou reputation.
When the Cuban crunch came in 1962, relatively few
Americans, including some near the throne, saw anything

---

[46] The history of the United States is one of the great success stories
of all time, and Americans have let success go to their heads. A slogan in
World War II used by a branch of the United States forces was: "The
difficult we do immediately. The impossible takes a little longer."

inconsistent about encircling the Soviet Union with missiles, while denying Moscow the right to emplace missiles in Cuba.[47]

The Munich myth has likewise borne a lush harvest of evil fruit. Before 1938 the word "appeasement" was in reasonably good odor; after Munich it became a dirty word. The Munich agreement was a compromise, although lopsided and morally vulnerable. Peacetime negotiation, as we know, is normally impossible without mutual compromise and concession. But after Munich countless two-fisted Americans inevitably branded all compromise as appeasement. One basic reason why we refused to sign the Geneva Accords of 1954 regarding Vietnam was that cries of base surrender were being raised in the United States. Bad though the Munich sellout was, the misapplication of its so-called lessons since then may already have caused even greater damage.[48]

Perhaps more harmful has been the myth of the Communist monolith, which has flourished not only in patriotic textbooks but among the planners on the Potomac. Fearful of this Kremlin-directed behemoth, we have fought two undeclared wars and disbursed over 100 billion dollars in foreign aid. But international Communism was never a

[47] This inconsistency seems all the more curious in view of President Kennedy's willingness to risk a nuclear holocaust rather than agree to withdraw from Turkey the obsolescent Jupiter missiles which he had ordered removed some two months earlier. Elie Abel, *The Missile Crisis* (Philadelphia, 1966), p. 191. The withdrawal had been recommended in 1961 by both the Congressional Committee on Atomic Energy and the Secretary of Defense. Schlesinger, *A Thousand Days*, p. 807. The Jupiter missiles were removed from Turkey April 15–26, 1963, some six months later. Assistant Secretary of Defense Warnke to Representative Charles S. Gubser, January 8, 1968 (letter in possession of author).

[48] Secretary of State Dean Rusk, publicly defending his Vietnam policy, repeated in classic form the Hitler-appeasement analogy. New York *Times,* December 9, 1967.

monolith, and most of the time not even communistic. Lenin, Trotsky, and Stalin were never in complete accord, and Trotsky paid for his dissent with exile and a smashed skull. But after China fell to the Reds in 1949, the monolith seemed all the more menacing. The next year, in May, 1950, President Harry S. Truman committed the United States to support the French in Vietnam with dollars and military hardware, and since then we have sunk ever deeper into the bottomless bed of snakes.

The irony is that the absence of a monolith was noisily advertised when Red China openly split with Red Russia in the 1960's. The men of Moscow had every reason to believe that they had reared up a nuclear Frankenstein's monster. "Who lost China?" was a question that could be more appropriately asked in the Kremlin than in Congress. The Sino-Soviet split removed the basic reason for our being in Vietnam, yet by this time we were too heavily bemired in the monsoon mud to pull out and had to stress other reasons for remaining. The crack in the so-called monolith presented Washington with a heaven-sent opportunity, yet our Vietnam policies, based in part on false assumptions, tended to narrow, rather than widen, the split between the once-intimate ideological bedfellows.

This by no means exhausts the list of costly or dangerous myths in the field of foreign affairs. Their persistence is a pointed reminder that the historian is involved in much more than art for art's sake. History *does* repeat itself, with variations, and the price seems to go up each time. As trustees of the nation's past, we historians have a special obligation to set the record straight and keep it straight. We cannot muzzle the poets, the playwrights, the pedagogues, the "patrioteers," the press, the politicians, and other muddiers of historical waters; but we can, if we will, control ourselves. The republic has wrought so many mighty deeds since independence that our people no longer need to be proud of history that never happened.

*The following paper is the author's address as presi-
dent of the Pacific Coast Branch of the American Historical
Association, delivered in Seattle, September 8, 1960. It was
designed to keep the audience awake and to provoke
thought by advancing a controversial interpretation. It has
been widely distributed, in reprint form, to stimulate classroom discussion. Much, of course, depends on semantics: on
how one defines "power," "world power," "great power,"
"superpower." The views here expressed have not commanded universal acceptance. They run counter to or-
thodoxy, for European-oriented historians are usually
reluctant to accord to Americans a status that European
powers were unwilling to grant until about 1898, if then.
Adolf Hitler did not regard the United States as a world
power, but his contempt did not erase realities, as he ultimately learned to his sorrow.*

# 2.

# AMERICA'S EMERGENCE
# AS A WORLD POWER:
# THE MYTH AND THE VERITY

"And so it has come to pass that in a few short months we have become a world power. . . ."
—President McKinley, 1899

"For over ten decades our nation has been a world power."
—William J. Bryan, 1899

I

Every American schoolboy knows—or would know if he bothered to read his textbook—that the United States did not become a world power until 1898. Commodore Dewey, according to the traditional tale, staged our memorable coming-out party at Manila Bay on May Day of that year. At the risk of arousing the United Spanish War Veterans, I venture to take issue with this melodramatic inter-

*Pacific Historical Review*, XXX (February, 1961), 1–16. Reprinted by permission.

pretation and to suggest that the United States became a world power 122 years earlier, on the day of its official birth, July 2—not July 4—1776.

I have collected the titles or subtitles of more than a dozen books that associate America's so-called spectacular eruption with the era of the Spanish-American War. This formidable phalanx of error does not include the scores of chapter titles or subtitles or magazine articles that reaffirm the May Day myth. I shall not name names, lest I redden the faces of certain scholars present, while magnifying my own sin. The embarrassing truth is that for eighteen years I further misled the youth of this land with a chapter title which I have since then unobtrusively corrected.

I cannot exculpate myself completely by pleading that at a tender age I was misled by my elders and betters, or that I later erred in distinguished company. By the time I became a graduate student I should have realized that cataclysmic changes, especially in the power position of a nation, seldom or never occur overnight. I should also have known that the very first obligation of the scholar is to examine critically all basic assumptions—the more basic the more critically. The majority is often wrong, and repetition does not make things so.

The pitfalls of periodization have no doubt contributed richly to our misunderstanding. Watershed dates like 1898 are useful as pedagogical landmarks, and although the careful historian has mental reservations while using them, the rote-minded student is likely to accept them as gospel.

More misleading is the singular indifference of many scholars to precision in terminology. Unabridged lexicons exist for standardizing the language, and we historians would do well to thumb them occasionally. The least un-

satisfactory definition of a "world power" that I have un-
covered is given by Webster (second edition) as follows:
"A state or organization powerful enough to affect world
politics by its influence or actions." This concept is obviously too broad, and I therefore propose to narrow it to
exclude "nuisance value" power, such as that exerted by
Serbia in 1914. My rewriting reads: "A nation with sufficient power in being, or capable of being mobilized, to
affect world politics positively and over a period of time." [1]
The term "great power," as distinguished from the less
exalted "world power," will be considered later.

Did the United States in 1776 measure up to the world-
power formula that I have just propounded? The answer,
in my judgment, is an emphatic affirmative.

II

First of all, what are the components of national
power? I have made up a detailed list of about one hundred items, major and minor, tangible and intangible, but
I shall not inflict them all on you. Let us examine a few
of the more noteworthy with reference to the United States
during the era of the American Revolution.

In territory, we exceeded all the European states, except Russia. In population, we outranked many of the
European nations, and possibly excelled them all in birth
rate. In quality of population, we could boast what was perhaps the most literate people in the world, and certainly

---

[1] The *New Standard Dictionary of the English Language* (Funk and
Wagnalls) defines a world power as "A state whose policy and action are
of world-wide influence or concern." Professor A. C. Coolidge defined
the world powers in 1908 as "powers which are directly interested in all
parts of the world and whose voices must be listened to everywhere."
*The United States as a World Power* (New York, 1908), p. 7. A literal
application of this definition would have disqualified all nations.

one of the more ingenious. In moral force we were from the outset probably the most influential power of all—the lodestar of liberals and the mecca of the masses. In statecraft and diplomacy we could point pridefully to Franklin, Washington, Adams, Jay, and Jefferson, to name only a corporal's guard of the Founding Fathers. In military strength we could muster adequate militia for defense, though shunning large professional armies. In the capacity to attract allies we could offer economic concessions and diversionary or additive military strength. In richness of soil, salubrity of climate, abundance of natural resources, and general self-sufficiency we were almost certainly the most blessed of all peoples.

Finally, in merchant shipping we were from the beginning a leader, ranking in the same top bracket with Britain, France, Spain, and Holland. In the days of the windjammer and smoothbore cannon an amphibious nation could so easily improvise a navy that a great maritime power could hardly escape being a world power.[2] Privateers played a devastating role in our two wars with Britain, and although we lost about as many ships as we captured, we bloodied our enemy's nose while getting our own bloodied. The menace of more privateers gave Downing Street nightmares during every Anglo-American crisis of the nineteenth century.

The power position of the United States, already formidable, was immensely strengthened by six fortunate circumstances. First, we had between us and Europe the watery vastness of the Atlantic Ocean—America's greatest

---

[2] President John Adams told Congress in 1797, on the eve of the crisis with France: "However we may consider ourselves, the maritime and commercial powers of the world will consider the United States of America as forming a weight in that balance of power in Europe which never can be forgotten or neglected." J. D. Richardson, comp., *Messages and Papers of the Presidents* (Washington, D.C., 1896), I, 238.

liquid asset. Second, we had defense in depth, as the foot-
sore British redcoats learned to their dismay in two frustrating wars. Third, we had the precarious European balance
of power, which caused our potential adversaries to fear
the dagger thrust of an envious neighbor. Fourth, we had
an imbalance of power in the Americas, with the United
States enjoying the top-dog position from the outset, and
with our weak neighbors dreading us rather than our people dreading them. Fifth, we had Canada under the muzzles
of our muskets, as a hostage unwittingly given to us by the
British for their good behavior. Finally, we had mountain-
ous surpluses of foodstuffs, cotton, and other raw materials,
upon which our most redoubtable diplomatic rivals, notably Britain, developed a dangerous dependence. Every
time the British faced up to the prospect of again fighting
the Yankees, they had to reckon with the sobering consequences of cutting their own economic throats. All this
adds up to the conclusion that from its birth the United
States has been incomparably the luckiest of all the great
nations—so far.

III

I have said that the United Colonies became a world
power in July, 1776, when the Continental Congress solemnly severed the umbilical cord. I might start even earlier
and assert that in a broad sense we had become a power
before we became a nation.[3] Charles and Mary Beard dated
America's birth as a "world power" from Edmund Burke's
masterly speech of 1775 on conciliation—an appeal in which
the orator revealed that the resources of the colonies were

[3] Colonial military and naval contributions in the Seven Years' War
indirectly affected the fall of both India and the Philippines to the British.

so boundless as to render them unconquerable.[4] I do not accept this particular date, primarily because Burke's views did not prevail with Parliament, and because his speech neither added to nor subtracted from our power potential.

But America's strength was already considerable by 1775. Her trade, as Burke revealed, was nearly equal to that of England's with the entire world in 1700. Her manufacturing, despite the frowns of the Mother Country, was prospering; in fact, her iron foundries, though smaller, were more numerous than those of England. Her economic coercive power was such as to force Parliament to repeal the detested Stamp Act in 1766. Her nautical biceps were bulging. Benjamin Franklin noted that the total tonnage, gunnage, and manpower of the colonial privateering fleets in the war with France ending in 1748 equaled the entire English navy which had defeated the Spanish Armada in 1588.

In manpower and military strength—the conventional criteria of world power—the homespun colonials were far from contemptible. Thomas Paine, referring in *Common Sense* (1776) to the veterans of the recent French and Indian War, numbering about 25,000, could boast with obvious exaggeration that we had "the largest body of armed and disciplined men of any power under Heaven." After Lexington, Washington commanded an army of about 20,000 men that trapped the British in Boston and finally ejected them. In the winter of 1775–76, some seven months before independence, the brash Americans, not content with purely defensive operations against perhaps the

4 Charles A. and Mary R. Beard, *History of the United States* (New York, 1921), p. 477. The Beards asserted that the United States (even during the Critical Period) was continuously a world power from March, 1775, "to the settlement at Versailles in 1919." The curious implication is that the United States ceased to be a world power after 1919.

world's greatest power, launched a two-pronged invasion of Canada which narrowly missed capturing the Fourteenth Colony.

## IV

In my view the most satisfying date for emergence is July, 1776, when the United States formalized a clean break with Britain. The Founding Fathers themselves believed that they were launching a new world power on the turbulent sea of international politics. The proud Preamble of the Declaration of Independence proclaimed an intention "to assume among the Powers of the earth the separate and *equal* station to which the Laws of Nature and of Nature's God entitle them." John Adams, who quarreled in Paris with Foreign Minister Vergennes, informed him in 1780, "The United States of America are a great and powerful people, whatever European statesmen may think of them." [5]

But actions speak louder than verbs. The strength of the upstart colonials was so apparent that France, seeking to redress the world balance of power, undertook to wean them away from their imperial apron strings and embrace them as allies. This move, the French reasoned, would have a double-barreled impact. It would not only add to the strength of France but it would subtract correspondingly from that of Britain. The French consequently provided secret aid for about three years, and in 1778 finally came out into the open with twin treaties of alliance and commerce. One of the most striking features of these pacts was

[5] The passage continues: "If we take into our estimate the numbers and the character of her people, the extent, variety, and fertility of her soil, her commerce, and her skill and materials for ship-building, and her seamen, excepting France, Spain, England, Germany [?] and Russia, there is not a state in Europe so powerful." C. F. Adams, ed., *The Works of John Adams* (Boston, 1852), VII, 226–27 (July 13, 1780).

that in tone and terminology they implied an agreement between two equal and long-established powers.

The British, unwilling to lose their most prized overseas possessions, had countered belatedly with an offer of home rule. The two most powerful nations of the world were thus openly bidding for the favor of the robust young republic. The anxiety of both rivals indicates that America's strength was regarded as crucial in tipping the balance.

But the embattled British, outbid in 1778, turned the tables in 1782. Fighting desperately against a fearsome coalition, they in effect seduced America from the French alliance—a counter-seduction if you will—by offering incredibly generous terms of peace. These concessions were both the measure of Britain's desperation and of America's substantial weight in the world balance of power.

Yet many historians, awed by the magnitude of open French aid, are apt to downgrade the basic strength of the Americans. The truth is that the ex-colonials carried the burden of battle alone for three years—and against two nations. So tough was the colonial nut that the British were forced to seek assistance abroad, and in hiring some 30,000 so-called Hessians made what amounted to a military alliance with a second power. American privateers, whitening the seas, established a partial blockade of the British Isles during the three years before France tore off the mask of neutrality. After Lexington, the raw colonials pinned down tens of thousands of British troops, and in 1777, at Saratoga, compelled the surrender of the largest force that Britain had yet yielded to a foreign foe.

I would be the last to discount the French role during the American Revolution, especially secret aid and the naval contribution at Yorktown. But the United States could conceivably have won its independence without open assistance from France. After the signing of the alliance of 1778, a kind of let-François-do-it attitude began to prevail, and American enlistments declined in a ratio roughly corresponding to the size of the French expeditionary forces. If we gained from the alliance, so did the French. If they had not calculated that we would be of about as much value to them as they would be to us, they almost certainly would not have struck so perilous a bargain.

### V

More than a century later, when the Philippines fell as a gift from Heaven—or was it Heaven?—American imperialists insisted that we had to keep the islands to prove that we were a world power. To this argument the anti-imperialist Carl Schurz replied early in 1899: "Well, we *are* a world power now, and have been for many years." [6] William Jennings Bryan, in his acceptance speech of 1900, was more specific: "The forcible annexation of the Philippine Islands is not necessary to make the United States a world power. For over ten decades our Nation has been a world power." [7] But both Schurz and Bryan, the one a professional calamity howler and the other a hardy quadrennial, were voices crying in the cornfields.

Of different stature was Professor A. B. Hart of Harvard, who published a challenging article in *Harper's Magazine* in February, 1899.[8] He cogently argued that the United States had been a world power from 1776 on, and he may have conveyed this notion dimly to Bryan. But the

[6] Carl Schurz, *American Imperialism* (n.p., 1899), p. 28.

[7] W. J. Bryan, ed., *Speeches of William Jennings Bryan* (New York, 1909), II, 14.

[8] Later published in expanded form as Chapter 1 of A. B. Hart, *The Foundations of American Foreign Policy* (New York, 1901).

idea apparently wilted in the feverish imperialistic atmosphere of the era, and Professor Hart himself evidently
weakened in the faith. In 1907, eight years later, he edited
as one of the volumes of the *American Nation Series* a
contribution by Professor John H. Latané, entitled *America as a World Power, 1897–1907*. Professor Latané himself
declared cautiously (p. 318) that "the United States has always been a world power *in a sense.*" He then went on to
discuss our influence in shaping civil liberties and international law the world over.[9] But Professor Hart is the only
spokesman whom I have found, historian or layman, who
precisely dates our birth as a world power from the
declaring of independence.

## VI

Try as I may, I cannot escape the unflattering conclusion that we historians are largely responsible for the per-
petuation of the Manila Bay hallucination. Certainly the
Fourth of July orator never doubted for one moment that
we were not only the greatest power of all time from the
very beginning, but had twice whipped the next greatest
power.[10] How did the trained scholar—the professional
custodian of our traditions—get so far off the track?

[9] Italics inserted. Seth Low, former president of Columbia University,
wrote two years earlier with similar qualifications: "From the beginning
of its history the United States has been a world power, *in the sense* that
it has profoundly affected the movements of thought and of action outside of itself." He refers to our influence on the French Revolution, our
stand for neutral rights and arbitration, our example of fair dealing with
neighbors, our reception of immigrants, and our contributions to education. *Annals of the American Academy of Political and Social Science,*
XXVI (1905), 6.

[10] Col. A. L. Snowden, in an Independence Day address delivered in
1895 before Independence Hall, attributed American superiority largely
to a superior national character. "The Foremost Nation of the World,"
*American Historical Register,* III (1895), 65–70.

First of all, we historians have been unduly swayed by the smallness of our army and navy.[11] We tend to judge national power by the size of armed forces *in being*. Until the present century the United States relied heavily on land militia and sea militia, and although amateurs rarely do as well as professionals, we somehow managed to muddle through with a minimum of disaster. Huge military establishments, contrary to popular fancy, are a source of weakness rather than of strength. They reduce productive employment, burden the taxpayer, and unless assembled for blatantly aggressive purposes, are an almost infallible symptom of insecurity and fear.

The United States was the only first-rate nation that until recent times could afford the luxury of a third-rate army. In 1812 Madison invaded Canada with some 6,000 men; simultaneously Napoleon invaded Russia with some 600,000 men. The erroneous assumption is that France was one hundred times stronger than the United States. The fact is that we may not have had much of an army but what we had we had here, and Napoleon, hemmed in by the British navy, was powerless to come to grips with us. He was more than one hundred times stronger than we were in Europe, but we were stronger than he was in America.[12]

[11] Even so acute an observer as James Bryce, writing in 1901, could refer to the United States in 1834 as follows: "Already a great nation, it could become a great power as soon as it cared to spend money on fleets and armies." James Bryce, *Studies in History and Jurisprudence* (Oxford, 1901), I, 395. An unwillingness to recognize the power position of the United States did not negate that power, as Mexico learned to her sorrow in the war of 1846–48.

[12] Such a concept inspired this piece of extravagance in a speech by young Abraham Lincoln in 1838: "Shall we expect some transatlantic military giant to step the Ocean and crush us at a blow? Never! All the armies of Europe, Asia and Africa combined, with all the treasure of the earth (our own excepted) in their military chest; with a Buonaparte for a commander, could not by force, take a drink from the Ohio, or make a track on the Blue Ridge, in a trial of a thousand years." R. P. Basler, ed., *Collected Works of Abraham Lincoln* (New Brunswick, 1953), I, 109.

A two-way provincialism thus continues to curse American historiography. If American historians are too America-centered, many European historians are too European-centered. A true perspective lies between these extremes.

### VII

Certain historians have also misinterpreted our early isolationism. We did not want to become one of the great powers of Europe, not so much because we were weak as because we thought it prudent to take full advantage of our unique geographical location and our phenomenal fecundity. Lord Castlereagh was quoted as saying that the fortunate Americans won their victories not on the battlefield but in the bedchamber. Certainly to play for time, to avoid unnecessary entanglements, to fatten as feeders while the Europeans famished as fighters—all this was statesmanship rather than timidity.[13]

The Monroe Doctrine has further muddied the waters. Some writers have hailed it as a virtual alliance with England, which it emphatically was not—quite the reverse.[14] In 1823 the British and the Americans, both intent on keeping inviolate the newly opened trade of Latin America, were pursuing a parallel policy. This meant that the mighty British navy, yardarm-to-yardarm with the modest American navy, was prepared to thwart possible intervention by the so-called Holy Alliance. The legend has there-

[13] Washington's Farewell Address, in urging the desirability of staying out of European embroilments, tended to overemphasize the weakness of the United States.

[14] See Walter Lippmann, *U.S. Foreign Policy: Shield of the Republic* (Boston, 1943), pp. 16–22, for a statement of the legend. Secretary Adams' famous remark about a "cockboat" coming in "in the wake of the British man-of-war" was obviously phrased to stress not so much our weakness as the desirability of pursuing an independent course. C. F. Adams, ed., *Memoirs of John Quincy Adams* (Philadelphia, 1875), VI, 179.

fore taken root that the Monroe Doctrine was upheld by the British navy throughout the nineteenth century and beyond. We thus have a mental image of the Yankee cringing behind the oaken petticoats of the Mother Country—a posture that hardly suggests world power. The disillusioning truth is that the British navy upheld the Monroe Doctrine only when the policies of Downing Street and Washington ran parallel, as they definitely did not during much of the nineteenth century. The sacred dictum of Monroe was flouted—or allegedly flouted—a score or so of times before 1904; and the British were involved in many of these infractions, either actively or passively. Beyond a doubt, the Royal Navy could have hamstrung or halted all such encroachments, had it been the protector-in-chief of the Monroe Doctrine. And as far as defending the United States was concerned, during the dozen or so Anglo-American crises between 1823 and 1898, we rightly regarded the British navy as our most formidable single adversary.[15]

VIII

Still another source of misunderstanding was the alleged absence of a far-flung American colonial empire until 1898. An authentic world power seemingly had to be burdened with overseas liabilities, as well as huge armies,

[15] On this point see Theodore Roosevelt's remarkable letter of November 30, 1918, in E. E. Morison, ed., *The Letters of Theodore Roosevelt* (Cambridge, Mass., 1954), VIII, 1407–09. A writer in the Manchester *Guardian Weekly* recently stated that "American security was, in fact, a by-product of the strength of the British fleet." LXXXII, 10 (June 30, 1960). It is true that Britain helped preserve the balance of power in Europe, to our incidental advantage, but if there had been no British navy, the balance would presumably have been redressed by other navies, or by a stronger American navy. Similarly, if there had been no United States navy to back the Monroe Doctrine, the Latin American republics would have had to maintain larger navies.

navies, and national debts. The point is often missed that during the nineteenth century the United States practiced internal colonialism and imperialism on a continental scale. When the Western European nations expanded, they had to go overseas; when we expanded, we had to go west.[16] We self-righteously preened ourselves on not becoming an imperialistic power until 1898, when we acquired Spanish real estate in the Philippines, Guam, and Puerto Rico. Yet hundreds of Spanish place names pepper the land from California to Texas, all of which, curiously enough, somehow managed to come under our nonimperialistic flag a half century earlier. As for the claim that the Philippines added to our national strength, the troublesome islands proved to be a perennial liability—militarily, economically, politically, and morally.

Another misleading cliché of the nineteenth century was that the United States, though still a lusty adolescent, loomed as *the* great power of the future. British editors condescendingly conceded that in the fullness of time— and thanks largely to our British blood and breeding—we would arrive.[17] Long after we had indubitably "arrived," the misleading habit persisted of referring cheerfully to America as the nation of the future.

[16] Tariffs to protect our domestic market were in some degree the equivalent of European imperialism for establishing overseas markets. Both American tariffs and European imperialism affected foreign peoples adversely.

[17] For examples of British opinion see *Scots Magazine,* LXXVII (1815), 63; *Edinburgh Review,* XXIV (1814), 262; *ibid.,* LXXXVI (1847), 395–96. Whig, rather than Tory, journals were disposed to play up the actual or potential power of the United States. See Richard S. Cramer, "British Magazines and the United States, 1815–1848" (unpublished doctoral dissertation, Stanford University). In 1765, eleven years before independence, the London *Gazette* remarked: "Little doubt can be entertained that America will in time be the greatest and most prosperous empire that perhaps the world has ever seen." Quoted in Hart, *Foundations of American Foreign Policy,* p. 12.

Additional confusion came from British travelers and others who harped on the youthfulness of America. We started as the youngest of modern republics, and we revealed a boyishness of spirit as we proceeded to crystallize our dreams into realities. But as the nineteenth century lengthened, as dozens of new nations sprang into existence, and as we developed a continental spread, critics continued to comment on our youth. Oscar Wilde, writing in 1893, had one of his characters quip, "The youth of America is their oldest tradition. It has been going on now for three hundred years." The juvenile behavior of some Americans, especially when abroad, still gives support to this illusion.

IX

A false estimate of our power position has also contributed lushly to the legend of 1898. I have already said that the United States, from the very day of its legal birth, was the strongest nation in the Western Hemisphere—a basic fact often overlooked.[18] In the pubescent period of the republic, France, Britain, Russia, Prussia, Austria, Spain—to name no others—could all marshal larger armed forces *in Europe,* but not effectively against us. As for the other sister republics of the Americas, the epithet "Colossus of the North" carries its own power-laden implications.

The United States from the outset was a European power—on those infrequent occasions when it chose to exert its power in Europe.[19] The panic-inspiring raids of John

[18] In 1856 a writer in *Blackwood's Edinburgh Magazine* thus described the United States: "The dominant power of the New World, and with three thousand miles of sea separating it from the great military states of Europe, the Union has found on its own continent no power which unaided can check its aggressions, and as yet no European state but Great Britain has had either an interest or the power to enter the lists against it." LXXX (1856), 116–17.

[19] The Czar of Russia thought well enough of the United States to invite it to join the Holy Alliance in 1819.

Paul Jones on the British coasts, to say nothing of the ravages of American privateers in British waters during two Anglo-American wars, are twice-told tales. Less familiar was the damaging effect of the American Embargo Act and the Non-intercourse Act, which together forced the British to suspend their infuriating orders in council before we declared war on them in 1812. The simple fact is that in the years before the Civil War the coercive power of King Cotton on British textile manufacturers was so potent that in an economic sense alone America was a world power.

The United States was also an African power in the nineteenth century, when it chose to be one. Most Americans have forgotten, if they ever knew, that William Eaton, the incredible Connecticut Yankee, led a motley army of some 500 men across the desert from Egypt to Tripoli and captured Derne in 1805. Most Americans have forgotten, if they ever knew, that the United States was the nation that chastised the cutthroats of Morocco, Algiers, Tunis, and Tripoli in naval campaigns extending from 1801 to 1815. Most Americans have forgotten, if they ever knew, that the United States launched Liberia in the 1820's, and in 1884, following the spectacular explorations of the American journalist Henry M. Stanley, joined the other great powers by invitation at the Berlin Conference on the Congo.

The United States was a Far Eastern power in the nineteenth century—fifty years or so before our ill-informed expansionists clamored for the Philippines so as to make America an active force in the Eastern Hemisphere. It was Commodore Perry who, with seven warships and the velvet glove, forced open the bamboo portals of Japan in 1854. It was "Blood-is-thicker-than-water" Tattnall who went to the rescue of the British off the Chinese forts in 1859. It was an American warship, in the midst of our own Civil War, that helped punish the Japanese feudal lord at Shimonoseki in 1864. It was a fleet of five American warships that demolished several Korean forts and killed some two hundred Koreans in 1871. And it was Commodore Shufeldt who initiated our diplomatic relations with Korea in 1882.[20] On the other side of Asia, it was an American man-of-war in Turkish waters that forced an Austrian warship to release the Hungarian refugee Martin Koszta in 1853. Nor does this catalogue take into account the moral influence of America through educational and missionary establishments, ranging all the way from the missions of China and Japan to Robert College at Constantinople.

In short, critics have often failed to recognize our three-ply policies in the nineteenth century: voluntary abstentionism, as a rule, in Europe; unilateral intervention in the Americas and Africa; and unilateral or joint-power intervention in the Far East. One reason for associating our advent as a world power with 1898 is the popular but erroneous assumption that the acquisition of the Philippines marked a complete break with the past. We are told that hitherto we had shunned colonizing (which is untrue), that we had formerly been isolated (which is untrue), and that thereafter we were internationalist (which is also untrue).

The May Day misconception can further be traced to the testimony of contemporary Americans and Britons— our esteemed primary sources. In 1898 a number of editors, further proving that propinquity often dulls perception,

[20] As far as the nineteenth century as a whole was concerned, Britain, and possibly Russia and France, were the only powers that exerted more influence than the United States in the Far East. Germany, Italy, and Austria-Hungary, the other three great powers of Europe, certainly exerted less.

hailed America's sudden and sensational advent as a world power.[21] Americans are notoriously afflicted with "hurry-upitis," and the concept of emerging overnight chimed in with the national psychology. President McKinley himself remarked in 1899 that "in a few short months we have become a world power." [22] But let us bear in mind that McKinley, to put it charitably, was slightly confused. Ex-President Benjamin Harrison, writing in 1901, and thinking of our unchallenged primacy in the Americas, declared that before 1898 we had been a half world power—as though world power could be divided and compartmented.[23]

## X

If my reasoning is sound, the United States became a world power in 1776 and has never fallen below that exalted status, except for the six-year hiatus of the so-called Critical Period following the Revolution. A nation that was militarily impotent, diplomatically despised, financially bankrupt, and politically fragmented ceased to be a power, much less a world power. We almost ceased to be a nation, for British and Spanish forces held or controlled about one half of our territory. The Constitution of 1787 was in part designed—and successfully so—to restore and strengthen American prestige.[24]

21 See *Public Opinion,* XXIV (May 12, 1898), 580; *ibid.* (May 19, 1898), 615; *Westminster Review,* CL (1898), 168; *Nineteenth Century,* XLIV (1898), 194. A British comment ran: "Unless all signs deceive, the American Republic breaks from her old moorings, and sails out to be a 'world power'." *Blackwood's Edinburgh Magazine,* CLXIII (1898), 703.

22 Cortelyou's Diary, August 17, 1899, quoted in Margaret Leech, *In the Days of McKinley* (New York, 1959), p. 464.

23 *North American Review,* CLXXII (1901), 177–90.

24 Modern scholarship has undertaken to show that domestic conditions under the Articles of Confederation were not so bad as traditionally pictured, but the nation's posture in foreign affairs was still weak.

The next question is: When did we step up a rung and become a great power? Webster (second edition), apparently the only dictionary to spell out this distinction, defines the great powers as "The most powerful nations of the world, especially in political influence, resources, and military and naval strength." The "Great Powers of Europe," as the pat phrase went, formed a kind of exclusive club, and by the 1890's included Britain, France, Russia, Germany, Italy, and Austria-Hungary. When did the United States deserve the status of a great power in its own right, rather than as an influential counterweight in the world balance?

A possible date is 1803, when we dramatically doubled our original birthright by the windfall of Louisiana. "From this day," exulted Minister Livingston in Paris, "the United States take their place among the powers of the *first* rank." [25] But this self-congratulatory assessment seems unduly optimistic.

I likewise reject the miserable little War of 1812, from which we were lucky to escape with a relatively whole skin. Yet forty-seven years ago the historian Charles Francis Adams, Jr., published an article strangely entitled: "Wednesday, August 19, 1812, 6:30 P.M.: The Birth of a World Power." [26] He referred, of course, to the first frigate duel of the War of 1812, in which "Old Ironsides" partially restored American self-esteem by smashing the aged and overmatched *Guerrière*. But the tiny United States Navy, despite heroic individual efforts on the high seas, was ultimately wiped out. The Americans did manage to win a

[25] François Barbé-Marbois, *The History of Louisiana* (Philadelphia, 1830), pp. 310–11. Italics inserted.

[26] *American Historical Review*, XVIII (1913), 513–21. Adams, oddly enough, refers to the United States in 1812 as "a power of the third class," ranking below Portugal and "more nearly on the level of Algiers" (p. 514).

grudging degree of diplomatic and naval respect, particularly for their postwar chastisement of the Barbary states, yet on balance the War of 1812 added little, if anything, to our overall strength.

I also reject the enunciation of the Monroe Doctrine, which likewise added nothing substantial to our national power. Much as it tickled our own fancy in 1823, it annoyed rather than alarmed Europeans. In their eyes, we seemed to be shaking our fists behind the stout wooden walls of the British navy.

A good case can be made out for the Mexican War as marking the emergence of the United States as a great power—and an imperialistic power at that. We impressed European skeptics, but we impressed ourselves even more. Henry David Thoreau ceased communion with the woodchucks long enough to mention in *Walden* the current discussion of America's being "a first rate power." [27] In an imperialistic coup worthy of the Romans, we sheared away one-half of Mexico, assumed sway over thousands of Spanish-speaking peoples, added one-third again to our continental domain, won a panoramic Pacific frontage, and further validated our claims to being both a Pacific and a Far Eastern power. While still one month deep in the war with Mexico, we stared the British down over the issue of the Oregon boundary, and forced them to yield the disputed triangle north of the Columbia River. This in itself

[27] Henry David Thoreau, *Walden* (Mt. Vernon, N.Y. [1956]), p. 317. The British scientist Alexander Mackay wrote in 1849 of the United States as being in "the first rank amongst the powers of the earth." *The Western World, or, Travels in the United States in 1846–1847* (London, 1849), II, 284. A British consul in Japan in the late 1850's informed the Japanese that "there were five great nations, viz. France, the Germanic Confederation, Great Britain, Russia, and the United States." C. P. Hodgson, *A Residence at Nagasaki and Hakodate in 1859–1860* (London, 1861), p. 308.

was no mean feat, especially when one considers the booming broadsides of the British navy. But again the European balance of power and the might of the rival French fleet strengthened our hand.[28]

The end of the Civil War, in my judgment, marks the arrival of the United States as a great power. We were now the third most populous white nation, ranking behind only Russia and France. We had achieved peaceful coexistence among the sections by the greatest constitutional decision of them all: that handed down by Grant at Appomattox Court House. We had washed away the moral incubus of slavery in a bath of blood. We had attained a staggering agricultural productivity, while our smokestacks ranked second only to Britain's. We had an immense navy of about 500 ships, with numerous ironclads, and we boasted the largest standing army in the world—a battle-singed army at that. When Secretary of State Seward demanded that the French clear out of Mexico, he spoke with the voice of one million bayonets—and Napoleon III, for reasons both foreign and domestic, took French leave of his ill-starred puppet Maximilian.

The Civil War had presented both Britain and France with the opportunity of the century. They had long distrusted our expansive power in this hemisphere, they had since 1783 pursued a policy of containment, and they had prayed for the day when they could engage in the hoary game of divide and dominate. But such was the strength of the United States—even a disunited United States locked

---

[28] British statesmen feared that hostilities with America might prompt the French, whose new steam navy was about as strong as Britain's, to invade England with a powerful steamer-borne army. John S. Galbraith, "France as a Factor in the Oregon Negotiations," *Pacific Northwest Quarterly,* XLIV (1953), 69–73. For a contrary view, see Frederick Merk, *The Oregon Question* (Cambridge, Mass., 1967), pp. 347–63.

in the throes of fratricidal conflict—that the two greatest powers of Europe, individually and collectively, shrank from the bloody consequences of armed intervention.[29]

## XI

After the Civil War, America turned inward. The Navy fell prey to worms and decay. Not until the end of the century did we have a modern steel fleet that had forged into about sixth place.[30] The standing army had dwindled to some 28,000 men by 1890, and ranked about thirteenth, below the armies of Belgium, Bulgaria, and Sweden. The usual overreliance of Europe-centered scholars on military force recently prompted a gifted young diplomatic historian to write for the Voice of America, "Before 1890 the United States was at most a second-rate power." [31]

Let us take a hard look at this "second-rate power" in the eight or so years before the Spanish-American War. By 1890 we were the number two white nation in population,

[29] A writer in the London *Spectator* (March 16, 1861) conceded that the North alone would have enough strength left to "be entitled to rank as a first-class power." XXXIV, 273. Richard Cobden wrote to Charles Sumner in March, 1865, that it was "nothing but your great *power* that has kept the hands of Europe off you." *American Historical Review*, II (1897), 318. The *Spectator* declared in February, 1866, "Nobody doubts any more that the Union is a power of the first class, a nation which it is very dangerous to offend and almost impossible to attack." XXXIX, 177. The same journal conceded in February, 1869, that America was "the greatest power in the whole world." *Ibid.*, XLII, 250. Ignorance of such views prompted the German General Friedrich von Bernhardi to condemn Britain's "unpardonable blunder" in not supporting the South. *Germany and the Next War,* trans. A. H. Powles (London, 1914), p. 94.

[30] Such estimates can be only approximations, owing to differences in types of ships, guns, armor, crews, bases, and other factors. Many European warships were built for short-range operations, and consequently lacked the bunker capacity to cross the Atlantic and engage the American Navy.

[31] Program of October 15, 1959. Ex-Secretary of State Richard Olney, writing in the *Atlantic Monthly* of May, 1898 (and presumably shortly before Dewey's victory), declared, "The United States is certainly now entitled to rank among the great Powers of the world." LXXXI, 578.

still trying to catch up with the Russians. We had bounded into first place in total manufacturing, including top rank in iron and steel—the standard indices of military potential. In addition, we held either first or second places in railroads, telegraphs, telephones, merchant marine, and in the production of cattle, coal, gold, copper, lead, petroleum, cotton, corn, wheat, and rye. The armies and navies were not there, but we had the means of creating them when we needed them—and did.

The diplomatic box score is most revealing. In a series of breathtaking crises, we forced our adversaries—three of them "great powers"—to come to terms or knuckle under: Germany over the Samoa scramble in 1889; Italy over the New Orleans lynching bee of 1891; Chile over the *Baltimore* brawl in 1891; Britain over the Venezuela boundary imbroglio in 1896.[32] Spain capitulated diplomatically over Cuba in 1898, at least substantially, but we picked a fight with her anyhow and forced her to capitulate militarily.

The flash of Dewey's guns merely spotlighted a maturation that had long since taken place. The irony is that we finally won belated acceptance into the great power "club" by thrashing a second-rate power in two naval engagements that cost us only one life.[33]

[32] As early as 1879 the London *Saturday Review* had referred to the United States as "A Power of the first rank." XLVIII (1879), 226. Five years later it bracketed America with "all other great Powers." *Ibid.*, LVII (1884), 333. See also the *Nineteenth Century*, XXI (1887), 799; *Spectator*, LXVII (1889), 532; *Westminster Review*, CXXXI (1889), 508; *Public Opinion*, VII, 229 (June 22, 1889). For an unfavorable view of America's power position, see *Nineteenth Century*, XXXIX (1896), 906–13.

[33] In 1909 Professor F. A. Ogg discerned three schools of thought: (1) we had always been a world power, (2) we became a world power with the Spanish-American War, (3) we had never become a world power. *Dial*, XLVI (1909), 44. Some scholars, mostly European or Europe-centered, would not accord the United States great power status until 1917–18, if then. They have been misled in part by the reluctance of American isolationist elements to face up to the responsibilities of world leadership.

## XII

I fear that some critics will regard my remarks this evening as academic hairsplitting. Power, world power, great power, superpower—what difference does it all make?

First of all, a failure to read and heed our history contributed to our costly overseas aberration in 1898. If enough of our historians—and their former students—had been able to say at the time that we had been a world power since 1776, that we had always been a colonizing nation, and that we did not have to wallow in the cesspool of overseas imperialism to prove our stature, we might have spared ourselves the tribulations of keeping up with the imperialistic Joneses by acquiring the Philippines and other overseas headaches.

A misreading of our history likewise accelerated the deadly isolationist drift of the 1920's and 1930's. With uncharacteristic modesty, we Americans confessed that we were greenhorns at the poker table of world politics. We were content to let the white-spatted British and French, old hands at the diplomatic game, breathe life into the stillborn League of Nations. If we had only realized how long, and in what varied areas, we had in fact been a great power, we probably would have been more willing to play a role commensurate with our monstrous strength.

A further misreading of our history has caused us to forget that national power is moral as well as physical. In the formative years of the republic, the three most feared "isms" in the world were probably American republicanism, constitutionalism, and liberalism. They no longer are. Unless we can rekindle some of the dynamic faith in our democracy that we displayed in the nineteenth century, our adversaries will bury us.

Finally, many Americans—including some in high places—evidently have not examined our past with sufficient care to appreciate the extent to which national power is relative. In 1789 we were absolutely weak but relatively strong. Today we are absolutely strong but relatively vulnerable. We can blow up more people than ever before, yet we were never in such mortal danger of annihilation. If we are a supercolossal power under these terrifying conditions, one can hardly avoid a degree of nostalgic respect for the United States of 1776. We were then only a newcomer in the family of nations, but we were, I submit, a world power, and within less than a century we were destined to become a great power.

*The author has long been impressed with the unfairness of comparing unlikes—that is, comparing men of different epochs confronted with different problems and clothed with different powers. He has ventilated his views on this subject at length in* Presidential Greatness *(1966). With some of these limitations in mind, he here makes an attempt to pick out America's six most distinguished diplomats, treating them in chronological order, without undertaking to rank them in descending order of distinction. The guidelines laid down could be employed in the selection of future ambassadors, and are much more fully developed in Bailey's* The Art of Diplomacy *(1968).*

# 3.

# A HALL OF FAME
# FOR AMERICAN DIPLOMATS

⌒⌒

"Successful diplomacy, like successful marriage, is
not much publicized."
—John P. Davies, ex-foreign service officer, 1965

I

Diplomats are often caricatured as frock-coated bunglers
whose chief occupation is to get us into wars, or at
least to stir up more trouble than they settle. They are also
supposed to have thick heads, further thickened by alcohol.
Zealous members of the Woman's Christian Temperance
Union have long insisted that America's so-called diplomatic defeats at Yalta in 1945 were due to the devastating
effects of Stalin's secret weapon—vodka.

What in fact should be the qualifications of the ideal
American ambassador?

Without being a stuffed shirt, he must first of all have
presence and dignity. He must in his person convey some-

The Virginia Quarterly Review, XXXVI (Summer, 1960), 390–404.
Reprinted by permission.

thing of the grandeur of the country he represents, as Commodore Perry succeeded in doing in Japan in the 1850's. If he cannot command respect, he is not likely to receive respect. He must be courteous, gracious, tactful, tolerant. He must have simple good manners and not emulate John Randolph, who, when presented to the Russian Czar in 1830, allegedly blurted out, "Howaya Emperor? And how's the madam?"

A diplomat must possess the necessary social graces and entertain appropriately, although Mrs. Perle Mesta in Luxembourg, with superabundant private means, recently left the impression that this was all she was doing. The ambassador abroad is the eyes, ears, mouth, and even nose of his government in Washington. The more he can get around, the more information he can pick up, especially after the fourth round of cocktails. As Secretary of State Robert Lansing once remarked, the individual whom you see in your office the day after a successful social affair is likely to be more accommodating than one whom you have never met socially.

Above all, the diplomat must avoid bad taste. He should on all occasions dress appropriately, and never appear at his office, as one of our representatives in the Caribbean once did, clad in a bare red undershirt. He must not ruin valuable Persian rugs by spitting tobacco juice on them, as at least one of our less polished envoys once did. If he drinks, he must hold his liquor like a gentleman. (Unfortunately the record reveals embarrassing departures from this rule, notably when one of our ministers in Germany was so drunk that he could not be officially presented to the Emperor.) Whatever the provocation, he must not become involved in fist fights, as did our Minister to Russia (Cassius M. Clay) in the 1860's, nor in café brawls, as did our Minister to Bulgaria (George H. Earle) in 1941. His relations with the opposite sex must be conventional or, if not, exceptionally discreet. General Daniel E. Sickles, who had lost a leg at Gettysburg, not only did his best to provoke war as Minister to Spain in the 1870's, but created a scandal by becoming the paramour of the adulterous ex-Queen Isabella, then exiled in Paris.

II

The ambassador must be highly resourceful and intelligent. It is reassuring to note how many, including John Quincy Adams, John Hay, and Dwight W. Morrow, could wear the key of Phi Beta Kappa. The diplomat must be literate and usually is, although Romulus M. Saunders in Spain in the 1840's, according to the Secretary of State, "sometimes murders" the English language. The envoy should be articulate and able to represent the nation properly at the unveiling of monuments and other ceremonial occasions. If he has a flair for oratory, he should hold himself in leash; if he must make speeches, he would do well to confine himself to platitudes about home, mother, and the flag. In the 1890's Ambassador Thomas F. Bayard in London delivered several addresses that were so pro-British as to infuriate the Irish-Americans at home and elicit a vote of censure from the House of Representatives. Above all, the ambassador must avoid important new pronouncements on policy, unless specifically instructed to do otherwise. Policy should be made in Washington and implemented by the man in the field.

The diplomat must not only be gifted with keen intelligence but also must be broadly informed. If he is to observe as well as see, he cannot know too much about too many different areas of human activity—government, politics, economics, psychology. A comprehensive historical background, including that of the United States and that of the country to which he is accredited, is especially desirable, and in this respect historians like George Bancroft in Prussia and Andrew D. White in Germany had an advantage over their predecessors. Less fortunate was Minister Denby in China in the 1890's; he believed that the Cossacks came from Corsica.

The envoy must not only have the capacity to learn quickly and adjust himself mentally to new situations, but he must possess an uncommon amount of common sense. Canny old Benjamin Franklin, the compiler of Poor Richard's sayings, was wise enough in the ways of men to do a superlative job as American commissioner and minister in Paris during the anxious years of the American War of Independence.

Common sense should be combined with creative imagination and with foresight—the capacity to foresee, as a good chess player must, more than one move ahead. Associated with this quality is perceptiveness, sometimes called "political sense." A cynic once remarked that fortunately many diplomats have long noses because they cannot see beyond the ends of them. Ambassador to Russia Joseph E. Davies, whose *Mission to Moscow* became one of the most insidious weapons of Soviet propaganda in World War II, was badly taken in by the purge trials of the 1930's, even though he was a lawyer by profession.

Ranking high also among the attributes of the superior diplomat is reportorial skill. One would be hard put to name a single qualification for a first-class foreign correspondent that one would not also seek in a first-class foreign envoy. The ambassador, who has long been regarded as a kind of licensed spy, must report the information, plus recommendations, on which his government in Washington can base its policy. The dispatches of Andrew D. White from Berlin in the 1890's were models of penetrating reporting; those of Thomas F. Bayard in London, who had been Secretary of State and who should have known better, consisted largely of pasted-up clippings from British journals. The foreign service has no place for the lazy man or the windy man.

Finally, the diplomat must be an objective reporter. He should tell the truth as he sees it, however unpopular, and even though the way to promotion and pay may lie in sending home rose-colored accounts designed to please his superiors. His assessment may later prove to be erroneous but it must be honest. One of the many unfortunate effects of McCarthyism was to put pressure on the man in the field not to report probable Communist successes lest he later be denounced, demoted, dismissed, and disgraced.

### III

General Charles G. Dawes, with his underslung pipe and picturesque profanity, was sent to the Court of St. James's in the Hoover era, and he reported with some bitterness that "American diplomacy is easy on the brain but hell on the feet." Henry P. Fletcher, ex-ambassador to Italy, counterquipped, "It depends on which you use."

Both men were stressing an important truth. The diplomatic service is no place for weaklings: it demands good health, physical and mental. Despite the illusion of glamor, it can be, and often is, grueling work. Standing at the head of a reception line for hours with a frozen smile, attending countless functions, trying to be pleasant at all times to all men—this takes a heavy toll. One also needs a cast-iron digestion to accommodate the strange foods—including stewed cat—that may be served. Many a man has regretted that he had only one stomach to give for his country.

Physical courage is also a prime requisite. One must face strange diseases in the tropics, pneumonia in Bolivia and Russia (many men succumbed in prepenicillin days), and physical injury at the hands of plotters and mobs. Ambassador Robert M. McClintock in Lebanon in 1958 had several close calls from bullets and bombs, while in 1924 Major Robert W. Imbrie, American Vice-Consul in Persia, was beaten to death by a mob of religious fanatics. On the walls of the State Department hangs a plaque commemorating the sixty or so diplomats in our history who were killed while serving on foreign soil.

In the good old horse-and-buggy days, campaign contributors often requested foreign posts for rather irrelevant reasons, including cultural opportunities for wives or daughters, or a more salubrious climate for their own rheumatism or other ailments. President Lincoln is supposed to have told a Congressman who was seeking a foreign post for one of his constituents, "There are nine candidates for the place ahead of you, and every one of them is sicker than yours." One may doubt if the best interests of the United States were being served when John Randolph, then dying of tuberculosis, was sent to chill St. Petersburg in 1830.

IV

The American representative must be a man or woman of the highest integrity. An ambassador has long since been cynically defined as "an honest man, sent to lie abroad for the good of the country." This ancient concept does not square with the American tradition, although there have been painful exceptions. "Tell the truth," replied Sir Henry Wotton when asked by a young diplomatist how best to confuse his adversaries. American diplomacy, which has often been described as of the shirt-sleeves or housetop variety, has generally avoided the devious. Men of sterling integrity, like Charles Francis Adams in London during the Civil War, have helped their cause by speaking out with vigor and candor.

If integrity is such a prime requisite, we serve the short-range interests of the party rather than the long-range interests of the country by sending abroad men of shady character. President Lincoln bundled Secretary of War Simon Cameron off to St. Petersburg in 1862, when embarrassing scandals began to erupt in the War Department. In 1943 President Franklin Roosevelt, seeking a refuge for the Bronx boss Edward J. Flynn, appointed him minister to Australia, then threatened by Japanese invasion. The resulting public uproar forced a withdrawal of the nomination.

v

Certain qualities of temperament are essential. The diplomat must be patient, able to stand the boredom of routine with equanimity, as Townsend Harris did in the 1850's in his lonely Japanese outpost. He must be inoffensively persistent, as Robert R. Livingston was in Paris in 1803 while pressing for the acquisition of Louisiana. (One French official offered to give him a certificate as the most importunate diplomat he had ever met.) He must display humility and evenness of temper, as Albert Gallatin conspicuously did during the Ghent negotiations of 1814. The diplomatic service has no place for hotheads like the French expatriate Pierre Soulé, American minister to Spain in the 1850's. He wounded the French ambassador in a duel, handed down an unauthorized ultimatum, and tried to pick a war with Spain over the *Black Warrior* affair. One critic observed that he was more of a matador than an ambassador.

The diplomat must be nonpartisan in representing the interests of his country, even though he be a party man at home. The outspoken George Harvey, in his Pilgrims' Club speech in England in 1921, delivered a violent harangue in which he presented the Republican case against the League of Nations. Although he spoke with President Harding's private blessing, he evoked a bitter outcry from the Democrats, whose taxes were helping to pay his salary.

The envoy must be dedicated to his job, and not regard it merely as a plum for political service or for a lush campaign contribution. He must also be devoted to the interests of his own country, and if he is, he will not lose the respect of foreigners. Many a man has fallen into the pit, as was true of Walter Hines Page in England during World War I, of currying favor with his hosts by embracing their viewpoint too wholeheartedly. Page's dispatches home became so pro-British that in effect the British had two ambassadors to the United States: one in Washington on their payroll, and one in London on ours. The ideal ambassador should not be too popular, unless, like Franklin in France, he can keep his head. Nor should he be unpopular; he should try to steer a safe middle course.

He must also be discreet: the diplomatic service needs no blabbermouths. Frederick Van Dyne—brave man indeed —opined in 1909 that one reason why so few women have risen in the service is their notorious inability to keep a secret. And when the diplomat says something, he must avoid statements that are twistable. The brilliant Ambassador George F. Kennan, provoked beyond endurance, let slip a remark in 1952 about the internment-camp isolation of Western diplomats in Moscow. The Kremlin was quick to seize upon this indiscretion as a pretext for demanding his recall.

The diplomat must be a loyal subordinate, willing to take orders and execute them promptly in the chain of command. John Jay deliberately violated his instructions in Paris and entered upon separate negotiations with the British in 1782. The result in this case turned out to be happy, but complete chaos would result if each envoy were a law unto himself.

The ideal ambassador must be flexible and adaptable, as Anson Burlingame was in Peking in the 1860's. He must be willing, if necessary, to wear knee breeches and walk backward in leaving the presence of royalty. No amount of nonconformity or rebellion, as John Adams noted, will change ancient customs abroad. He must be willing to yield a little while taking perhaps a little more; and he must be sparing in his use of the flat negative. As the old saying goes, "When a diplomat says 'yes' he means 'perhaps'; when he says 'perhaps' he means 'no'; when he says 'no' he is no diplomat." This observation had more validity before the ungentlemanly Bolsheviks appeared on the scene with short and ugly words and emphatic noes.

No one should enter the diplomatic service who does not like mankind in general and his potential hosts in particular. Handsome, kindly Myron T. Herrick, an able politician, banker, and organizer, distinguished himself in Paris from 1912 to 1914 and again from 1921 to 1929. Such

were his qualities of heart and head, particularly as revealed during the hectic invasion summer of 1914, that the
French conferred upon him the Grand Cross of the Legion
of Honor and conveyed his remains to America in a French
warship after he had died at his post.

VI

Experience must take a high place among the desired
qualifications, although no one wants a life-tenure snob-
ocracy. In the morning years of the republic, when we
dispatched  ill-trained militiamen to the fighting front, we
tapped able but inexperienced men like John Adams and
John Jay for the diplomatic front. The system worked sur-
prisingly well, partly because men who have achieved distinction in a profession often have the capacity to adjust
themselves to diplomacy. The good lawyer in fact can rather
quickly acquire the essentials of international law, without
which he is definitely handicapped.

But the militia days are gone and the complexities of
international life are such that there is little place for the
well-meaning amateur, however gifted. We must discard
the naïve notion that diplomacy is the only profession that
requires neither preparation nor experience. American diplomacy has now become deeply entangled with power
politics, and this largely explains why we train selected
career diplomats at the National War College. Significantly,
the roster of American ambassadors to Moscow since 1942
includes two admirals (Standley, Kirk) and one general
(Smith). The chief of mission often finds himself the co-
ordinator of a complex organization involving economic
aid, military aid, propaganda efforts, and other activities,
all of which call for both business experience and admin-

istrative skill. In such a capacity, and with the aid of the permanent career staff, an able politician-businessman, like Chester Bowles in India, has often acquitted himself creditably.

Knowledge of the relevant foreign languages is likewise eminently desirable. If a Turkish ambassador were to come to Washington knowing no English, we can imagine how seriously handicapped he would be in attempting to sample newspaper opinion, secure the views of the American in the street, discharge his social obligations, and communicate orally with the Secretary of State. Similar difficulties would beset the American Ambassador in Ankara if he knew no Turkish. Linguistic gifts in themselves are no guarantee of diplomatic competence, but if the envoy has the other essential qualifications he can add immeasurably to his effectiveness by communicating with his hosts in their own tongue.

Prestige can also be helpful. Robert Todd Lincoln, the somewhat disappointing son of the Great Emancipator, went to the Court of St. James's in 1889, and there found his influence greater because of the name he bore. A distinguished general, like the late George C. Marshall in China after World War II, normally finds his path made smoother, especially if he is known, as was true in this case, to have the ear of the President.

Finally, the top-ranking American ambassador should have money—made, married, or inherited. One of the supreme paradoxes of our vaunted democracy is that in the upper diplomatic reaches, thanks to a penny-pinching Congress, we are a plutocracy. The outlay for entertainment at a half dozen or so of our key embassies—notably London, Paris, and Rome—is such that only a wealthy man can provide the additional forty to seventy thousand dollars a year.

For such posts the first question is not: Does he have the attributes herein outlined? It is: Does he have money? The list of ambassadors to London since the late 1920's reads like a millionaires' club: the Daweses, the Mellons, the Binghams, the Kennedys, the Harrimans, the Aldrichs, the Whitneys. Many a man of the highest capabilities has been compelled to decline the honor of bankrupting himself in the service of his rich but parsimonious country.

VII

Before unveiling my nominees for a Hall of Fame, I must first of all explain why certain names will not appear.

A man of exceptional ability, like the famed lawyer Joseph H. Choate in London (1899–1905), may have the ill fortune to be serving at a time when routine is the order of the day. On the other hand, Robert R. Livingston happened to be minister to France in 1803 when Napoleon, for reasons purely realistic, decided to dump all of Louisiana into the lap of the United States. This lucky windfall has enshrined Livingston in our textbooks, while Choate is embalmed in the achives of the Department of State.

We shall also have to keep in mind whether we are considering the B.C. or the post-B.C. era—before the cable or after the cable. Livingston, in violation of his specific instructions, could take it upon himself to sign the Louisiana purchase treaties because the bargain was too overwhelming and time was too short. "Thim was th' days," remarked the droll Mr. Dooley, "whin ye'd have a good time as an ambassadure." But the wire and then the wireless wrought a vast change. When ex-Secretary of State Richard Olney declined the ambassadorship to Britain in his seventy-eighth year, he supposedly declared, "An ambassador is nobody these days; he sits at the other end of a cable and does what he is told." The grain of truth in this complaint has sprouted into the myth that today the envoy is nothing but a white-spatted puppet dancing to the strings pulled in Washington. The fact is that there is still no substitute for a personable and perceptive diplomat on the ground, particularly one who has a delicate sense of timing.

An additional cause of confusion is the reflected glamor of distinction in another high office or field of endeavor. John Marshall was a distinguished Chief Justice, but hardly a distinguished envoy to France in 1797–98. John Quincy Adams was an eminent Secretary of State, but less eminent earlier as a diplomat abroad. During the nineteenth century, in the absence of Fulbright grants, the authorities in Washington would rather frequently send abroad literary luminaries—"damn literary fellers" Simon Cameron dubbed them. Washington Irving served as minister to Spain and James Russell Lowell as minister to Britain; Nathaniel Hawthorne, Bret Harte, and William D. Howells all occupied consular posts. John Hay, himself a minor literary figure, ultimately achieved a global reputation as Secretary of State, but his earlier career as ambassador in London was unspectacular.

Another source of misunderstanding lies in the behind-the-scenes nature of diplomacy. The most successful diplomat, like the most successful secret-service agent, usually works the most quietly, as Townsend Harris did in Japan. The headline hog—like theatrical Pierre Soulé in Spain in the 1850's—has no place in the foreign service. If he crows over his triumphs, his diplomatic adversaries will be doubly vigilant to prevent further loss of face. The highly skilled negotiator achieves many of his successes without either his opponents or the mass of his contemporary countrymen knowing they are successes.

The career diplomat, who knows the value of prudence, is at a disadvantage in attaining fame. Men like

Henry White and Joseph C. Grew, both of whom served for many years at varied posts, were the victims of day-to-day routine and professional discretion. On the other hand, politicians like the noisy George Harvey at the Court of St. James's in the 1920's, need have little concern for their diplomatic career. It presumably will last no longer than the incumbent administration, which in turn is at the mercy of both the ballot and the bullet.

VIII

With the foregoing qualifications in mind, I herewith propose six names as the nucleus of an American Diplomatic Hall of Fame.

First chronologically, and still towering above all others, stands Benjamin Franklin, the canny and urbane jack-of-all-trades. His spectacular experiments with electricity, to say nothing of his other notable achievements, had already marked him as one of the giants of the age. Dedicating the tag end of a busy life to his country, he played a vital rôle in securing the crucially important French Alliance of 1778 and the Peace Treaty of 1783. He had virtually all of the major qualifications herein set forth, including a quaint knowledge of French and more than a decade of diplomatic experience as a colonial agent. His fur-cap showmanship caught the fancy of the French, and further established him as our first great public-relations expert. His wife had died—and a socially conscious wife can be a valuable asset—but this presumed handicap merely increased his mobility and popularity among the French ladies. His intellect was still razor sharp; his tact was Chesterfieldian; his writing skill superb. His only major weakness was a diminution of energy resulting from gout, bladder stone, and other infirmities of old age. But an ailing

Franklin in his seventies had enough left to qualify him easily for our first place.

Albert Gallatin, though Swiss born and speaking with a foreign accent, ranks as a statesman in the same bracket with Jefferson, Hamilton, John Adams, and John Quincy Adams. For sheer nobility of character he had few equals and no superiors among his contemporaries. His greatest diplomatic achievement came at the peace table of Ghent, where he held together the quarreling American quintet long enough to extract an unexpectedly favorable treaty from the British negotiators at the end of the War of 1812. Highly intelligent and literate, moderate and conciliatory, patient and persistent, yet withal tactful, he continued to serve his adopted country admirably both in Paris and in London. His only real handicap was an unfounded suspicion among his countrymen that he had never become truly Americanized.

Charles Francis Adams—a son of John Quincy Adams, and a grandson of John Adams—was born with diplomacy in his blood. While a boy with his father in St. Petersburg, he had mastered French so thoroughly as to prefer it to English. Ultimately graduating from Harvard (Phi Beta Kappa honors), he became a prominent lawyer and politician, and in 1861 was sent by President Lincoln to London. Armed with a famous name, an English-like reserve, and a knowledge of British character growing out of two rugged years in an English boarding school, he raised the prestige of American diplomacy not only in England but also on the Continent. Through four desperate years of the Civil War he labored valiantly and successfully to stave off the British intervention which would have guaranteed the success of the Confederacy. In handling a series of harrowing crises, his foot almost never slipped. He commanded respect by his outstanding ability, his balance of mind (in which he excelled both his father and grandfather), his logic, his moderation, his reasonableness, his evenness of temper, his persistence, his directness, his sincerity, and his transparent integrity. While valiantly upholding the interests of his own country, he won the admiration of his hosts. In 1868, when his name was mentioned during a debate in the House of Commons, the assemblage broke into cheers.

## IX

Townsend Harris, a largely self-educated New York merchant who helped found the College of the City of New York, served as consul general and then minister in Japan from 1855 to 1862. A bachelor and formerly an intemperate drinker, he became a total abstainer, and despite bad food, rats, cockroaches, cholera, and lonesomeness—for one stretch he did not see an American ship for fourteen months—he finally won the confidence of the Shogun's régime by his frankness, tact, patience, persistence, and forbearance. His great achievement was concluding the epochal commercial treaty of 1858 with Japan during an era of nerve-racking domestic turmoil. The remarkable influence that he exercised on the Japanese government stemmed in part from his determination, unlike that of some of his Western colleagues, not to take undue advantage of Japan's weakness.

Anson Burlingame, a prominent Massachusetts Congressman, lawyer, orator, and politician, was sent to Peking in 1861 as a reward for having helped elect Lincoln President. Magnetic, urbane, candid, tolerant, and devoted to the cause of the underdog, he developed a strong admiration for the Chinese. Such were his qualities of personality that, although a novice, he almost immediately assumed leadership of the diplomatic corps in Peking during a period of acute East–West tension. Although best known for the Treaty of 1868 regulating Chinese immigration, he probably staved off the partition of China by the European powers, or at least a serious encroachment on her sovereignty. When he was about to resign, the Peking government appointed him head of a special diplomatic mission of Chinese to the principal Western powers, even though he spoke no Chinese. This compliment was not only unique but eloquent testimony to the impression he had made by his fairness, sympathy, and absence of race prejudice.

Dwight W. Morrow is a prime example of how a gifted amateur may become a professional almost overnight. A graduate of Amherst with Phi Beta Kappa distinction, he enjoyed a remarkable career as a lawyer, a House of Morgan banker, a politician, a humanitarian, and an organizer. (He received the Distinguished Service Medal for work in organizing Allied transport in World War I.) One of his great gifts was an uncanny knack of finding the common ground on which differences could be resolved. Appointed Ambassador to Mexico in 1927 by his former Amherst classmate President Coolidge, he stepped into a seemingly hopeless imbroglio over oil and agrarian rights. "I know what I can do for the Mexicans," he remarked. "I can *like* them." No wonder the masses greeted him on his travels with enthusiastic cries of approval. Morrow's intelligence, tact, sympathetic understanding, and a capacity to inspire trust wrought a diplomatic miracle in an incredibly short time.

Other names are no doubt deserving of a place in our Hall of Fame. Some critics will miss John Quincy Adams, who may properly be reserved for high rank among the great secretaries of state. But the immortal six here listed may serve as a beginning. Though mostly amateurs at the outset, they were all diplomats in the finest tradition and worthy of grateful remembrance by their debtors—the American people.

*Intimately related to the goodwill generated by the visits of the Russian fleets in 1863 was the purchase of Alaska from Russia in 1867. The following article is one of the author's earliest excursions into the area of public opinion as related to American foreign policy. These views, when first published, were somewhat unconventional, but they seem less so now. They have been substantially confirmed by other researches, notably those of Richard E. Welch, Jr., in "American Public Opinion and the Purchase of Russian America,"* American Slavic and East European Review, XVII (1958), 481–94. *Dr. Glyndon G. Van Deusen's new* William Henry Seward *(New York, 1967) presents a scholarly portrait but does not alter the conclusions here propounded.*

# 4.

# WHY THE UNITED STATES PURCHASED ALASKA

"... I feel ... warmly toward Russia, because when the fate of our Government was trembling in the balance, when she saw our people animated in a fearful struggle ... [she] sent her fleets into our western waters."
—Representative Mullins, in 1868 debate on Alaska appropriation

I

It would not be difficult to make up a list of thirty arguments that were advanced by proponents of the purchase of Alaska. But to determine which of these arguments weighed most heavily with the American people is quite another matter. Numerous commentators have made half-hearted attempts to solve this problem, but their results have been sadly lacking in uniformity. A historian of

*Pacific Historical Review*, III (March, 1934), 39–49. Reprinted by permission.

Alaska merely added to the confusion when he came to "the inevitable conclusion that the chief reason for the United States buying Alaska was William H. Seward." [1]

Although no one will deny that Seward was chiefly responsible for the negotiation of the purchase treaty, the fact is all too frequently overlooked that secretaries of state do not and cannot buy vast tracts of foreign territory. In the case under consideration, Seward had to secure the approval of President Johnson and his Cabinet, of two-thirds of the Senate, and of a majority of the House of Representatives. Nor can we stop here. It is axiomatic, as Seward himself remarked in discussing his ill-fated attempt to purchase the Danish West Indies,[2] that treaties have little chance of running the senatorial gauntlet unless they are supported by public sentiment. In the last analysis, then, the American people bought Alaska, and we shall go a long way toward solving our problem if we can discover why they reacted as they did to the transaction.

The whole subject has been confused by the findings of historical scholarship. Up until 1915 it was supposed that gratitude to Russia for her friendliness to us during the Civil War had played an important part in persuading us to relieve her of a hyperborean liability. Then Professor Frank A. Golder came along and exploded one of the prettiest and most tenacious myths in American history. He demonstrated conclusively that the Russian fleets were sent to America during a critical period of the Civil War not so much as a gesture of friendship as a means of serving the

---

[1] Henry W. Clark, *History of Alaska* (New York, 1930), p. 79.
[2] Frederick W. Seward, *Seward at Washington as Senator and Secretary of State* (New York, 1891), p. 369.

Czar's own ends.[3] In a subsequent article, Professor Golder concluded that "friendship between America and Russia had nothing whatever to do with the selling or with the buying of Alaska, *at least not with the state departments.*" [4]

It will be observed that his statement is carefully qualified, and in no way refers to the Senate, to the House of Representatives, or to American public opinion. Nevertheless, the unwary have been led astray. The author of a respected college textbook on American diplomatic history, to cite only one example, leaves one with the impression that Russian friendship can no longer be considered an important factor in the purchase of Alaska.[5] It would seem, therefore, as if this phase of the question warrants further examination.

Why Russia should have seen fit to dispose of a territory that had become increasingly burdensome does not fall within the purview of our subject. Nor need the question of Seward's motives detain us for long; this aspect of the problem has already been developed in some detail by Professor Golder and others. There seems to be no reason for doubting that Seward acted to satisfy his own insatiable passion for territorial expansion, to improve the strategic position of the United States in the Pacific, and at the same time to revive the decaying popularity of the State Depart-

[3] Frank A. Golder, "The Russian Fleet and the Civil War," *American Historical Review*, XX (1915), 801–12. See also E. A. Adamov, "Russia and the United States at the Time of the Civil War," *Journal of Modern History*, II (1930), 586–602. The rumor that $5,800,000 of the purchase price of Alaska went to reimburse Russia for the expense of sending her fleets to America rests upon inadequate historical data. See B. P. Thomas, *Russo-American Relations, 1815–1867* (Baltimore, 1930), pp. 162–64.

[4] Frank A. Golder, "The Purchase of Alaska," *American Historical Review*, XXV (1920), 425. Italics mine.

[5] John H. Latané, *A History of American Foreign Policy* (Garden City, N.Y., 1927), pp. 424–25.

ment, which was sharing the opprobrium being heaped upon the head of Johnson. In the end, the Secretary of State was able to secure the approval of the President and the Cabinet, and on March 30, 1867, the treaty was submitted to the Senate.

II

The American people were astonished when the announcement of what had been done was forthcoming. Preoccupied as the country was with vexatious problems growing out of the Civil War, there was no popular demand whatsoever for more territory, let alone this inhospitable region. The unexpectedness of the transaction, the immensity of the domain involved, and an utter ignorance of its nature and resources left the editorial mind groping, but bewilderment, as we shall see, should not be mistaken for opposition. The first reports of the Washington correspondents appear to have been practically unanimous in agreeing that there was little chance of obtaining the necessary two-thirds vote. Charles Sumner, later the leading advocate of the purchase in the Senate, even urged the Russian minister to withdraw the treaty rather than risk the humiliation of almost certain defeat. In certain quarters, however, it was observed that the senators were cautious in speaking of the purchase, for they desired to obtain an expression of public opinion before taking a definite stand.[6]

At this point we must guard against a fundamental error. Many of the secondary accounts state that the treaty encountered from the first an overwhelming storm of opposition, and the writer of one standard text remarked

[6] New York *Herald*, April 1, 2, 3, 1867; Sacramento *Union*, April 2, 4, 1867; San Francisco *Alta California*, April 9, May 17, 1867; Golder, "The Purchase of Alaska," 421.

simply that "the majority of American newspapers . . .
condemned it." [7] For the purpose of checking such statements, the present writer canvassed the views of twenty-one
representative American dailies, and although he found
much indifference and a considerable amount of lukewarm-
ness, he discovered that only one important newspaper
really fought the treaty.[8] This was the New York *Tribune,*
whose editor, the inimitable Horace Greeley, was carrying
on a private feud with Secretary Seward. The data used in
this study would indicate, therefore, that not even during
the period of bewilderment immediately following the announcement of the treaty did a majority of the American
newspapers actually oppose the purchase; and public sentiment, for reasons we shall observe, became increasingly
favorable to the transaction during the ensuing ten days.

There are several reasons why the extent and intensity
of the opposition to the treaty have been exaggerated. The
Secretary of State had incurred a tremendous amount of
unpopularity by siding with President Johnson, and although a number of Radical Republican editors favored
the purchase, they were distressed beyond measure to see
Seward get credit for it. Furthermore, Alaska lent itself to
picturesque objections, which attracted and still attract
much more attention than the matter-of-fact arguments of
its supporters. Such expressions as "Seward's folly," "Es-
quimaux senators," "Walrussia," "Seward's ice box," and
"Johnson's polar bear garden," illustrate this point.[9]

In fact, Alaska was such a fertile field for the punster
that many a newspaper which advocated the purchase

[7] Asa E. Martin, *History of the United States* (Boston, 1931), II, 83.

[8] Nine of these newspapers were Eastern, six Middle Western, and
six Pacific Coast. Two weeklies, the New York *Nation* and *Harper's
Weekly,* opposed the purchase.

[9] For a list of such expressions, see Seward, *op. cit.,* p. 367.

could not refrain from facetious comment—remarks which have since then been interpreted as indicating opposition. An outstanding example is the New York *Herald.* Its erratic editor, James Gordon Bennett, supported the treaty in his editorial columns, but just below them he inserted numerous fictitious advertisements to the effect that impecunious European sovereigns with worthless territory for sale might apply to W. H. Seward, Washington, D.C., and secure a handsome price.[10]

It should further be noted that much of the indifference to the purchase wore off as authentic accounts of the resources of Alaska were made known to the public. This circumstance would suggest that many of the immediate objections were grounded on ignorance. Illustrations of this point are not difficult to find. Contemporary analyses of public opinion agreed that of all the sections of the United States the Pacific Coast area, because of obvious commercial advantages, was most warmly in favor of securing Alaska. Yet the San Francisco *Alta California,* representing a seaport city that stood to gain heavily by the purchase, remarked in its first editorial that Russian America "is intrinsically of no value to us whatever. . . ." After an interval of two days, during which there was doubtless much dusting off of almanacs and admittedly much consulting with merchants and traders who had had direct dealings with Alaska, this same journal took an entirely different stand, and in its succeeding editorials waxed enthusiastic over the economic and commercial possibilities of the contemplated purchase.[11] Discounting for the moment selfish motives, the Pacific Coast appears to have been more favorable to the transaction than the other sections

10 *E.g.,* New York *Herald,* April 12, 1867.
11 San Francisco *Alta California,* March 31, April 3–5, 1867.

because it had more firsthand knowledge of the territory. In other words, the greater the ignorance, the stronger the opposition.

### III

During the early stages of the discussion it appeared that the treaty had more to fear from indifference and lack of information than from active opposition. But Secretary Seward, who was keenly alive to the necessity of enlisting public sentiment on his side, sprang to the breach and carried on a campaign of education (or propaganda), the extent and value of which have not been fully recognized. From the many communications favoring Alaska that came into the Department of State, Seward selected those from influential men like General Halleck, Commodore Rodgers, and Quartermaster General Meigs, and handed them over to the press for publication.[12]

When the Secretary of State learned that the opposition was voicing the same objections that had been used against Louisiana, he went to some expense to have such material copied from the newspapers of 1803, and in turn made it available to the press. With Department of State funds, Seward purchased a number of copies of Sumner's highly informative speech, which he distributed judiciously, and he also sent quantities of useful information to Congress to be printed in public documents.[13] At the same time columns of material provided by the Smithsonian Institution began to appear in the newspapers, and more than one commentator professed to see therein the hand of the Secretary of State.

[12] See Washington *Daily Morning Chronicle*, April 6, 1867.
[13] *House Reports,* 40 Cong., 3 sess., no. 35; *House Executive Documents,* 40 Cong., 2 sess., no. 177.

This assiduous campaign of education did not escape
the attention of alert observers. The New York *Herald*
remarked that "the illustrious Premier is working the telegraphs and the Associated Press in the manufacture of public opinion night and day. . . ." [14] On the floor of Congress
much dissatisfaction was expressed with what Representative Williams termed "a subsidized Press." [15] Before an in-
vestigating committee of the House of Representatives,
Seward later denied vigorously that he had spent more than
$500 of State Department funds for such purposes,[16] and
the smallness of this figure probably accounts for the failure
to attach much significance to his activities. At the time,
however, the effectiveness of the Secretary's campaign was
recognized, for the New York *Herald,* in referring to the
mass of information made public shortly after the announcement of the purchase, observed that, as a consequence, the prospect of ratification was much better than
it had been a week before.[17] A prominent Pacific Coast
newspaper remarked that when the treaty was about to
ground on the shoals of ignorance, Seward gave out the
light.[18]

IV

The situation with regard to the Senate was complex.
The reconstruction controversy, shortly to culminate in the
impeachment trial of President Johnson, had just entered
upon its most acute phase, and the Alaska treaty was re-

14 New York *Herald,* April 9, 1867.
15 *Congressional Globe,* 40 Cong., 2 sess. (Appendix), 485.
16 *House Reports,* 40 Cong., 3 sess., no. 35, 10.
17 New York *Herald,* April 8, 1867.
18 Sacramento *Union,* April 9, 1867.

garded as not only an annoying interruption but as an effort on the part of the harassed Administration to cover its blunders at home with a spectacular triumph in the field of diplomacy. Seward shared the bitterness directed against his superior, and, in addition, his personal enemies were legion. Senators even came to the Russian minister in Washington and asserted that they would vote against the treaty for no other reason than because it bore the Secretary's name.[19] But strong as was this feeling against Seward, the Radical Republicans in the Senate had no desire to fly into the face of public opinion, and, merely to gratify their spite, incur the odium of depriving the United States of a vast and valuable accession to its territorial domain.

It is not surprising, then, that the senatorial ear sought the ground to ascertain what the people wanted. Only the most obtuse and perverse members could have ignored the fact that public sentiment, responding to Seward's campaign of education and other sources of information, was gradually crystallizing behind the treaty. In fact, a number of newspapers called upon the senators in no uncertain terms to lay aside partisanship and vote for the good of the country. As a result of these developments, it was generally observed by April 6, 1867, almost exactly a week after the purchase had been announced, that the chances of ratification, which at first had seemed poor, were decidedly better.[20]

It is against this background that we must consider the part played by Charles Sumner. As chairman of the powerful Senate Committee on Foreign Relations he was in a

---

[19] Golder, "The Purchase of Alaska," 421.

[20] New York *Herald*, April 7, 1867; San Francisco *Evening Bulletin*, April 8, 9, 1867. See also excerpts from Eastern newspapers in Sacramento *Union*, April 9, 1867.

position to make or break the treaty. Although a bitter opponent of Johnson and personally unenthusiastic about Alaska, Sumner was persuaded to support the purchase, and once he had made this decision he went about his task in no halfhearted way. Beyond a doubt his influence, more than that of any other man, carried the treaty through the Senate. It is always difficult to disentangle the motives of men, but an examination of the evidence leads one to conclude with James Ford Rhodes that (1) Sumner was desirous of helping Russia attain her end because of her friendliness during the Civil War and (2) he had some idea of the value of the territory.[21] In any event, it is evident that Russian friendship can not be entirely disregarded as a factor in facilitating the ratification of the treaty.

On April 8, 1867, the treaty was reported out of committee, but on the floor of the Senate it encountered more opposition than is generally known or than the final vote would indicate. A motion for postponement mustered twelve votes, and a half-dozen or so senators who spoke against the treaty pusillanimously abstained from voting or voted affirmatively.[22] Their action indicates a recognition of the gathering public sentiment behind the purchase and an unwillingness to espouse an unpopular cause. Sumner's magnificent three-hour speech was the highlight of the discussion. He outlined at great length the economic aspects of the transaction and he stressed above all the desirability of stealing a march on our ancient foe, Britain, and at the

21 See Edward L. Pierce, *Memoirs and Letters of Charles Sumner* (Boston, 1894), IV, 325; *The Works of Charles Sumner* (Boston, 1875–1883), XI, 183, 216, *et seq.*

22 *Journal of the Executive Proceedings of the Senate of the United States of America*, XV, 675; *Diary of Gideon Welles* (Boston, 1911), III, 83–84; New York *Tribune*, April 10, 1867, cited in Sacramento *Union*, April 12, 1867.

same time doing our ancient friend, Russia, a substantial favor.[23]

Sumner's exposition played an important part in senatorial approval. Also influential were a growing appreciation of Alaska's resources, an unwillingness to affront a friend by failing to complete a negotiation we had initiated, a fear that the Democrats would make political capital out of a rejection of the treaty, and a sensitiveness to an increasingly articulate public opinion.[24] But which of these considerations weighed most heavily with the senatorial mind one can not determine with any degree of definiteness, for the debates took place in secret session. It is clear, however, that Seward lobbied with the utmost assiduity, calling in and making confidants of the more tractable senators, and bringing various kinds of pressure to bear on others. He even held sumptuous banquets for a number of the members, at which it was reported that both solid and liquid refreshments were liberally served.[25] Perhaps the Lord Elgin treaty of 1854 was not the only one in history to be "floated through on champagne." Finally, on April 9, 1867, the Senate consented to ratification, 37 to 2, the negative votes coming from New England, a section which rather feared the competition of the Alaska fisheries.

## V

It was assumed that the House of Representatives would vote the $7,200,000 involved without any question.

---

[23] Sumner, *Works*, XI, 186, *et seq.*

[24] New York *Nation*, April 18, 1867, 305; New York *Evening Post*, April 11, 1867, cited in Sacramento *Union*, April 13, 1867; *House Executive Documents*, 40 Cong., 2 sess., no. 177, 38.

[25] *Memoirs of Cornelius Cole* (New York, 1908), p. 284; Welles, *Diary*, III, 75; New York *Herald*, April 9, 1867.

After a number of delays, among them the unsuccessful impeachment trial, the House turned to this responsibility in an ugly temper. Many of the members deeply resented the failure of the Secretary of State and the Senate to consult them in advance regarding the appropriation. There was also a strong suspicion that Seward had hurried through the official transfer of Alaska so as to be able to confront the House with a *fait accompli*. The resulting debates were prolonged and bitter; but a great deal of the opposition, as has been indicated, was grounded on motives that had nothing at all to do with the merits of the newly acquired territory. In the end, the appropriation carried, 113 to 43.[26]

The debates in the House of Representatives are of vital importance to this study. If one resorts to the simple expedient of listing every argument advanced in support of the purchase, and recording a check every time that argument was repeated, one can obtain a fairly reliable index as to what was uppermost in the minds of the Congressmen. Two general considerations stand so far above all the other two dozen or so arguments presented that it is not necessary to discuss a third.[27] (1) Alaska was economically and commercially valuable, and would augment

[26] Only five dissentient votes came from trans-Mississippi states, and only one of these came from a trans-Rocky state. *Congressional Globe,* 40 Cong., 2 sess., 4055. Much of the opposition centered in New England, with its rival fishing interests, and much of it centered in the upper Mississippi Valley, where there was a provincial outlook and a feeling that the money could better be spent on the improvement of the river.

[27] The chief preoccupation of the House was whether or not it was constitutionally or morally bound to vote an appropriation without having been previously consulted. These considerations had nothing to do with the merits of the territory and are consequently not taken into account in this study.

the national strength. (2) We could not offend Russia, which had evidenced her friendship for us by sending her fleets to America during the Civil War, by throwing a territory which we had solicited back into her face. The first of these arguments was repeated in one form or another about twice as many times as the Russian friendship argument, but the latter was a major concern of both advocates and opponents of the purchase. Many of the Congressmen who opposed the appropriation felt it necessary to point out that although Russia had been and was a friend, she could take no legitimate offense at our refusing to carry through a transaction which was contrary to American interests.

In view of all these facts, it would seem as if not enough emphasis has been placed upon the statement of James G. Blaine, then a member of the House, that there was "little doubt that a like offer from any other European government would have been rejected." [28] The fate of Seward's treaty for the purchase of the Danish West Indies, which was submitted to the Senate in December, 1867, lends support to this view. Although these islands were of considerable strategic value, the treaty, unable to command a single supporter in the Senate Committee on Foreign Relations, died a lingering death.[29]

VI

A prolonged congressional debate will frequently represent with a fair degree of accuracy what the people

---

[28] James G. Blaine, *Twenty Years of Congress from Lincoln to Garfield* (Norwich, Conn., 1886), II, 333.
[29] Pierce, *Sumner*, IV, 328–29.

throughout the country are thinking on a given subject. It is self-evident that the representative who does not make some effort to keep in touch with the currents of public opinion in his district usually does not remain in Congress for long. Fortunately, however, we are not entirely dependent upon statements made in the House of Representatives regarding Alaska for a cross section of public sentiment. The present writer analyzed the arguments presented in twenty-one representative newspapers in exactly the same fashion as he analyzed those in the House. The results are astonishingly similar. Economic considerations lead by a wide margin, with Russian friendship, in almost precisely the same ratio, a good second. There was, however, some little difference in emphasis on the minor arguments,[30] but this development has no important bearing on the main lines of the present study.

It is not unreasonable to conclude that the American people bought Alaska primarily because they thought it was worth the money. Yankee love for a bargain and a highly developed speculative instinct were not to be gainsaid. Russian friendship was of great importance in facilitating the transaction, and it is quite possible that if Russia had not sent her fleets to America during the Civil War the treaty would have failed of ratification. If Professor Golder's revelations had been common knowledge in 1867, the story might well have been different. As it was, a majority of the American people were convinced that disinterestedness and friendship had prompted the course of the Czar in 1863, and they formed their opinions accordingly.

[30] A third argument, which was repeated about half as many times as that regarding Russian friendship, was that the purchase of Alaska would sandwich British Columbia between American territory and make inevitable its annexation.

The whole transaction is but one more example of the unfortunate fact that under a popular government the important thing is frequently not what happened but what the people thought happened.

*This article is significant partly because it was one of the author's earliest forays into American diplomatic history. His interest in the general field was first kindled at Stanford by courses under Professor E. D. Adams; and subsequent residence in Hawaii facilitated access to the manuscript resources of the territorial archives. After this initial taste, Bailey increasingly swung away from political to diplomatic history, with emphasis on public pressures and reactions. Such a backdoor introduction to the field doubtless had much to do with his multidimensional approach to a subject that was traditionally concentrated on formal diplomatic interchanges. The following article, to which an updating commentary is appended, probes annexation sentiment in both the United States and Hawaii.†*

† The companion article, not reprinted because of space limitations, is "Japan's Protest Against the Annexation of Hawaii," *Journal of Modern History*, III (March, 1931), 46–61.

# 5.

# THE UNITED STATES AND HAWAII DURING THE SPANISH-AMERICAN WAR

"We need Hawaii just as much and a good deal more than we did California. It is manifest destiny."
—President McKinley, 1898

I

In 1893 the white property owners in Hawaii, chiefly American or American descended, forcibly overthrew the decadent Hawaiian monarchy and established a republic. Their coup might have failed without the open support, both moral and military, of the United States minister in Honolulu, representing the Republican Administration of President Harrison. A treaty of annexation, hastily drafted in Washington with representatives of Hawaii, was rushed to the United States Senate. But the sands of the Harrison

*The American Historical Review,* XXXVI (April, 1931), 552–60. Reprinted by permission.

Administration ran out, and President Cleveland, a Democrat, took over. Suspecting foul play, he withdrew the pact from the Senate and subsequently revealed such strong opposition to the acquisition of the islands that the annexationists, both in Hawaii and in the United States, abandoned all hope of attaining their objective while he occupied the White House.

On June 16, 1897, the recently inaugurated President McKinley, a Republican, submitted a new treaty of annexation. Although supported by a majority of the senators, it was unable to command the necessary two-thirds vote. It was still languishing in the Senate nearly a year later, when war between Spain and the United States appeared imminent; and the Hawaiian authorities themselves conceded that approval was virtually impossible.[1] In the event of Spanish-American hostilities, several courses lay open to the Honolulu government: first, a proclamation of neutrality; second, silence and passivity; third, acquiescence in a wartime occupation of Hawaii by the Americans; and fourth, active assistance to the United States.

A large and influential group in Hawaii, composed chiefly of royalists and foreigners, feared property losses through Spanish reprisals or postwar claims. They therefore demanded an immediate proclamation of neutrality, even going so far as to urge foreign residents to appeal to their respective governments for protection.[2] The French commissioner in Honolulu announced his intention of joining the representatives of the other powers in action

---

[1] Hatch (Hawaiian minister to the United States) to Cooper (Hawaiian minister of foreign affairs), April 14, 1898. All correspondence herein cited, unless otherwise noted, is to be found in the Archives of Hawaii.

[2] Honolulu *Independent*, April 14, May 6, 9, 1898.

that would insure adequate protection of foreigners in Hawaii. This, of course, would be a kind of interference that the United States could not have viewed with equanimity.[3]

But the Hawaiian government had no assurance that Spain would respect a declaration of neutrality. Madrid could argue with considerable force that since Hawaii had officially consented to a treaty surrendering her sovereignty to the United States, she was, in spirit if not in fact, a part of the United States.[4] The Hawaiian officials agreed, moreover, that a positive stand for neutrality would be interpreted by Americans as nothing short of a slap in the face. It might ruin whatever chances remained of annexation, the specific end for which the existing Honolulu regime had been formed.[5]

## II

For a time a policy of silence and passivity on the part of Hawaii received some, although not very serious, consideration. Such a course, although somewhat objectionable, was preferable to avowed neutrality.[6] But with the outbreak of hostilities active measures were considered more desirable. The Hawaiian representatives in Washington were especially concerned about protecting their tiny republic until such time as annexation could be consummated, while securing for the United States the stra-

[3] Sewall to Sherman (confidential), April 30, 1898, Department of State, Despatches, Hawaii, XXX.

[4] Hatch to Cooper, April 14, 1898; Honolulu *Pacific Commercial Advertiser*, June 10, 1898.

[5] Cooper to Hatch, March 30, 1898; Hatch to Cooper, April 28, 1898; *Advertiser*, June 10, 1898.

[6] Cooper to Hatch, March 30, 1898; Hatch to Cooper, May 4, 1898; *Advertiser*, June 10, 1898.

tegic advantages of the islands. They therefore drafted
a bill authorizing McKinley to use Hawaii for war purposes, and sent it on to Honolulu for approval.[7] But the
scheme met with such serious opposition, both in the
Hawaiian cabinet and in the legislature, that it was not
even submitted to the latter body for approval. Among
the objections were doubts as to the precise meaning of
this proposed measure, an inability to discover whether it
had the approval of Washington, differences of opinion as
to its constitutionality from the standpoint of both America and Hawaii, and fear that such a step would permanently endanger annexation by permitting the United
States in the future to assume control over the islands only
when it was convenient and profitable to do so.[8]

The joint resolution of annexation subsequently introduced into Congress appeared to be a far more satisfactory substitute, although in the event of its failure to
pass, President McKinley might find authority to use Honolulu for war purposes under the provisions of existing
treaties. McKinley may in fact have entertained the idea
of resorting to occupation by executive action as a last
expedient. When the Senate minority was opposing the
passage of the joint resolution, Henry Cabot Lodge wrote:
". . . I do not believe the Senate can hold out very long,
for the President has been very firm about it and means to
annex the Islands any way. I consider the Hawaiian business as practically settled." [9]

[7] *Ibid.*, December 24, 1898.

[8] Sewall to Sherman, May 16, 1898, Department of State, Despatches,
Hawaii, XXXI; Cooper to Hatch, March 30, 1898; Hatch to Cooper,
April 14, 1898; Cooper to Hatch, May 10, 1898; *Advertiser*, May 16, De-
cember 24, 1898.

[9] Lodge to Roosevelt, June 15, 1898, in *Selections from the Correspondence of Theodore Roosevelt and Henry Cabot Lodge*, ed. H. C.
Lodge, I, 311.

### III

The fourth possible course—and the one eventually adopted by the Hawaiian government—was the rendering of active assistance prior to and without any definite assurance of annexation. As a matter of fact, the Honolulu regime at no time favored neutrality, and from the beginning of hostilities was eager to do everything within its power to aid the United States.[10] Nevertheless, there were several problems that had seriously to be considered before an actual proffer of assistance could be made. The oldest pro-annexation newspaper in the islands, although favoring an abandonment of neutrality, wondered how far "we the annexationists and the dominant power here, numbering a small percentage of the inhabitants, have the right to push men, women, and children, who largely outnumber us and do not agree with us, into the risks of war. . . ." [11]

The Honolulu government itself was chiefly puzzled to know whether outspoken adherence to the fortunes of the United States would embarrass that nation by increasing its war responsibilities. Not desiring to take any steps without ascertaining American wishes, President Dole addressed two dispatches to the Hawaiian minister in Washington, F. M. Hatch, instructing him to sound out McKinley. But before a reply was received, news of the outbreak of war reached Hawaii on May 7, 1898. On the following day, Dole, as a result of several conferences with his cabinet, sent a telegram requesting Hatch to ascertain what McKinley wanted the Hawaiian government to do.

---

[10] Undated holograph memorandum of Dole, probably written in January, 1899, and now in the possession of the Historical Commission of the Territory of Hawaii; Cooper to Hatch, May 10, 1898.

[11] *Advertiser,* June 10, 1898.

In case McKinley appeared to favor such a course, Hatch was to "tender to the President the support of this Government in the pending conflict," even to the extent of negotiating a treaty of alliance.[12]

President McKinley greatly appreciated the attitude of the Hawaiian government and promised to make known the wishes of the United States as circumstances developed. But he did not care to go into details about the formal offer just at that time because he believed that Congress would speedily annex the islands. This proffer of assistance before the news of Dewey's victory had come to Hawaii, and in the face of strong local opposition, aroused much more sympathy for the Hawaiian cause in the United States than would otherwise have been possible. It undoubtedly had much to do with the passing of the joint resolution of annexation.[13]

IV

Several weeks before the outbreak of hostilities, L. A. Thurston, a Hawaiian treaty commissioner in Washington who hoped to score a point for annexation, suggested to the Navy Department the desirability of buying all of the available coal in Honolulu for war purposes. Immediately Theodore Roosevelt, then Assistant Secretary of the Navy, began to dictate letters and send off dispatches for that purpose. The purchases were made, and on April 12, 1898, the Hawaiian executive council, on application from the United States consul general, voted to allow four addi-

[12] Cooper to Hatch, May 10, 1898.

[13] Hatch to Cooper, May 22, 26, 1898; Cooper to Hatch, June 10, 1898; Hatch to Cooper, May 22, June 12, 1898; Sewall to Sherman, May 16, 1898, Department of State, Despatches, Hawaii, XXXI; *Congressional Record*, 55 Cong., 2 sess., 5773.

tional esplanade lots for storage purposes.[14] Dole considered this action, if not an actual breach of neutrality, a definite commitment to the side of the United States. With the outbreak of hostilities, the republic of Hawaii, realizing that it would have to pay the price if a Spanish cruiser should appear, extended every possible kind of help to the United States. The islands in fact became a base for operations against the Philippines. A movement to put a battalion of Hawaiian volunteers in Cuba was abandoned only when word came from Washington explaining that more troops could not be used. During the course of the conflict three Philippine-bound transport fleets called at Honolulu, and on every occasion from 3,000 to 5,000 American soldiers were fed and entertained for several days. The civilian population did its utmost to cultivate annexation sentiment among the troops by a lavish display of sympathy and hospitality. The Hawaiian officials, hoping that the soldiers would indirectly impress upon Congress the desirability of possessing the islands, actually turned them loose with an abundance of writing material in the house and senate chambers.[15] The Spanish government was naturally aware of these violations of neutrality, but in the circumstances the forthcoming protest from its vice consul at Honolulu received scant attention.[16]

The position of Dewey after his victory at Manila gave an unexpected twist to the Hawaii question. As the annexation treaty before the Senate appeared to have no

[14] Hatch to Cooper, March 26, 1898; Dole, Memorandum.

[15] *Advertiser*, May 18, June 4, 25, July 6, 1898; Cooper to Hatch, June 10, 1898.

[16] Renjes to Cooper, June 1, 1898; Cooper to Renjes, June 6, 1898; Cooper to Hatch, June 10, 1898.

reasonable hope of success, the Administration proposed a joint resolution. It was promptly introduced into the House on May 4, 1898, and reported out by the Committee on Foreign Affairs on May 17, 1898. Significantly, another joint resolution, supplemented by an elaborate report, had been presented by the Senate Committee on Foreign Relations on March 16, 1898, but no further action had resulted. The failure of this joint resolution, and the introduction of the successful one almost immediately after the news of Dewey's victory, revealed a new appreciation of the strategic importance of Hawaii.

v

Throughout the ensuing debates in Congress, dozens of reasons were presented for and against the acquisition of Hawaii. But most of them had already been discussed at great length during the preceding five years. The position of the islands in relation to the war enabled the annexationists to emphasize three strong arguments, two of which were new and a third of which, although previously considered, appeared in a far stronger light. First, the attitude of the United States toward Hawaii was morally unsound; second, Hawaii was indispensable for the successful prosecution of the war; and third, Hawaii was necessary for the defense of the Pacific seaboard and the Philippines.

The moral argument had considerable force. The United States was flagrantly violating the neutrality of the islands, even though Washington had given formal notice of the existence of war to the other powers (so that they might proclaim neutrality), and was jealousy watching their behavior. The position of America was all the more reprehensible in that she was compelling a weak people to violate the international law that she had in large measure strengthened by her own stand on the *Alabama* claims of Civil War memory. Furthermore, in line with the precedent established by the Geneva arbitral award of 1872, Hawaii would be liable for every cent of damage caused by her dereliction as a neutral, and for the Americans to force her into this position was cowardly and ungrateful. At the end of the war, Spain or cooperating powers might occupy Hawaii indefinitely, if not permanently, to insure payment of damages, with a consequent jeopardizing of the defenses of the Pacific Coast.[17]

The reply of the anti-annexationists was that Hawaii, in return for past protection of independence and favorable tariff arrangements, owed many times over whatever favors she was conferring on the United States. Washington, moreover, was in a position to assume any claims for damages against Hawaii, or to compel prostrate Spain to free Hawaii from liability. To be sure, the payment of money by the United States would not right a wrong; but, on the other hand, Spain would experience difficulty in establishing a case. Although the islands were admittedly flouting neutrality, they had nothing to do with Dewey's victory, and it could not be demonstrated that they were responsible for the loss of the Philippines. One may conclude, therefore, that although the moral argument was undeniably a powerful one, its appeal was more emotional than practical.

---

[17] For these and the following arguments, see *Cong. Record,* 55 Cong., 2 sess., 5771–72, and *passim; Appendix,* 580, 604, 660, 670; *Advertiser,* July 1, 1898.

## VI

The argument that annexation was imperative for prosecuting the war in the Philippines carried, whatever its merits, great weight both in Congress and out. Dewey, surrounded by millions of Spanish subjects, was in grave need of reinforcements, and not to send them to him as speedily as possible would be an act of the basest ingratitude. A coaling station in the Pacific was necessary, for there were only two ships in the Navy that could steam from San Francisco to Manila without recoaling. Colliers might be used, but they were slow, uneconomical, and dangerously uncertain in rough weather. Although the United States had long-term rights to a coaling station at Pearl Harbor, there was no coal there and the inlet could not then be entered by warships. Furthermore, the islands were believed necessary for the health of the soldiers confined on the transports.

The anti-annexationists, on the other hand, pointed out that it would be possible to save more than 400 miles over the Hawaiian route by sailing from San Francisco to the Philippines by way of the Aleutian Islands. There the United States already had Kiska, a far more commodious harbor than that of Honolulu. Although there was no coaling station at Kiska, the Navy could rather easily send ahead a fleet of colliers and establish one. Furthermore, there were a number of ships in the service that could not sail all the way from Honolulu to Manila without exhausting their coal supply, but there was not a single ship that would have to recoal at sea if it went from San Francisco to Manila by way of Kiska. In addition, the chilly northern route would be a more healthful one for the troops.

The annexationists objected that the Kiska route was undesirable because of ice, shoals, fog, currents, and storms, whereas in Hawaii these drawbacks were absent. Besides, there were shops in Honolulu capable of handling almost any repairs. But the difficulties of the northerly voyage were evidently exaggerated. Anti-annexationists pointed out that the Canadian Pacific line, which had made the quickest recorded trips for the crossing of the Pacific, used the route a little south of the Aleutians summer and winter. Moreover, vessels leaving San Francisco for Japan did not waste the additional time necessary for touching at Honolulu unless they had special business there.

## VII

In evaluating the war-measure argument one should note that, assuming the usefulness of the islands for war purposes, there was no need to annex them. Without possession, the Americans were reaping every possible benefit they could have received had the islands been a part of their territory. And these favors, bestowed largely for the purpose of cultivating annexation sentiment, would probably not have been forthcoming so generously if the islands had been annexed.

One may also question the need for excessive haste in reinforcing Dewey. There was no Spanish fleet left in Asiatic waters, and Dewey had Manila at the mercy of his guns. The departure of Cámara's fleet from Cadiz on June 16, 1898,[18] had no appreciable bearing on annexation, for that event was not even mentioned in the debates. Nor was

[18] Cámara appears to have had no intention of attacking Dewey, even if he had reached the Philippines. F. E. Chadwick, *The Relations of the United States and Spain: The Spanish-American War,* II, 387–88.

the possibility of trouble from the German fleet at Manila more than suggested, and by the time the joint resolution passed the Senate, Dewey had received sufficient reinforcements to strengthen himself against a possible German attack. But even if these two threats had appeared to Congress to be serious, help could not have been rushed to Dewey sooner if Hawaii had been a part of the United States.

Nor could annexationists demonstrate that Hawaii was indispensable for the relief of Dewey. Colliers could have been employed, and a coaling station, although it had drawbacks, could have been established, as noted, on the shorter Kiska route. As one Congressman pointed out, if Britain had held the Hawaiian islands at the outbreak of the war, the United States would have sent relief to Dewey without unusual delay. In short, he added, Honolulu was merely a convenience, not a necessity.

One may therefore conclude that annexation was not necessary for the prosecution of the war. Enthusiasm for Dewey overbalanced the actualities of the situation, and the annexationists could hardly be blamed for capitalizing on this feeling. No better evidence of the fallacy of the war-measure argument can be adduced than to point out that with the defeat of Cervera in Cuban waters on July 3, 1898, the contest was won. Yet three days later, largely as a war measure, the Senate approved the joint resolution of annexation and on the next day McKinley signed it.


VIII


The defense argument, which probably received as much attention and carried as much weight as any, was not so much connected with the war then being fought as with a future one. For years eminent naval and military authorities, such as Captain A. T. Mahan, had been urging the acquisition of Hawaii as a first line of defense before some formidable power, say Japan, should seize it as a base against the Pacific Coast. Prior to the Spanish-American War this reasoning had carried little weight. But the operations of Cervera's fleet had so terrified the civilian population of the Atlantic Coast that the strategic importance of Hawaii came to be better appreciated than ever before. Throughout the debates in Congress the note was constantly struck that although the war had added nothing to the defense argument, it had enabled the public to appreciate its force.[19] Significantly, only two of the sixteen members of Congress from the Pacific Coast states voted against annexation.[20]

A less important phase of the defense argument was concerned with the Philippines. The possible retention of these islands at the close of the war would, many Americans believed, justify the annexation of Hawaii, which would allegedly be necessary as a base in holding them. But at the time of the passing of the joint resolution no one could be sure that McKinley would keep the Philippines.[21] One should likewise remember that the United States already had secured rights to a naval station at Pearl Harbor in 1887. The fear was expressed that some other nation might take Hawaii if we did not, and cut off communications with the Far East. But such a stroke would have meant nothing

[19] *Cong. Record*, 55 Cong., 2 sess., 5772, 5795, 5839; *Appendix*, 560, 561, 665.

[20] *Ibid.*, 6019, 6712.

[21] Lodge, *op. cit.*, I, 323, 330; A. L. P. Dennis, *Adventures in American Diplomacy, 1896–1906* (New York, 1928), pp. 80ff.

less than war, so definitely had the United States established what amounted to a protectorate over the islands.[22]

It is clear that if the war had not come when it did, and if Dewey had not triumphed where he did, Hawaii would not have been annexed for some years to come, if ever. The moral argument was more emotional than practical; the war-prosecution argument was fallacious; but the defense argument, as it related to the Pacific Coast, was relatively sound. This argument had been employed for decades, and although the war added nothing to its validity, it added much to its comprehensiveness and force.

∽

*The events of World War II justified the arguments of those American spokesmen who in 1898 had clamored for the Hawaiian Islands as a defensive measure. Even with this springboard of the Pacific under its feet, the United States in 1941–45 was able to prosecute the trans-Pacific war against Japan only with extreme difficulty. Had the Japanese been permitted to annex the islands, the Pearl Harbor attack might well have been launched from Pearl Harbor against the mainland cities of the Pacific Coast.*

*Subsequent writers on annexation have drawn on the author's conclusions, and in so doing have reinforced the essential outlines of the story herein given. Additional de-*

---

[22] *Senate Reports,* 55 Cong., 2 sess., no. 681; *Cong. Record,* 55 Cong., 2 sess., 6305.

*tails may be found in two useful works: William A. Russ, Jr.,* The Hawaiian Republic, 1894–1898 *(Selinsgrove, Pa., 1961), and Merze Tate,* The United States and the Hawaiian Kingdom: A Political History *(New Haven, 1965).*

*One of the prettiest and most persistent myths of American history is that the British "saved" Admiral Dewey from the Germans at Manila Bay in 1898 by a spectacular interposition of their fleet. The author first heard this tale of perfidy as a high school boy from the lips of a Liberty Loan orator in the spring of 1918. His interest still piqued, he later secured manuscript materials from the archives of Germany, Britain, and the United States, and then demolished the original tale (at least to his satisfaction) in 1939. But to his dismay (see quotation p. 105 and also p. 20 of the first essay in the present book), it continues tenaciously in the world of journalism and even historical scholarship. Some of the reasons for this remarkable longevity will become evident as the story unfolds—a story that concerns American, British, and German public sentiment.*

# 6.

# DEWEY AND THE GERMANS
# AT MANILA BAY

"... On 13 August 1898, when the American assault on Manila began, [Captain Sir Edward Chi-
chester] interposed his ships between the Americans
and the Germans, who showed every evidence of
trying to bluff Dewey into calling off the bombardment."
—Samuel E. Morison, *Oxford History of the
American People*, 1965

I

Shortly after the outbreak of the Spanish-American War,
Commodore George Dewey, in command of the
United States Asiatic squadron, left the coast of China for
Manila Bay, and there, on May 1, 1898, completely destroyed the Spanish fleet. Although the city lay at the mercy
of his guns, he could not hope to capture the land fortifica-
tions until troop reinforcements arrived from the United

*The American Historical Review*, XLV (October, 1939), 59–81. Reprinted by permission.

States. Meanwhile he found it necessary to establish a blockade of the bay to prevent succor from reaching the enemy.
These restrictions resulted in serious misunderstandings
with the commander of the German fleet. Reports of what
happened, both factual and fictitious, had such an important bearing on subsequent German–American and British–American relations that it seems desirable to reexamine
the developments at Manila in the light of important new
evidence.[1]

At the outset it must be borne in mind that Dewey was
in a difficult position. First of all, he had to be on constant
guard against possible mine or torpedo attacks from the
surviving officers and men of the defeated squadron. In
addition, he knew that the Spanish government was preparing a superior fleet under Admiral Cámara, who finally
left Cadiz on June 16 for the Philippines. To meet this
threat Dewey had an inadequate force and a seriously de-
pleted supply of ammunition; and despite his urgent appeals the Navy Department seemed to be assembling rein-

---

[1] This article is concerned primarily with the actual happenings at
Manila Bay and their results rather than with the larger aspects of German policy, a subject that has been treated by L. B. Shippee, "Germany
and the Spanish-American War," *American Historical Review*, XXX
(1925), 754–77; J. Fred Rippy, "The European Powers and the Spanish-
American War," *James Sprunt Historical Studies*, XIX (1927), no. 2,
22–52; and Alfred Vagts, *Deutschland und die Vereinigten Staaten in der
Weltpolitik* (New York, 1935), II, Chapter 12. See also *Die grosse Politik
der europäischen Kabinette, 1871–1914*, ed. Johannes Lepsius et al. (Berlin, 1922–27), XV, 3–105. Admiral Arno Spindler of the Kriegswissenschaftliche Abteilung der Marine, Berlin, generously made the entire file
of relevant German documents available to the writer. Except for the logs
of the German ships (photostatic copies of which were secured through
Admiral Spindler), they are contained in bound manuscript volumes entitled "Kriegsführung zwischen Amerika und Spanien" (Cap. II, Litr.
Am., No. 11a) and will hereafter be referred to by the volume number
only. Through the courtesy of the secretary of the British Admiralty
transcripts of all relevant British naval documents were obtained. Mr.
George Dewey, son of Admiral George Dewey, graciously permitted the
writer to examine his father's private papers, some of which are now in
the Dewey Papers at the Library of Congress.

forcements with undue deliberation. The strain on Dewey's nerves was further increased by the absence of cable communications, for it normally took about a week to send a ship to Hong Kong and receive a telegraphic reply from Washington. Moreover, the Filipino insurgents, under Aguinaldo, were attacking Manila, and it was Dewey's task to keep them from getting out of hand while encouraging them to continue their pressure against the enemy. As if all this were not enough, the danger of an epidemic of disease in the fleet was great and the heat almost intolerable. Dewey deserves credit for having kept his head as well as he did.[2]

On May 2, the day after the historic naval battle, a British gunboat, the *Linnet,* arrived in the bay, and during the ensuing weeks varying numbers of British, German, French, Japanese, and Austro-Hungarian warships entered or left the harbor. Since the city was subject to immediate bombardment and was being attacked by semi-civilized Filipinos, it was both necessary and proper for the neutral powers to have men-of-war at hand to protect their nationals and to evacuate them in the event of imminent danger.[3]

[2] A good picture of Dewey's difficulties, though inaccurate in some details, appears in the *Autobiography of George Dewey* (New York, 1913), pp. 234–82. The portions of this book that relate to operations in the Philippines are based on a manuscript prepared under Dewey's direction by Commander Nathan Sargent and entitled "The Preparations at Hong Kong, Battle of Manila Bay, Enforcement of Blockade, and Operations Resulting in the Surrender of Manila" (hereinafter cited as Dewey–Sargent Manuscript). On November 10, 1904, Dewey attested with his signature his approval of the contents. Dewey Papers, Library of Congress. In letters to his son Dewey repeatedly complained of the heat, writing on one occasion that the temperature rarely dropped below 90°. Dewey to George Dewey, June 30, 1898, Dewey Private Collection, Chicago.

[3] The commander of the *Linnet* reported that the single ship under his command "would probably be inadequate to afford efficient protection on shore." Smythe to Commodore Holland (Hong Kong), May 5, 1898, China Letters, 1898, British Admiralty.

The *Linnet* was reinforced on May 8 by the armored cruiser *Immortalité*, commanded by Captain Edward Chichester, who became senior British officer. During most of the month of May and part of June, Great Britain had the strongest neutral force in the Philippines—the two vessels mentioned and three gunboats. This presence caused no concern in the United States, for the British were the heaviest foreign investors in the island, and, disturbed by the growing rivalry with Germany, they were conspicuously friendly to the Americans. The Germans were represented by the second-class cruiser *Irene* and the third-class cruiser *Cormoran,* which, in response to an order issued by the Kaiser on April 28 to protect German nationals in the Philippines, had arrived on May 6 and May 9, respectively.[4] Several days later Prince Henry of Prussia, then in the Far East, and the German consul at Manila telegraphed the foreign office in Berlin that, according to the information they had received, the Filipinos might welcome a German protectorate. Foreign Secretary Bülow thereupon suggested to the Kaiser that a naval officer of high rank, Vice-Admiral Otto von Diederichs, be sent to Manila, where he could observe the situation at first hand and report on the sentiment and position of the natives.[5] The Kaiser gave his approval, but it was not until June 2 that the following orders were cabled to Diederichs, who was then refitting at Nagasaki, Japan:

His Majesty the Emperor and King orders the Commander of the Squadron to proceed to Manila in order to

---

[4] Summary of ship movements in commanding admiral (Berlin) to foreign office (copy), August 20, 1898, Band 3a. See also Admiral Otto von Diederichs, "Darstellung der Vorgänge vor Manila von Mai bis August 1898," *Marine Rundschau,* XXV (March, 1914), 253 (hereinafter cited as Diederichs, "Darstellung der Vorgänge").

[5] *Grosse Politik,* XV, 34–35.

form personally an opinion on the Spanish situation, mood of natives, and foreign influence upon the political changes. I shall leave it to you to travel either with the "Kaiser" [flagship] or by mail steamer and have the "Kaiser" follow later on. Also protect with the Squadron German interests in the West-Caroline Islands, Palaos Islands. Send a ship [there] as soon as the Americans do the same.[6]

An examination of the German naval records reveals that no further orders were dispatched to Diederichs from Berlin.[7] The published correspondence of the foreign office indicates that, from the standpoint of international politics, the German fleet was sent to Manila, not to interfere with the Americans, but to strengthen the German claim to the Philippines, in the event that the United States should decide not to annex them.[8]

II

On June 12 the German vice-admiral, having left the *Kaiser* to join him later, arrived at Manila on the first-class cruiser *Kaiserin Augusta.* The beleaguered Spaniards were greatly heartened by the presence of this distinguished offi-

[6] Commanding admiral to Diederichs, June 2, 1898, Band 1.

[7] On July 12 Diederichs informed Captain Chichester that he had received no orders from home since leaving Nagasaki. Chichester to Holland, July 14, 1898, China Letters, 1898. This report is published in *British Documents on the Origins of the War, 1898–1914,* ed. G. P. Gooch and Harold Temperley (London, 1927), I, 105–07. On July 19 the German foreign office informed the commanding admiral, in Berlin, that judging from the documents available there was no reason "to give political instructions to the chief of the squadron [Diederichs]." This would indicate that, up to this time at least, none had been sent. Richthofen to commanding admiral, July 19, 1898, Band 2. Diederichs himself later wrote that he had received no political instructions and only one order of a military nature from his immediate superior—"to maintain the strictest neutrality." Diederichs, "Darstellung der Vorgänge," p. 257.

[8] Shippee, "Germany and the Spanish-American War," 774; Vagts, II, 1327.

cer, who outranked Dewey, and it was widely rumored in Manila that he had come to take sides against the Americans. Although Diederichs attempted to discourage these wholly groundless reports, the Spaniards continued to regard the Germans as more friendly than the other neutrals, and paid marked attention to them.[9] On or about June 24 the Spanish governor general went so far as to propose to Diederichs that the neutral powers take over Manila *in deposito*. But the German commander, pleading lack of instructions and the American blockade, refused to have anything to do with the offer.[10]

Dewey was naturally displeased with the improvement of Spanish morale which had resulted from the arrival of the *Kaiserin Augusta* on June 12.[11] American relations with Germany had not been particularly cordial since the Samoan imbroglio of the 1880's, and Dewey's suspicions of the Germans had already been aroused by several unfortunate incidents at Hong Kong and by the unwillingness of

[9] Several purely accidental developments that gave rise to the false Spanish hopes are described in commander of *Irene* (Obenheimer) to Diederichs, May 17, 1898, Band 2; Diederichs to commanding admiral, June 25, 1898, Band 3a. Chichester reported that the Spaniards were "elated" by the arrival of the Germans and suspicious of the British. Chichester to Holland, May 12, June 16, June 23, 1898, China Letters, 1898.

[10] Diederichs to commanding admiral (telegram, Hong Kong), June 27, 1898, Band 2. See also *Grosse Politik*, XV, 44, 55–56. Diederichs' explanatory dispatch differs somewhat from the cablegram and indicates that the governor general proposed to offer a Spanish protectorate to the Filipinos; that they were to lay down their arms; and that the Germans were to take over the arms and guarantee a fulfillment of Spanish promises. Diederichs replied that he had no instructions to take such a step and that if it were undertaken all the neutrals would have to participate. Diederichs to commanding admiral, June 25, 1898, Band 3a.

[11] As late as November 10, 1898, the United States chargé in Berlin complained to a "high" official in the foreign office that it was "almost certain" that Spanish resistance had been prolonged by the hope of assistance which had resulted from the presence of the German fleet. Jackson to Day, November 10, 1898, Dispatches, Germany, LXVII. (All Department of State records for this period have been transferred to the National Archives.)

the German ships at Manila to respect his blockade.[12] Nor could he have failed to realize that the ultimate disposition of the Philippines was in doubt, that the Germans were on the prowl for colonies, and that their squadron at Manila was commanded by a forceful officer who had become something of a hero in Germany as a result of his occupation of Kiao-chau in 1897.[13] On the day of Diederichs' arrival, therefore, Dewey sent a cablegram to the Navy Department, in which he described the general situation as regards the insurgents and made his first reference to the Germans: "The German Commander-in-Chief arrived today. Three German, two British, one French, one Japanese man-of-war, now in port; another German man-of-war is expected. I request the departure of the *Monadnock* and the *Monterey* may be expedited." [14] Although a hasty reading of this message suggests that Dewey was urging reinforcements primarily because of a German threat, his private correspondence reveals that at this time he was much more concerned about the approaching Spanish fleet.[15] We should also observe that his own force of six cruisers and two smaller craft was probably more than a match for the three German men-of-war then in the harbor.

---

[12] Misunderstanding with the Germans at Hong Kong is described in Dewey's *Autobiography,* pp. 181–85, which omits a few details that appear in the Dewey–Sargent Manuscript. Both accounts indicate, however, that amicable relations were restored. See also the story in the New York *Tribune,* June 2, 1898. For Dewey's early difficulties with the Germans over the blockade see Dewey, *Autobiography,* pp. 254–56.

[13] White to Day, June 18, 1898, Dispatches, Germany, LXVI.

[14] Dewey to Secretary of Navy (telegram), June 17, 1898 (Hong Kong; June 12, Cavite), Ciphers Received, No. 2, Navy Department, Washington, D.C.

[15] See Edwin Wildman, "What Dewey Feared in Manila Bay," *Forum,* LIX (May, 1918), 518–19. In the Dewey–Sargent Manuscript Dewey states, with memory perhaps a bit clouded by the events of the intervening six years, that he had the Germans definitely in mind. He also expressed the belief that they had instructions to goad him into some overt act of which they could take advantage.

III

Late in the month of June the picture was changed by
the arrival of two additional German cruisers, the *Kaiser*
(June 18) and the *Prinzess Wilhelm* (June 20). The presence of Diederichs had caused considerable misgivings in
American quarters, and the increase of the fleet to five ships
was a blunder. The augmented force was not only out of
all proportion to the German commercial stake in the
Philippines, but it was so much stronger than Dewey's
squadron as to be regarded by the Americans as a grave
discourtesy.[16] Diederichs later explained the gathering of
the five cruisers at Manila as due to the necessity of meeting
a relief ship.[17] But the presence of this unnecessarily powerful force inevitably led to a misconstruction of Diederichs'
intentions.[18]

[16] The figures for 1896 and 1897, the most satisfactory available, indicate that Germany ranked sixth among the foreign nations in imports
from the Philippines, while Great Britain was first. In exports to the
islands Great Britain was first, with three times the trade of Germany,
which occupied second place. Bureau of Statistics, Treasury Department,
*Monthly Summary of Commerce and Finance of the United States* (Washington, D.C., 1899), p. 1315. On the basis of tonnage and weight of metal
the German fleet was perhaps 20 percent stronger than Dewey's. Diederichs' flagship, the *Kaiser,* was the only ship of the armored class in either
fleet. It had a displacement of 7,531 tons and the *Kaiserin Augusta,* 6,331
tons, as compared with Dewey's largest ship, the *Olympia* (5,800 tons).
T. A. Brassey, ed., *The Naval Annual, 1898* (Portsmouth, 1898), pp. 300,
303, 341–43.
[17] Diederichs, "Darstellung der Vorgänge," pp. 253–54. See also *Grosse
Politik,* XV, 40; *Brit. Documents,* I, 106.
[18] Diederichs repeatedly noted in his official reports that the presence
of so many German ships was a mistake. As early as June 25 he expressed
the hope that the sending away of a part of his squadron would quiet
the anti-German rumors. He also stated that he thought the presence
of a commanding officer of his high rank was unfortunate. Diederichs
to commanding admiral, June 25 (Band 3a), August 2, August 9, 1898
(Band 3b).

Meanwhile public opinion in the United States had become definitely disturbed by the presence of the German fleet at Manila. From time to time an occasional item had appeared in the press referring to the friendly relations between the Spaniards and the Germans and to the attempts of the latter to disregard Dewey's blockade. But not until the report reached the United States that Diederichs had been ordered to Manila did the press evidence anything like widespread solicitude.[19] On June 13 the German ambassador in Washington, Theodor von Holleben, cabled the foreign office that the news had made an unfortunate impression.[20] Five days later the Navy Department published Dewey's cablegram announcing the arrival of Diederichs and requesting that the monitors be expedited. This added to the public disquietude, as did the increase of the German squadron to five ships. But such interest quickly faded away, for the main preoccupation was with operations in Cuban waters.[21]

Late in June, Dewey began to show more anxiety about Diederichs' force. Admiral Cámara was approaching the

[19] The following newspapers were examined in connection with this study: New York *Herald,* New York *Journal,* New York *World,* New York *Times,* Chicago *Tribune,* Chicago *Record,* and London *Times.* The symposia published in the *Literary Digest* and *Public Opinion* proved useful. New England sentiment is emphasized in Clara Eve Schieber, *The Transformation of American Sentiment toward Germany, 1870–1914* (Boston, 1923), Chapter 3.

[20] *Grosse Politik,* XV, 40. See also Holleben's dispatch of June 17, 1898, *ibid.,* pp. 40–42.

[21] See particularly New York *Herald,* June 18, 1898; *Public Opinion,* XV (July 7, 1898), 7–8. One explanation of the lack of interest in the Germans at Manila is that Dewey placed the newspaper correspondents attached to the fleet on their honor not to give a sensational interpretation to the happenings and thus make his position more difficult. John Barrett (one of the correspondents in question), "Admiral George Dewey," *Harper's Monthly Magazine,* XCIX (October, 1899), 806–07. Some of the German newspapers resented American criticism of Diederichs' strong force. See Vagts, II, 1332.

Suez Canal (he arrived on June 26); the Germans were maintaining cordial relations with the French naval force in the bay; and they were apparently fraternizing with the Spaniards.[22] The German squadron in its comings and goings was evincing a disposition to ignore the American blockade, especially at night; and several disagreeable incidents occurred, such as firing over German ships to bring them to a stop.[23] Diederichs maintained, then and later, that since no blockade had been announced in the conventional manner, there was no blockade. Nevertheless he reported that such restrictions as existed were very considerate of neutrals and that he was taking every precaution to avoid irritating Dewey and causing him to become more exacting.[24]

Diederichs may have been sincere in declaring that he was doing his best to keep on good terms with the Ameri-

[22] Diederichs referred at some length to his relations with the French commander in his report of August 28, 1898, Band 4. The present writer's request to examine the French naval documents elicited the reply that they were not open beyond 1870. Such intercourse as there was between the Germans and the Spaniards probably would not have excited undue comment had it not been for the international situation and the rumors of German intervention.

[23] Dewey's *Autobiography*, pp. 252–67. On July 9 Chichester reported that the German ships had been constantly leaving and arriving at Manila at night and burning searchlights and "making flashing signals" between the ships at Manila and those approaching from Mariveles. "Their ways," he added, "are certainly mysterious, but the American officials look on the same as a 'game of Bluff.'" Chichester to Holland, July 9, 1898, China Letters, 1898. The covering report of Vice-Admiral Seymour stated: "The proceedings of the German Ships in the Philippines, regardless of the wishes and interests of the United States Admiral, are certainly a breach of courtesy towards him, if not indeed more serious." Seymour to secretary of admiralty, July 30, 1898, *ibid*. The reports of Chichester and of his superiors at Hong Kong indicate that the British were annoyed by the attitude of the Germans toward the Americans. See particularly Chichester to Holland, July 25, 1898, *ibid*.

[24] Diederichs to commanding admiral, June 27, 1898 (telegram, Band 2), July 7, 1898 (Band 3a); July 25, August 9, 1898 (Band 3b).

cans, yet the simple fact is that he did not succeed in doing so. If the German vice-admiral had been more willing to yield form to expediency as regards the blockade, if he had not been conscious of the superiority of his fleet, and if he had entertained more respect for American discipline and fighting prowess, he probably would not have given the Americans so definite an impression that he was deliberately trying to flout their authority.[25]

## IV

The growing tension came to a head early in July. At that time the Filipino insurgents, tacit allies of Dewey, were attacking a Spanish force at Isla Grande, in Subic Bay. The German cruiser *Irene* arrived and, for what its commander claimed were humanitarian reasons, began to evacuate some of the noncombatants.[26] Informed of this apparent interference in behalf of the enemy, Dewey dispatched the *Raleigh* and the *Concord* to end German intervention. When the American ships entered the bay on July 7 they passed the *Irene,* which was leaving, and nothing happened. Dewey believed, or professed to believe, that when the Germans saw the American ships approaching they slipped their cable and hurried out.[27] But the log of the *Irene* and the lengthy report of her commander in-

[25] Diederichs reported unfavorably on American marksmanship and discipline. To commanding admiral, August 28, 1898, Band 4.

[26] Commander of *Irene* (Obenheimer) to Diederichs, July 7, 1898, Band 3a.

[27] At the meetings of the General Board at Newport, R.I., during 1902 and 1903, Dewey excitedly related how he sent two of his smaller ships so that the *Irene* would not avoid a fight if looking for one. Statement of Lieut. Col. L. C. Lucas, January 30, 1930, File 00, Naval Records and Library, Navy Department, Washington, D.C. See also Dewey–Sargent Manuscript.

dicate that the possibility of hostilities with the Americans was not even considered.[28]

Dewey promptly telegraphed the following report of the *Irene* incident to the Navy Department:

Aguinaldo informed me his troops had taken all of Subic Bay except Isla Grande, which they were prevented from taking by the German man-of-war 'Irene.' On July 7th sent the 'Raleigh' and the 'Concord' there; they took the island and about 1,300 men, with arms and ammunition. No resistance. The 'Irene' retired from the bay on their arrival.[29]

The Navy Department released the telegram to the press on July 13, the day it was received. The suggestion that the Germans were trying to interfere with Dewey's conquest of the Philippines aroused a flurry of excitement in the American press—the greatest, in fact, created by any of the misunderstandings arising between Dewey and the Germans. It was even rumored on both sides of the Atlantic that the American commander was attempting to conceal the extreme gravity of the situation.[30] But public interest soon

[28] The log of the *Irene* has this matter-of-fact entry for July 7, 1898: "7.10 American cruiser Raleigh and gunboat Concord passed by" (Kriegswissenschaftliche Abteilung der Marine, Berlin). At the end of his nineteen-page report the commander of the *Irene* casually mentions the arrival of the American ships (Obenheimer to Diederichs, July 7, 1898, Band 3a). If the Germans had anticipated trouble with the Americans, they would undoubtedly have taken precautions, and this fact would have been recorded in the log. The *Raleigh* cleared for action before meeting the *Irene;* the *Concord* after. Since the Americans attacked the Spaniards upon arriving, this would indicate that their preparations were not made for the Germans. The *Concord* otherwise would have cleared for action earlier (logs of *Concord* and *Raleigh,* July 7, 1898, Bureau of Navigation, Navy Department).

[29] Dewey to Secretary of Navy (telegram), July 13, 1898 (Hong Kong), Ciphers Received, No. 2.

[30] New York *Journal,* July 14, 1898; New York *Herald,* July 14, 15, 16, 19, 1898; London *Times,* July 15, 16, 1898; *Literary Digest,* XVII (July 23, 1898), 91–93.

shifted from faraway Manila to the more exciting events connected with the surrender of Santiago, in Cuba.

v

News of the friction at Manila following the *Irene* incident came to the American public largely through rumor and exaggeration. Thoroughly aroused by the conduct of the Germans, Dewey sent Flag-Lieutenant Thomas M. Brumby to Diederichs later on that same day, July 7, with a summation of American grievances growing out of alleged infractions of the blockade. The vice-admiral expressed surprise on learning of these incidents, and this is not remarkable when one notes that there is no mention of some of them in his detailed reports or in those of his subordinates. Diederichs, according to Brumby, "disclaimed *any intention of interfering in the least with Admiral Dewey's operations* and said he would as far as possible avoid all movements of his ships etc. at night—that Admiral Dewey had conducted the blockade in the mildest way possible and he did not want to embaarrass [*sic*] him in the slightest." At the conclusion of his report Brumby added: "The Admiral was most polite. He repeated his statement that he did not wish to interfere in any way with Admiral Dewey's operations, and I was convinced of his sincerity and personal probity." [31]

[31] Typewritten report of Brumby, dated July 7, 1898, Dewey File, Naval Records and Library. The italics are Brumby's. Diederichs' report to the commanding admiral is dated July 14, 1898, Band 3a. Diederichs gives the date of Brumby's visit as July 8, but the 7th is confirmed by the log of the *Olympia*, Dewey's flagship. Captain Edward L. Beach, who was then a lieutenant on the *Baltimore*, remarked to the present writer (December 21, 1938) that the difficulties at Manila were largely due to the fact that the Germans had no naval tradition and lacked "sea manners."

On July 10, three days later, Diederichs sent Flag-Lieutenant Hintze to Dewey with a verbal explanation of the
complaints that had been presented by Brumby. Hintze
was also instructed to refer to the fact that the *Irene,* on
June 27, had been improperly stopped and boarded by the
United States revenue cutter, *McCulloch,* off Corregidor.
This was too much for Dewey, who, according to Hintze's
report, cried out:

> "Why, I shall stop each vessel whatever may be her colors!
> And if she does not stop I shall fire at her! And that means
> war, do you know, Sir? And I tell you if Germany wants war,
> all right, we are ready. With the English I have not the slight-
> est difficulty, they always communicate with me, etc." Ad-
> miral Dewey became more and more excited.
> When the phrases: "If Germany wants war," etc., began
> to recur the flaglieutenant [Hintze] left.[32]

Diederichs, who fortunately realized that Dewey was
laboring under a great strain, appears not to have been
unduly disturbed by this outburst and took no immediate
action.[33] By the next day, July 11, Dewey had apparently

[32] Diederichs (countersigned by Hintze) to commanding admiral,
July 14, 1898, Band 3a. A part of this conversation appears in *Grosse
Politik,* XV, 62, n. In 1904 Dewey described the scene as follows in the
Dewey–Sargent Manuscript:

> "Do you want war with us?" asked the Admiral impressively.
> "Certainly not," replied the German.
> "Well, it looks like it, and you are very near it; and"—his voice ris-
> ing in pitch and intensity until it could be heard in the officers' quarters
> below—"and you can have it, sir, as soon as you like."
> The German backed in consternation away from the Admiral, and
> in an awed voice said to Lieutenant Brumby, "Your Admiral seems to
> be much in earnest."
> "Yes," replied Brumby, "and you can be certain that he means every
> word he says."

The Hintze account is the only one the writer has found that was
set down immediately after the incident. All the numerous versions, some
of which emanated from men present, agree that Dewey threatened war.

[33] Diederichs to commanding admiral, July 14, 1898, Band 3a.

recovered himself, and he replied by letter to Hintze's inquiries regarding the *Irene,* insisting that as commander of the blocking squadron he had a right, in the case of any vessel, to make "such inquiries as are necessary to establish her identity." Diederichs interpreted this as meaning that Dewey was going so far as to claim the *droit de visite* for men-of-war. He thereupon communicated with the commanders of the other neutral squadrons to ascertain their interpretation of this point. Those who gave definite replies—and this list included Captain Chichester—agreed that the ordinary rules of visit and search did not apply to men-of-war, even in a blockade. The tension was relieved on July 14 when Dewey wrote that by "inquiries" to "establish identity" he did not necessarily mean visit and search but rather the ordinary means of communication between vessels.[34] With this clarification Diederichs apparently abandoned his efforts to interest the other neutral commanders, and eventually went so far as to concede that Dewey might board his ships at night when identification was otherwise difficult.[35]

The week following the *Irene* incident, July 7 to 14, was undoubtedly the most critical period in the controversy between Dewey and the Germans. Diederichs issued explicit orders to the captains of his ships to repel, by force if necessary, any attempt on the part of the Americans to board them, except at night.[36] If Dewey had attempted to

---

[34] The correspondence between Diederichs and the neutral commanders appears in summary form or enclosures in *ibid.* Diederichs' report squares with that of Chichester, who wrote (July 14) that visits to establish nationality were "quite legitimate" but that ordinary search was "inadmissible and resentable." *Brit. Documents,* I, 106. There were also difficulties between the Germans and the Americans over the blockade of Cuba. See Vagts, II, 1351, n.

[35] Diederichs to commanding admiral, August 9, 1898, Band 3b.

[36] Diederichs to cruiser commanders, July 11, 1898 (copy), Band 3a.

exercise at this time the right that he apparently claimed, he would have been fired on. And there can be no doubt that he was in a mood to fight back.[37] Yet it seems unlikely that with his inferior force and other handicaps he would have provoked hostilities. Diederichs apparently did not fear serious developments, for on July 9, two days after the Subic Bay incident and one day before Dewey's outburst, the *Irene* left the Philippines. It is also significant that Captain Chichester, in reporting the dispute, referred to it as "a slight case of friction." [38]

VI

The attitude of Chichester throughout this period appears to have had a quieting effect. Although the British maintained a strict neutrality during the war, there could be no doubt that their sympathies lay with the Americans and that they viewed with suspicion the activities of the Germans in Philippine waters.[39] Chichester was under

[37] Suspecting the worst of German intentions, Dewey had already worked out a plan for engaging the superior German force, as any prudent commander would have done in the circumstances, but with less prudence he had discussed it in the presence of newspaper correspondents (John Barrett, *Admiral George Dewey* [New York, 1899], pp. 103, 130ff.; Oscar King Davis, *Released for Publication* [Boston, 1925], pp. 12–13). Frederick Palmer, who ghosted Dewey's *Autobiography*, remembers that this is one of the two things that Dewey wanted omitted. The other was what he had told Hintze. (Conversation with writer, March 25, 1937.) Dewey said to the French admiral, when the latter was about to leave Manila, that he had made one mistake—" 'I should have sunk that squadron over there'—pointing to the Germans" (Dewey–Sargent Manuscript).

[38] *Brit. Documents*, I, 105.

[39] On June 26 Dewey cabled (from Cavite): "The British Consul informed me today he has orders to telegraph in cipher his Government movements of the German men-of-war in the Philippines." Dewey to Secretary of Navy (telegram), July 1, 1898 (Hong Kong), Ciphers Received, No. 2. The present writer was informed by Sir Stephen Gaselee, head librarian of the British foreign office, that the British consul did not officially report anything relevant to German–American friction.

orders to pursue a neutral course, and, although he apparently did not depart from the strict letter of his instructions, he and his men maintained most cordial personal relations with the Americans—a relationship displeasing to the German commander.[40] It was widely rumored, as Diederichs probably knew, that in the event of a clash between Dewey and the Germans, the British would be ranged on the side of the Americans.[41] Whatever the basis for these reports—and there appears to have been none—American morale was undoubtedly improved by the presence of the British and by their sympathetic attitude. Chichester's generally correct course at this time won the warm commendation of his superior at Hong Kong, and, in January, 1899, the Order of St. Michael and St. George.[42]

Diederichs repeatedly complained that Captain Chichester and other British officers, as well as the British consul, were circulating vicious anti-German rumors. He further charged that the English newspapers of Eastern Asia picked up these reports and embroidered them.[43]

[40] Chichester to Holland, May 20, 1898, China Letters, 1898; Diederichs to commanding admiral, August 28, 1898, Band 4.

[41] One reporter related that when Diederichs asked Chichester what he would do if the Germans interfered with the Americans, the latter replied "There is but one man who knows what I would do, and his name is Dewey" (New York *Tribune*, July 20, 1898). This story was widely circulated.

[42] London *Gazette*, January 10, 1899. Vice-Admiral E. H. Seymour, Commander-in-Chief, China (Hong Kong), concurred "in the opinion expressed by Commodore Holland as to the very zealous, tactful, and efficient way in which Captain Sir Edward Chichester has carried out his duties. . . . Not only did Captain Chichester well maintain British interests, but I have reason to know that he was looked up to and consulted by Foreign Officers, and greatly contributed at times to the soothing of excited feelings" (Seymour to secretary of admiralty, September 8, 1898, China Letters, 1898).

[43] To commanding admiral, July 14, 1898 (Band 3a); July 25, August 2, August 9, 1898 (Band 3b). In one of his last reports Diederichs recommended that the Germans buy a Far Eastern newspaper for the purpose of counteracting British propaganda. To commanding admiral, August 28, 1898, Band 4.

There was doubtless much substance to this accusation.[44] Although the European press (particularly that of Germany) gave loud warning that British propagandists were poisoning the wells of German–American amity, and although American newspapers advised their readers to make due allowances, such colored or false reports doubtless had considerable influence on opinion in the United States.[45]

It is also to be noted that during these months a number of German newspapers were outspoken in their desire for the Philippines and in their dislike of the Americans. The British republished many such statements,[46] which in turn found their way through the Associated Press and other channels into the American journals, thus providing a lurid background for Diederichs' activities.[47] The Germans complained bitterly, but without effect, of this practice; and the American ambassador in Berlin, Andrew D. White, repeatedly advised the Department of State to be on its guard.[48]

[44] Vice-Admiral Seymour admitted that the Hong Kong press contributed to German–American misunderstanding (to secretary of admiralty, June 30, 1898, China Letters, 1898). Diederichs quotes a letter from Dewey (April 16, 1899) in which the latter states that their differences were of "newspaper manufacture" ("Darstellung der Vorgänge," p. 278).

[45] The Shanghai *Mercury,* whose reporter claimed to represent the London *Central News,* printed a story about the Germans "slobbering over the Spanish" so false that Joseph Stickney, Manila correspondent of the New York *Herald,* warned his readers to be on their guard (New York *Herald,* June 4, 1898); see also another warning from Stickney (*ibid.,* July 19).

[46] See the London *Times,* June 4, 13, 15, July 2, 4, 7, 8, 15, 1898.

[47] New York *Herald,* May 3, 5, 12, 13, June 15, 16, 18, 20, 29, July 1, 1898; New York *Tribune,* May 13, June 12, 1898.

[48] White reported that the "English journals and news agencies" had been ready to circulate and develop "everything which could arouse prejudice in the United States against Germany, and that one of them, on at least one occasion, resorted to the invention of fictitious news for this purpose" (to Day, August 12, 1898, Dispatches, Germany, LXVI). Secretary of State Day also tried to counteract these rumors (Rippy, *Sprunt Hist. Studies,* XIX, 31, n.; Vagts, II, 1330ff.). See the complaint of Holleben (*Grosse Politik,* XV, 40–42).

VII

Following the mid-July crisis at Manila, all danger of a clash seems to have passed.[49] Dewey's position was considerably strengthened by the destruction of Cervera's squadron off Santiago on July 3 and by Cámara's recall from Suez on July 5. The first American transports had arrived on June 30 and with them the cruiser *Charleston,* which strengthened Dewey's fleet and brought much-needed ammunition. The departure of the *Irene* on July 9 reduced the German squadron to four ships, and the second contingent of American troops reached Manila on July 17. The third arrived on July 31, and on August 4 the powerful monitor *Monterey,* with two twelve-inch and two ten-inch guns, steamed into the harbor. Dewey felt stronger than the Germans for the first time since their fleet had been augmented.[50]

All these developments contributed to an improvement of the atmosphere at Manila. Diederichs made virtually no references to the Americans in his lengthy reports, except to complain of the machinations of the British and

[49] On July 26 Dewey cabled from Cavite: "Hope monitor [*Monterey*] will be here before the surrender [of Manila] to prevent possible interference by the Germans" (Dewey to Secretary of Navy, July 26, 1898 [July 30 from Hong Kong], Ciphers Received, No. 2). It is unlikely that Dewey was as seriously concerned about the Germans at this late date as the telegram suggests; it is more probable that he was using the German menace as a means of hastening the *Monterey,* which he needed for reducing the defenses of the city. His private letters to Consul General Wildman, at Hong Kong, reveal that he was relieved by the improvement of relations with the Germans. Wildman, *Forum,* LIX, 513–35.

[50] Dewey, *Autobiography,* p. 272. The other monitor, the *Monadnock,* arrived on August 16. Diederichs learned that Chichester expressed satisfaction at her arrival and that the British commander and Dewey both regarded the reinforced American fleet as stronger than that of the Germans (Diederichs to commanding admiral, August 28, 1898, Band 4).

to note that the attitude of the German officers and men toward the Americans was "formal but not unfriendly." [51] Personal intercourse between Diederichs and Dewey developed increased cordiality, and the American told the German consul that reports of friction were largely lies. [52] The German commander was apparently trying to be conciliatory, and he even advised his superiors against entertaining any hope of acquiring the Philippines. [53]

The Department of State appears to have been cognizant of this changed atmosphere. In fact, one of the most surprising things about the whole episode is the apparent lack of concern in official Washington. Not until July 22, more than a month after Diederichs had arrived at Manila and about ten days after the *Irene* excitement had flared up and died down, did the Department of State send to Ambassador White, in Berlin, its only instruction relating to the German fleet. This was as follows:

> Personal and confidential. German Ambassador made a friendly call on President today. All indications seem favorable to good relations. Presence of so large a German fleet at Manila is the subject of much comment in the press and among our people. Can you give us your view as to whether it is intended to keep fleet at Manila, and whether it is likely to be recalled or reduced, without making embarrassing inquiries, official or otherwise? [54]

This, it will be observed, was far from being a protest.

[51] Same to same, July 25, 1898 (Band 3b); July 30, 1898 (telegram, Band 2); August 9, 1898 (Band 3b).

[52] Same to same, August 28, 1898, Band 4. See also Vagts, II, 1353.

[53] Diederichs to commanding admiral, August 2, 1898, Band 3b. Diederichs was careful to inform Dewey of the arrival and departure of German ships (August 9, 1898, Band 3b). He also permitted the Americans to send officers aboard his ships at night (August 9, 1898 [telegram], Band 3b).

[54] Day to White (telegram), July 22, 1898, Germany, Instructions, XX.

Eight days later, on July 30, White was able to report the result of a conference with the acting minister for foreign affairs, Baron von Richthofen.

He declared, with every appearance of sincerity, that the only reason for sending the five ships originally and for retaining the three [four] ships in that harbor now has been that, the reason for their remaining at Kiao Chou having ceased, public opinion here as well as at Manila earnestly insisted on a demonstration that Germany intends fully to protect her subjects; that there is not a word of truth in the statement that orders had been issued to their admiral or that permission had been given to any person to interfere in any respect with the United States, or to thwart her policy in those waters in the slightest degree; that, on the contrary, strict orders had been given and constantly renewed to the effect that all pains should be taken to maintain the best relations with the Americans in those regions.

White added that, speaking for himself, he had suggested to Richthofen that the anxiety produced in America by the presence of Diederichs' fleet would be relieved if the German ships should come and go rather than remain at Manila in a concentrated force.[55] When Bülow, to whom this proposal was conveyed, remarked that the Kaiser would not be pleased with the suggestion, White hastened to say that his hint was purely informal.[56]

[55] White to Day, July 30, 1898, Dispatches, Germany, LXVI, no. 506. For additional evidence on the German public demand for the fleet see Stephen Gwynn, ed., *The Letters and Friendships of Sir Cecil Spring-Rice* (Boston, 1929), I, 251–52.

[56] White to Day, July 30, 1898, Dispatches, Germany, LXVI, no. 507. Richthofen records that White withdrew his suggestion very apologetically (*Grosse Politik,* XV, 67–68). Vagts concludes that the absence of the Kaiser and other high German officials on their vacations had something to do with the continued presence of the fleet; also, that Dewey's remark to Diederichs that the United States did not intend to keep the islands made inadvisable the withdrawal of the squadron (II, 1336–37, 1349). The frequent and detailed reports to the Kaiser, copies of which appear in the naval records, indicate his interest in the situation at Manila.

At this point two questions naturally arise: Why did not the Department of State take action earlier, particularly in view of the expressions of dissatisfaction in the press, and why did it not lodge at least an informal protest? In the first place, Ambassador White's lengthy dispatches placed a favorable interpretation on the motives and conduct of the Germans.[57] In addition, statements emanating from the government in Berlin, as well as from the German ambassador in Washington, indicated that Germany had no desire to interfere with American operations.[58] Finally, Dewey's four sketchy telegrams, from which the pertinent passages have been quoted and which apparently constitute all that he ever officially reported regarding the alleged German menace, were not so worded as to indicate that diplomatic pressure was necessary.[59]

[57] White to Day, June 18, 1898, Dispatches, Germany, LXVI. On July 12 White cabled that he had been advised by the foreign office that "Germany had thus far repelled all approaches of other European powers looking to interference, and that German admiral under orders from his Government resisted tempting offer made him at Manila" (to Day, *ibid.*). This, of course, refers to the proposal to take over Manila *in deposito*.

[58] The Department of State records reveal that no notes were exchanged on this subject though there were informal conversations with Holleben (*Grosse Politik*, XV, 41–42, 46; Day to White [telegram], July 22, 1898, Germany, Instructions, XX; White to Day, July 30, 1898, Dispatches, Germany, LXVI). Only one of Dewey's cablegrams, that of June 12, regarding the increase of the German fleet, was officially communicated to the Department of State.

[59] This statement is based upon a careful search through the files and registers of the Navy Department. See also Dewey's *Autobiography*, p. 252. Dewey was self-reliant; cabling was difficult; he disliked writing; there was no point in sending lengthy dispatches that were some six weeks in transit; and he was not so much concerned about the Germans then as he apparently believed, at a later day, that he had been. In letters to his son he did not mention them once, and in his personal letters to the United States Consul at Hong Kong he revealed only a secondary solicitude. Wildman, *Forum*, LIX, 513–35.

Approximate positions of ships off Manila, at 11 A.M., August 13, 1898, from the logs of the vessels and the reports of their commanders.

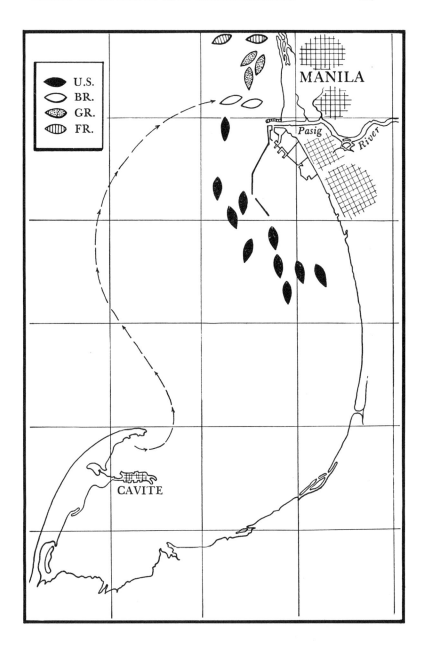

VIII

Early in August, American preparations for storming Manila neared completion. On August 7 Dewey notified the foreign ships, which were anchored off the city, to change their positions by noon of the 9th so as to be out of the line of fire. The British men-of-war, with their refugee-laden steamers, moved about eight miles south of Cavite, where Dewey was then stationed.[60] The one Japanese warship, with one vessel in charge, did likewise. The two French cruisers moved past the mouth of the Pasig River to the north and west of the city, with three shiploads of refugees, as did the three German men-of-war. The fourth remaining German warship, the *Cormoran,* was left in charge of four steamers of German refugees in Mariveles Bay, a harbor some twenty miles southwest of Manila.[61]

Much significance has been attached to the fact, particularly in later years, that the British and Japanese, who were known to be friendly to the Americans, anchored near them, while the Germans and the French, who were believed to be less well disposed, drew off together where they were in a better position to interfere with Dewey's operations. But Diederichs reported at the time that he did not go to Cavite because the place was already crowded with

[60] Numerous secondary accounts relate that on this occasion the British flagship played the "Star-Spangled Banner." The writer has found several contemporary references to such an incident. New York *Herald,* August 18, 1898; *Japan Weekly Mail,* September 3, 1898; letter of Lieut. Col. Charles L. Jewett, quoted in Henry Watterson, *History of the Spanish-American War* (San Francisco, 1898), p. 371. It is significant, however, that no mention of band music is made in the reports or logs of either fleet, although it was not unusual to record such courtesies.

[61] Chichester to Holland, August 14, 1898, China Letters, 1898; Diederichs to commanding admiral, August 28, 1898, Band 4; log of *Olympia,* August 9, 1898, Bureau of Navigation.

American, Japanese, and British ships and because he thought that Mariveles, which was distant from the scene of hostilities, would be a better place for the refugees.[62] The action of the French seems to have been dictated by convenience rather than by design, for the anchorage they chose was considerably closer than Cavite, and it enabled them to watch the operations of the Americans to better advantage.

On the morning of August 13 Dewey's fleet left Cavite to bombard the defenses of Manila.[63] Shortly thereafter the two British cruisers, the *Immortalité* and the *Iphigenia,* circled around Dewey's fleet and came to a stop in a position roughly between the German and American squadrons. This movement was later interpreted as an effective warning to the Germans, who were allegedly about to attack Dewey on his flank, that the British were prepared to fight on the side of the Americans.

The evidence against this interpretation is overwhelming. First of all, the crisis in German–American relations at Manila had passed almost exactly a month before. If Diederichs had wished to violate his instructions and try conclusions with Dewey he certainly would have done so before the arrival of the powerful *Monterey* and before the reduction of his own squadron from five to three ships.

[62] Diederichs also reported that Dewey expressed his gratitude that the Germans did not come to already crowded Cavite (to commanding admiral, August 28, 1898, Band 4).

[63] It was stated that as the fleet got under way the band of the *Immortalité* played patriotic airs in honor of the Americans. Chicago *Record,* August 19, 1898; New York *Herald,* August 18, 1898, 4; Dewey, *Autobiography,* p. 277 (also Dewey–Sargent Manuscript); Davis, *Released for Publication,* p. 17 (he was there at the time); Oscar Williams (former consul general at Manila, then on U.S.S. *Baltimore*) to Department of State, August 13, 1898, Consular Letters, Manila (now in the National Archives), XIII. Neither the British nor the American reports or logs refer to the playing of the band.

As for the German cruisers supposedly preparing to attack the Americans, their logs reveal that they were anchored and that they were not cleared for action. Nor do the three German logs and Diederichs' official report reveal any concern about the approaching British.[64] The log of the *Prinzess Wilhelm* did not even mention this movement; and Diederichs, in his eighty-three page dispatch, merely noted: "The English ships 'Immortalité' and 'Iphigenia' anchored near the German and French vessels, the latter [English] obstructing my view so nonchalantly that I was compelled to order S.M.S. 'Kaiser' to change anchorage."[65]

From the British point of view certain facts are conclusive. The two gunboats were left behind at Cavite, and neither the *Immortalité* nor the *Iphigenia*, as the logs reveal, cleared for action. The two British warships proceeded over the eight-mile course at ordinary cruising speed,[66] which does not indicate that Dewey was in desperate need of protection. During this maneuver Chichester watched the firing of the American fleet with such care that he could hardly have been thinking of action with the Germans.[67] On arriving at their new station the two British ships dropped anchor, the last thing they would have done if preparing for hostilities. In short, Chichester simply

[64] Logs of *Kaiser, Kaiserin Augusta,* and *Prinzess Wilhelm,* August 13, 1898 (Kriegswissenschaftliche Abteilung der Marine).

[65] To commanding admiral, August 28, 1898, Band 4. Diederichs did not mention the British movement in his telegram to the commanding admiral of August 15, 1898, Band 3a.

[66] At ten knots (60 revolutions). The *Immortalité* was capable of 18 knots; the *Iphigenia,* of 19.75. Brassey, *Naval Annual,* 1898, pp. 257, 267.

[67] For example, Chichester reported that he did not see the *Monterey* fire a single shot during the entire engagement (to Holland, August 14, 1898, China Letters, 1898).

shifted position, as his records indicate, so as to watch more advantageously the progress of the battle.[68]

In view of the great significance later attached to the British change of anchorage, the present writer was surprised to find no strictly contemporary mention of it outside of the brief references in the official German and British records. Not a single one of the seven logs preserved from the American fleet refers to the movement, though they meticulously record the comings and goings of ships in the harbor, particularly the shift of positions on the 9th.[69] Nor do Dewey's sketchy official reports contain any reference to the British maneuver. There were twenty-four newspaper correspondents at Manila, several of them actually on the ships of the American fleet, and not one of them, so far as has been discovered, described the movement at the time.[70] Both the London *Times* and Reuters news agency had representatives on the ground, and one wonders how they overlooked the opportunity to capitalize on the incident, particularly at a time when Great Britain was

[68] Chichester reported: "On the American Squadron weighing [anchor] this ship [*Immortalité*] and 'Iphigenia' weighed and proceeded to an anchorage North of the Passig [*sic*] River to watch proceedings" (*ibid.*). The log of the *Iphigenia* reads: "9.0 Weighed and proceeded 60 revns [revolutions] course as reqte [requisite] for anchorage Northward of Manila town" (logs of *Iphigenia* and *Immortalité*). The voluminous British and German reports on the battle of May 1, as well as other data, indicate that the neutral naval powers were keenly interested in technical aspects of this war.

[69] *Olympia, Baltimore, Raleigh, Petrel, Concord, Boston, Monterey,* Bureau of Navigation. The logs of the cruiser *Charleston*, the gunboat *Callao*, and the revenue cutter *McCulloch* have not been preserved.

[70] The New York *Herald* correspondent did go so far as to report that the two British ships, "whose commanders kept them in motion, watched the fight from a favorable position." The same issue of the *Herald* published a map showing the position of the British after they had completed their movement ("as described by the Herald's correspondents") but not explaining how they got there or attaching any significance to their presence at that spot. New York *Herald*, August 18, 1898.

so obviously seeking the friendship of the United States.[71]

There are two basic reasons for the silence of the newspaper correspondents. First, all eyes were focused on the bombardment by the American fleet and the assault of the troops.[72] Second, no one apparently was expecting, or had reason to expect, that the Germans would attempt to interfere. The British movement, therefore, had no special significance and consequently no news value.

IX

Late in the afternoon of the same day, August 13, after the city had surrendered, the German cruiser *Kaiserin Augusta* slipped out of the harbor for Hong Kong carrying General Augustín, who had been removed as governor general of the Philippines on August 5. The Americans at Manila were annoyed by Diederichs' failure to extend the usual courtesy of offering to carry dispatches, and the rumor spread that Dewey had been robbed of a legitimate prisoner of war.[73] Upon arriving at Hong Kong the Germans attempted to keep secret the fall of Manila, much to the annoyance of the British, but the news leaked out. Both the American and the British press expressed resentment

[71] The Reuters dispatch in the London *Times* had only this to say: "The bombardment was watched by the ships of the foreign Powers stationed here" (London *Times*, August 17, 1898).

[72] Bradley A. Fiske, later rear admiral, who was then at Manila, subsequently referred to the British maneuver but added, "I did not notice it myself." B. A. Fiske, *War Time in Manila* (Boston, 1913), p. 128. It is to be noted that Dewey's informal press censorship was lifted on August 13. Barrett, *Dewey*, p. 117.

[73] The German discourtesy seemed all the greater because the *Kaiserin Augusta* was a fast ship, and the Americans were eager to get news of the fall of Manila to the United States.

at such conduct, and the German newspapers lashed back with hot retorts.[74] This, it will be observed, was the third flurry of excitement growing out of German–American relations at Manila.

The German foreign office, presumably anticipating a protest from the United States, caused a telegraphic inquiry to be sent to the commander of the *Kaiserin Augusta*. He promptly replied that he had brought General Augustín with the permission of the Americans.[75] Diederichs explained his action by saying that he wanted to be the first to report the fall of Manila and that if he had stopped to pick up dispatches from all the foreign ships the departure of the *Kaiserin Augusta* would have been greatly delayed. Besides, he assumed that Dewey would send one of his own vessels to Hong Kong.[76] In any event, the Department of State files do not indicate that protests were lodged, and the incident was quickly forgotten.

On August 14, the day after the fall of the city, the German ships returned to their former anchorage. On August 15 the British did likewise, and the *Immortalité* fired a salute of twenty-one guns in honor of the United States flag, which then waved over Manila—an exhibition that somewhat annoyed the German commander.[77] She was the only ship to accord this honor to the Americans. On the same day Diederichs received orders, in response to a suggestion that he had himself telegraphed, to proceed to Batavia and

[74] New York *Herald*, August 17, 18, 1898; Chicago *Record*, August 18, 1898; London *Times*, August 17, 18, 1898.

[75] Commanding admiral to Köllner (telegram), August 17, 1898; Köllner to commanding admiral (telegram), August 17, 18, 1898, Band 3a; Diederichs to commanding admiral, August 28, 1898, Band 4.

[76] *Ibid.*

[77] *Ibid.*

there take part in the coronation ceremonies in honor of Queen Wilhelmina. At the same time the Kaiser congratulated Diederichs on his handling of the situation at Manila.[78] The next day, August 16, news reached the Philippines of the signing of the peace protocol.[79]

German–American misunderstanding growing out of the events in the Philippines did not end with the war. Although space limitations preclude a full treatment of this aspect of the story, the most significant developments may be noted. In April, 1899, Captain Coghlin of the *Raleigh*, speaking before the Union League Club in New York, attracted international attention when he described German–American friction at Manila and dramatically repeated what the American commander had told Hintze.[80] Dewey himself unwittingly contributed to the flames on his voyage home when, at Trieste, he remarked to a man who happened to be a correspondent of the New York *Herald* that "our next war will be with Germany." The story was widely published on both sides of the Atlantic, and the bitterness of this experience, combined with suspicions of Germany which arose from the Venezuela incident of 1902–03,

[78] Diederichs to commanding admiral, August 15, 1898 (telegram); Wilhelm I.R. to Oberkommando der Marine, August 15, 1898 (telegram); commanding admiral to Diederichs, August 15, 1898 (telegram), Band 3a.

[79] In view of Dewey's laconic and matter-of-fact telegrams about the Germans during the war, it is interesting that he cabled the following complaint nearly three months after hostilities had ended: "German cruiser *Irene* arrived yesterday and did not salute Port no German man of war has yet done so" (to Secretary of Navy, November 17, 1898, Bureau of Navigation). This would indicate that recent events were beginning to rankle and that the renewal of cable connections with Manila made it easier to report unimportant developments.

[80] For details of the incident see the New York *Herald*, April 23, 1899, and issues following. The German government made official representations (Vagts, II, 1385–86, n.).

probably further colored Dewey's recollection of the events at Manila.[81]

X

Late in 1898 and early in 1899 a considerable number of writers, some of whom had just returned from the Philippines, published magazine articles and books in which they described the recent events at Manila Bay. Several of these correspondents appear to have discovered for the first time that there had been a British ship movement.[82] Drawing upon these accounts and presumably also upon his imagination, Henry Cabot Lodge published in 1899 the first full-blown version of the legend that the writer has found.[83] According to this account, (1) the Germans were threatening Dewey with annihilation, (2) Chichester rapidly steamed in between the Germans and Dewey, (3) the Germans took the hint, (4) Dewey was saved by the British. This, in outline, is the story that came to be accepted.[84]

[81] New York *Herald*, July 29, 1899, and issues following. The evidence is strong that Dewey was quoted correctly, or substantially so. A sheaf of cablegrams asking for confirmation attests to general interest in the incident (Dewey Papers, Library of Congress). At the time of the Venezuela excitement Dewey gave out another anti-German interview, which elicited a tactful reprimand from President Roosevelt. Joseph Bucklin Bishop, *Theodore Roosevelt and his Time* (New York, 1920), I, 239. See also Vagts, II, 1555, 1593, 1610, n.

[82] See particularly Joseph L. Stickney, *Life and Glorious Deeds of Admiral Dewey* (Chicago, 1898), p. 110; Edward W. Harden, "Dewey at Manila," *McClure's Magazine*, XII (February, 1899), 369–84; John T. McCutcheon, "The Surrender of Manila," *Century Magazine*, LVII (April, 1899), 940. All these writers had been at Manila.

[83] *The War with Spain* (New York, 1899), pp. 215–16.

[84] See the rather confused account of Edgar Stanton Maclay, *A History of the United States Navy from 1775 to 1902* (new and enl. ed., New York, 1902), III, 429. John D. Long, ex-Secretary of the Navy, placed a semi-official stamp on the story when he repeated it in a rather prosaic fashion in *The New American Navy* (London, 1904), II, 112. See also the lurid account in Harry Thurston Peck, *Twenty Years of the Republic, 1885–1905* (New York, 1906), p. 589.

The principals in the drama generally kept silent throughout the decade following the events at Manila. Chichester, however, was not loath to refer on occasion to the good feeling that had existed between the Americans and the British; [85] and his death, in 1906, recalled his sympathy during the trying days of 1898.[86] In September, 1913, Dewey published his *Autobiography,* and, although he described in considerable detail the petty points of friction with the Germans, he mentioned the British ship movement somewhat casually.[87] German naval circles and to a lesser extent the press were aroused by Dewey's animadversions, and with the sanction, if not the active encouragement, of the admiralty Diederichs published a lengthy and circumstantial rebuttal in the *Marine Rundschau.* He had available his diary and detailed reports, and was able to find a number of errors in Dewey's account, which was based to a considerable extent on memory. The episode, which received some notice in the American press for about two weeks, served to stir anew the embers of 1898. [88]

[85] See his speech at Algeciras, reported in the New York *Times,* January 17, 1906.

[86] London *Times,* September 18, 1906; see an anecdote in *Harper's Weekly,* L (October 6, 1906), 1415.

[87] In his *Autobiography* (p. 277) Dewey states: ". . . Captain Chichester got under way also and with the *Immortalité* and the *Iphigenia* steamed over toward the city and took up a position which placed his vessels between ours and those of the foreign fleet." In the Dewey–Sargent Manuscript "significantly" appears before "took up a position"; and there is also this statement: "This manoeuvre was quietly executed, but it meant much, and no doubt was as thoroughly understood by the foreign men-of-war as it was appreciated by our own."

[88] The Diederichs account ("Darstellung der Vorgänge") was translated in slightly abridged form in the *Journal of the Royal United Service Institution,* LIX (November, 1914), 421–46. For the press accounts of the Dewey–Diederichs debate see New York *Times,* February 18, 19, 20, 21, 25, 26, 28, March 1, 4, 1914.

The Dewey–Diederichs debate had not been entirely forgotten when, in August, 1914, the Germans invaded Belgium. Many Americans, especially those with pro-Ally leanings, were quick to remember German hostility and British sympathy at Manila Bay. Magazine writers and orators in the United States exploited this theme—with what effect it is difficult to say—both before and after America entered the war.[89] But the British, with Belgian atrocity stories at hand, did not make the Manila Bay imbroglio a major point in their propaganda campaign, though the writer has found one pamphlet devoted to it.[90] During the years following 1918 the story of German unfriendliness and British support continued to appear in hands-across-the-seas propaganda, the reminiscences of newspaper correspondents, and the observations of radio commentators.[91] It was too good a tale to let die.

In retrospect it appears that the German–American friction at Manila Bay grew primarily out of a misunderstanding of German actions and motives. Although Diederichs had no orders to interfere with the Americans and

[89] In 1918 *Forum* featured a series of letters written by Dewey from Manila to the United States consul general at Hong Kong. Dewey's few more or less innocuous observations about the Germans were heavily italicized by the editor, who added the Chichester legend in lurid form (Wildman, LIX, 513–35). See also James Middleton, "The Mailed Fist in American History," *World's Work*, XXXII (May, 1916), 145–52.

[90] Archibald Hurd, "An Incident of War: 'By Order of the Kaiser' " (London, 1916).

[91] See Owen Wister, *A Straight Deal or the Ancient Grudge* (New York, 1920), pp. 180–81; Davis, *Released for Publication,* pp. 6–19. In a radio broadcast on January 14, 1938, Miss Dorothy Thompson had the British save Dewey from the Germans just before the battle of Manila Bay, May 1, 1898. Mr. Westbrook Pegler, in his syndicated column of September 3, 1938, referred to the "British admiral who stood off the Germans at Manila Bay." In March, 1939, Mr. Preston Grover, also a newspaper columnist, became involved in a controversy in which he repeated the legend.

apparently had no intention of doing so, his insistence upon what he conceived to be his rights during a blockade, together with the disproportionate strength of his fleet, gave a sinister aspect to German intentions. This situation, coupled with other unfortunate incidents and contrasted with British friendliness for the Americans, created an atmosphere in which misrepresentation and legend found a rapid and tenacious growth.

∿

*A potentially dangerous use of this episode is mentioned in Dr. William L. Neumann's* America Encounters Japan *(Baltimore, 1963), p. 264. On October 12, 1940, when a blitzed Britain was reeling, Secretary of War Stimson wrote a lengthy letter to the President. He retold the hoary myth of how the British had saved Dewey from German perfidy by interposing their ships and thus preventing a possible war. He reasoned that an interposition of the American fleet at Singapore, between the Axis navies of Japan and those of Germany and Italy, would have a similarly salutary effect. There is no record of a reply by Roosevelt. Nearly six years later Stimson appended a note to his file copy of the letter saying that his calculations had not taken into account the unexpected superiority of Japanese air power. (It had proved disastrous to the British warships* Repulse *and* Prince of Wales *near Singapore in December,*

*1941, just following the Japanese attack on Pearl Harbor.)*
*A copy of this letter, the original of which is in the Yale Library, was provided through the courtesy of Dr. Neumann.*

*One of the most loosely used words in American politics is "mandate." All too often the victorious party claims that it has received a mandate to do just about anything that was discussed in the recent Presidential campaign— and even some things that were not discussed, including a "packing" of the Supreme Court (1936). The following essay is an examination of the impact of politics on foreign affairs and vice versa. Extrapolating from this case study, one may conclude, contrary to common misconceptions, that the results of the following elections could not have been clear-cut mandates: 1844 (to annex Texas); 1920 (to reject the League of Nations); 1964 (to deescalate the Vietnam War).*

# 7.

# *WAS THE PRESIDENTIAL ELECTION OF 1900 A MANDATE ON IMPERIALISM?*

"The [Republicans] . . . must not imagine that a
majority of the voters have set the seal of their approval upon the un-American colonial policy of
the Administration. . . ."

—Detroit *Free Press,* 1900

I

For a number of years a considerable body of historians
has assumed that imperialism was the "paramount"
issue in the campaign of 1900, and that McKinley's trium-
phant reelection was a generous endorsement of his policy

*The Mississippi Valley Historical Review,* XXIV (June, 1937), 43–52.
Reprinted by permission. This paper is based primarily upon the correspondence of Carl Schurz, Grover Cleveland, W. J. Bryan, Theodore
Roosevelt, J. C. Spooner, W. E. Chandler, Henry White, and W. A.
Croffut—all in the Library of Congress. Croffut was secretary of the Anti-
Imperialist League. The McKinley MSS. in the Library of Congress
yielded little. The editorial observations of ninety American newspapers
(twenty-four of which were consulted directly, the others secondhand
through magazines of opinion or other newspapers) proved useful.

of expansion. The origins of this interpretation are not difficult to trace. First of all, McKinley won by the largest popular plurality that a Presidential candidate had yet polled; and the party in power invariably but illogically interprets reelection as a blanket endorsement of all its deeds and misdeeds. Secondly, the Democratic platform stated unequivocally that imperialism was both the "burning" and the "paramount" issue. In his letter of acceptance Bryan stood squarely on this pronouncement, as did his running mate, Adlai E. Stevenson.[1] But, unfortunately for the historian, the "paramount" issue is not always what the platform and the candidates announce it is going to be.

Seldom has this truth been better illustrated than by the campaign of 1900. Unforeseen economic developments had destroyed the effectiveness of the silver issue; but Bryan, whether through principle or through what he regarded as expediency, forced a secondary free silver plank down the throats of a rebellious Democratic convention. This appears to have been a colossal blunder. It completely ruined whatever chances he may have had of securing the votes of the gold-standard East, particularly the pivotal Empire State. As Thomas B. Reed is reported to have drawled with his characteristic amiability, Bryan "had rather be wrong than president."

The silver plank was a godsend to the harassed Republicans. Driven into a defensive position by the embarrassing Philippine insurrection, they promptly and joyously assumed the offensive with the very weapon that Bryan had thrust into their hands. They could scarcely have asked for anything better than an opportunity to fight the campaign of 1896 over again. McKinley straightway took up

---

[1] Chicago *Record*, September 18, 28, 1900.

the challenge and in his letter of acceptance insisted that currency, not Bryan's charge of "imperialism," was the "immediate" issue. The cyclonic Roosevelt, the Republican Vice-Presidential candidate, echoed these words in his letter of acceptance, and proceeded to rattle the metallic and horrendous skeleton of free silver with unprecedented ferocity.[2] In other words, each party had its own paramount issue, the validity of which the opposition vehemently denied.

II

It might be argued that because the McKinley ticket won by approximately 800,000 votes, the sovereign American people decreed that money and not imperialism was the paramount issue. But such an explanation is far too simple to be satisfying. First of all, it is undeniable that in any Presidential campaign a large percentage of the electorate is not concerned with the issues at all. In the year 1900 several million Republicans and several million Democrats were going to vote the straight party ticket whatever (within reason) the candidates or the issues. But it is a time-honored American custom that parties must have issues. So millions of congenital Democrats worked up what enthusiasm they could over anti-imperialism; and millions of congenital Republicans became alarmed, or attempted to become alarmed, about free silver. The scholar's first task is to penetrate this jungle of verbiage and try to determine what issue or issues influenced the votes of those whose minds were open to conviction. In other words, what was the "decisive" issue?

[2] Chicago *Record*, September 10, 17, 1900. The Republicans probably would have stressed Bryan's free silver taint in any event, but the silver plank added immeasurably to the force of their counterattack.

This assignment is by no means a simple one, largely because of the multiplicity and confusion of the issues. Bryan opened the campaign with some heavy blasts about colonialism, imperialism, and militarism; but when he found his audiences singularly unresponsive, he swung heavily to trusts, plutocracy, and special privilege. The Republicans emphasized the gold standard, the full dinner pail, continued prosperity, the tariff, patriotism, Bryanistic vagaries, Populism, and class hatred. It would not in fact be difficult to make up a list of sixty subjects that were discussed during the campaign, ranging all the way from Crockerism to Pettigrewism and from the St. Louis riots to the Boer War. To add to the confusion ten different parties or political groups actively entered the canvass.

The quandary of the conscientious and intelligent voter cannot fail to arouse sympathy. Ex-President Cleveland wrote that he was "pestered to death" with anxious inquiries; and among his papers one may find dozens of letters from correspondents who asked not only for advice as to how to vote but for help in determining the issues.[3] The day before the election the New York *Evening Post* remarked editorially that it had never before received such a large number of letters on the issues of a Presidential campaign. One may say in all seriousness that one of the important issues in 1900 was: "What is the paramount issue?" [4]

There were many voters who earnestly desired to cast a ballot for both the gold standard and anti-imperialism.

---

[3] Cleveland to D. M. Dickinson, October 12, 1900; Cleveland to W. S. Bissell, September 16, 1900, Cleveland MSS. See particularly W. A. Ownby to Cleveland, October 18, 1900, on which appears the penciled annotation, "Dozens like this."

[4] New York *Evening Post*, November 5, 1900. One cartoonist represented the campaign as being the great game of finding the paramount issue. New York *Tribune*, November 2, 1900.

But to vote for McKinley and the gold standard was apparently to endorse imperialism; to vote for Bryan and anti-imperialism was presumably to endorse free silver. Such a militant sound money man as Carl Schurz concluded that imperialism was the more immediate evil, and found himself faced with the "horrible duty" of working for Bryan, or rather against McKinley. On the other hand, ardent anti-imperialists like Andrew Carnegie and Charles Francis Adams regarded economic chaos as the more imminent danger and threw their support to McKinley. It is a significant fact that four of the most effective campaigners for the Republican ticket were leading anti-imperialists: Senators Hoar and Hale, and Representatives Littlefield and McCall.

A large number of Gold Democrats—how many will never be known—heroically voted for McKinley. They concluded that after the United States had first set its own house in order there would be time enough to turn to the Philippine problem.[5] In postelection statements McKinley, Roosevelt, and Hanna freely acknowledged their indebtedness to Democratic support. In fact, so generally recognized was this defection that the press made repeated references to the nonpartisan character of the victory.[6]

## III

A considerable number of those who wished to cast a clear-cut vote against imperialism felt that their only op-

[5] See L. M. Beck to Cleveland, October 31, 1900, Cleveland MSS.; Schurz to E. M. Shepard, October 7, 1900, Schurz MSS.

[6] Philadelphia *Public Ledger,* November 7, 1900; New York *Evening Post,* November 10, 1900; Indianapolis *Journal,* November 7, 8, 1900; New York *World,* November 8, 1900. See also Roosevelt to James Bulloch, November 9, 1900; C. N. Douglas to Roosevelt, November 10, 1900; Roosevelt to Delos McCurdy, November 10, 1900, Roosevelt MSS.

portunity lay in a third party; but for reasons that need not be discussed here this movement fell through. Others urged Bryan to come out with a ringing pledge not to disturb the gold standard if elected, thus narrowing the paramount issue down to imperialism. But Bryan, foolishly it appears, turned a deaf ear to all such advances.[7] Daniel M. Lord, of the American Anti-Imperialist League, found many anti-imperialists who had decided to vote for McKinley because of their greater fear of free silver. He therefore suggested to Schurz that a protest signed by several hundred thousand such people before the election would convince McKinley that he had not received a mandate to go ahead with expansion. Schurz replied that this plan would be desirable after the election but, if executed earlier, it would merely serve to increase the McKinley vote by enabling the anti-imperialists to salve their consciences.[8] The Springfield *Republican* observed that the suggestion of voting for McKinley first and protesting afterwards won many votes for the Republicans, although, as this journal remarked, the cold figures in no way reflected the voters' "mental reservations."[9]

So obviously misleading were the election returns that a number of newspapers called upon McKinley not to interpret the results as an endorsement of imperialism. Indeed, there is some scattered evidence to support the thesis, which obviously can neither be proved nor disproved, that if the question had been placed before the electorate solely

[7] Schurz to Louis Ehrich, October 4, 1900; Schurz to E. B. Smith, October 7, 13, 1900, Schurz MSS.

[8] D. M. Lord to Schurz, October 25, 1900; Schurz to Smith, November 5, 1900; Smith to Schurz, November 7, 1900, Schurz MSS. Lord wrote that almost without exception some fifty Republicans whom he had approached had expressed a willingness to sign such a petition.

[9] Springfield *Republican,* November 7, 1900.

on its merits the American people would have voted against retaining the Philippines, at least permanently.[10]

In the minds of many voters the problem was one of choosing the lesser of two evils: the platitudinous and presumably malleable McKinley (Thomas B. Reed's "Emperor of Expediency") or the heretical and rattlebrained Bryan. "Bryanism and McKinleyism!" exclaimed Cleveland, "What a choice for a patriotic American!" In the end thousands of voters cast their ballots for McKinley in spite of his Philippine policy—and hoped for the best. They preferred the known weaknesses of McKinley to the wild theories of Bryan. As a Nebraska editor wrote to Cleveland, "It is a choice between evils, and I am going to shut my eyes, hold my nose, vote, go home and disinfect myself." The New York *Nation* suggested for a McKinley banner: "The Nation's Choice—of Evils." [11]

IV

Although it is obvious that any campaign following the colorful crusade of 1896 would seem a tame affair, one is impressed with the fact that there was a marked falling off of the vote in 1900.[12] The general confusion over the

---

[10] See similar view in A. C. Coolidge, *The United States as a World Power* (New York, 1908), p. 157; also Schurz to Howe, June 22, 1900, Schurz MSS.; Cleveland *Plain Dealer*, November 8, 1900. The New York *Herald* conducted a poll in fifteen of the largest cities in the United States. Of 726 voters interviewed, 324 favored and 333 opposed expansion. Figures cited in San Francisco *Argonaut*, July 23, 1900.

[11] Cleveland to C. S. Hamlin, September 13, 1900, in Allan Nevins, ed., *Letters of Grover Cleveland, 1850–1908* (Boston, 1933), p. 536; J. S. Morton to Cleveland, November 2, 1900, Cleveland MSS.; *Nation* (New York), CLXXI (1900), 302. See also R. F. Cutting to Herbert Welsh, October 2, 1900; Schurz to Shepard, October 7, 1900; C. W. Eliot to Schurz, October 4, 1900, Schurz MSS. The large protest vote polled by the minor parties is further evidence of disgust with the major party candidates.

issues, combined with a widespread disgust with both of the candidates, caused a considerable number of voters to stay away from the polls. This appears to have been the case with Grover Cleveland, who, according to one newspaper, planned to register his disgust by going duck shooting.[13]

The obvious lack of interest in the campaign was doubtless due in large measure to the fact that the Philippine issue was now more or less stale. The islands had already been under the Stars and Stripes for over two years; and the American public, leaping with characteristic avidity from one sensation to another, had apparently already begun to classify them among those things settled and accepted. E. V. Abbot noted the "languid interest" in the question of imperialism and observed that "the Republicans weariedly support the administration and the Democrats weariedly oppose it." [14] Moreover the Republicans were confident of victory; and Hanna, dissatisfied with his early efforts to "shake down" the plutocrats, complained that the big enemy of the party was none other than "General Apathy." Finally, in contrast with 1896, the country was pulsating and prosperous, too fat and contented to be aroused to a high pitch of crusading zeal.[15]

---

[12] That is, relative to the increase in population. Only 64,710 more votes were cast in 1900 than in 1896. For election figures see Edgar E. Robinson, *The Presidential Vote, 1896–1932* (Stanford University, 1934), *passim*.

[13] Boston *Evening Transcript*, November 2, 1900. T. B. Reed, W. G. Sumner, and W. S. Bissell all expressed a determination not to vote. See A. W. Thurman to Schurz, October 9, 1900, Schurz MSS.

[14] Abbot to Schurz, October 5, 1900, Schurz MSS. C. F. Adams wrote that he was enjoying "the repose of this presidential election." Adams to Schurz, July 14, 1900, Schurz MSS.

[15] Herbert Croly, *Marcus Alonzo Hanna* (New York, 1912), p. 328; Lodge to Henry White, September 3, 1900, White MSS.; Lodge to Roosevelt, August 30, 1900; H. C. Payne to Roosevelt, August 22, 1900, Roosevelt MSS.; Lodge to Roosevelt, August 18, 1900, Roosevelt to Lodge, August 22, 28, 1900, *Selections from the Correspondence of Theodore Roosevelt and Henry Cabot Lodge, 1884–1918* (New York, 1925), I, 473, 474, 475.

It would not, in fact, be too much to say that prosperity was the keynote of the campaign. The closing years of McKinley's term afforded a striking contrast to the widespread distress of Cleveland's second administration. Mark Hanna was not unaware of the potency of stand-pattism and the full dinner pail when he solemnly asserted in an Omaha speech, "There is only one issue in this campaign, my friends, and that is, let well enough alone." [16] The deep-seated fear of Bryan that had been instilled by two extraordinary campaigns of education was abundantly reflected by the stock market, which experienced a tremendous boom immediately after the election. In the contest between the heart and the stomach the "belly vote," as one journal put it, won. The American people were interested primarily in hogs, corn, and wheat—only secondarily in the Filipinos. Shortly after the election Bryan received a remarkable letter from his campaign manager, Senator James K. Jones of Arkansas, who deplored the heavy falling off of Democratic majorities in his state, and added, "In my own county, men who have voted the Democratic ticket all their lives, voted the Republican this time, openly boasted of it, and gave as the reason, that they did not want any more '5 cent cotton.' " [17]

At this point it is possible to answer with some degree of confidence the question as to what was the "decisive" issue in the campaign. Assuming that Bryan had an outside chance to win, the issue that beat him was "Bryanism"—so-called by scores of opposition newspapers. Basically Bryanism was the fear that Bryan would destroy prosperity by overthrowing the gold standard and putting into effect his economic heresies. When the election was over dozens of newspapers insisted that the dread spectre of Bryanism had

---

[16] *Public Opinion* (Washington), XXIX (1900), 548.
[17] Jones to Bryan, December 1, 1900, Bryan MSS.

brought about the result. Even the ebullient Roosevelt wrote with unaccustomed modesty that above McKinley, Hanna, and even himself, "it was Bryan . . . who did most" to bring about the result. That Bryan was a burden to the Democratic cause is further attested by the fact that in general he ran behind his ticket. The "great Commoner" himself admitted, after the election, that the prosperity argument was the most effective one used against him by the Republicans.[18]

v

One final word about imperialism. If it had been the only issue in the campaign, would the reelection of Mc-Kinley have been a clear-cut mandate? The answer is still, no. First of all "imperialism" and "anti-imperialism" were but vague catchwords that meant all things to all men, ranging from a permanent occupation of the Philippines to an immediate and cowardly surrender to Aguinaldo. Bryan certainly did not advocate the latter of these alternatives, but this was the interpretation forced upon him by the opposition, notably Roosevelt, who stormed about the country decrying the dastardly attempt to haul down the flag. Thus imperialism became inextricably identified with patriotism, and a number of voters who wished for ultimate withdrawal supported McKinley because they did not wish to uphold the blood-drenched hands of the enemy. After the election, Bryan himself said that although the prosper-

---

18 Roosevelt to Lodge, November 9, 1900, *Roosevelt–Lodge Correspondence*, I, 479; *Nation*, CLXXI (1900), 437; Schurz to Welsh, October 5, 1900, Schurz MSS.; R. F. Pettigrew to Croffut, November 13, 1900, Croffut MSS.; William J. Bryan, "The Election of 1900," *North American Review* (New York), LXXI (1900), 789.

ity argument was the most potent one used against him, the Republican cry, "Stand by the President" won many votes.[19]

Even if imperialism had been clearly defined and had been the only issue, Bryan's record inspired no great confidence in his willingness to withdraw from the Philippines. Whatever may be said in defense of his rather unexpected course in securing the ratification of the treaty with Spain, it is undeniable that he had begun the campaign on the high note of anti-imperialism and then had shifted to trusts. Such chameleon-like conduct was roundly condemned by the Republicans, including Charles Francis Adams, who remarked in disgust, "I cannot make out whether he is a knave or a fool." [20] And Cleveland wrote, "How do you know what such an acrobat would do on that question [imperialism] if his personal ambition was in the balance?" [21] In other words, many voters concluded, whether correctly or not, that Bryan was just a professional Presidential candidate who was only paying lip service to a synthetic issue that might get him into office. The hands were the hands of Esau but the voice was the voice of Bryan.[22]

Even if Bryan had received a clear-cut mandate to withdraw from the Philippines, would his party have per-

---

[19] New York *World,* November 9, 1900. In the Roosevelt collection there are several letters from Democrats who deserted Bryan because they felt that he was encouraging the Filipinos to fire on the American uniform.

[20] Adams to Schurz, July 14, 1900; Edward Holden to Schurz, November 10, 1900, Schurz MSS.

[21] Cleveland to Judson Harmon, July 17, 1900, Cleveland MSS. Schurz later called Bryan the "evil genius" of the anti-imperialist cause. C. M. Fuess, *Carl Schurz, Reformer* (New York, 1932), p. 366.

[22] See M. E. Curti, "Bryan and World Peace," *Smith College Studies in History* (Northampton), XVI (1931), nos. 3–4, pp. 119ff., for a scholarly yet rather favorable interpretation of Bryan's course at this time.

mitted him to do so? The recent Spanish conflict, with its fortuitous insular fruits, had in large measure been brought about by Democratic pressure; and although the solid South, for obvious reasons, was going to support Bryan, there was a notoriously strong imperialist sentiment in this section.[23] In addition, the patronage-hungry Democratic party could scarcely have been expected to achieve the self-denial of surrendering these new territories, with their scores of offices for deserving Democrats.[24] Nor did newly developed solicitude of the Democrats for colored peoples ring true to those who knew of conditions in the South. Apparently, as the Republicans taunted their opponents, charity began abroad. Although the Democrats were denouncing imperialism, their platform advocated a protectorate for the Philippines; and was not that imperialism? In fact, a number of observers insisted that the difference between the avowed programs of the two parties was so slight as to amount to a discussion of tweedledum and tweedledee. So it was that many voters, regarding the pronouncements of both Bryan and his party as untrustworthy and insincere, cast their ballots for McKinley because they felt that under his leadership the United States would be able to get out of the Philippines sooner than under that of Bryan.[25]

[23] J. B. Henderson to Croffut, August 23, 1900; Erving Winslow to Croffut, November 8, 1900, Croffut MSS.; Schurz to Winslow, July 22, 1900; Abbot to Schurz, October 5, 1900; Adams to Schurz, October 11, 1900, Schurz MSS.; Roosevelt to Bulloch, November 9, 1900, Roosevelt MSS.; New York *Evening Post,* November 5, 7, 1900; Curti, "Bryan and World Peace," pp. 125–26.

[24] Franklin Carter to Welsh, October 2, 1900; W. G. Sumner to Welsh, October 2, 1900; Adams to Schurz, October 11, 1900, Schurz MSS.; Bissell to Cleveland, September 8, 1900, Cleveland MSS.

[25] Carter to Welsh, October 2, 1900, Schurz MSS.; F. C. Lowell to Roosevelt, November 7, 1900, Roosevelt MSS. See also Adams to Schurz, July 14, 1900, Schurz MSS.

It seems reasonable to conclude that the election of 1900 could not have been an endorsement either of McKinley's leadership in general or of his policy of expansion.[26] One is even tempted to go a step further and add that because of partisan, personal, sectional, and a host of other domestic considerations, Presidential elections have never been and can never be a mandate on any question of foreign policy. Indeed, one wonders if these great quadrennial convulsions can ever be a mandate on anything.

[26] As compared with 1896 Bryan's popular vote showed large gains in the East, particularly in Massachusetts, the stronghold of the anti-imperialists. But much of this was merely the return of disaffected elements to the party. McKinley gained heavily in the Rocky Mountain and Pacific Coast states, where it was presumed that the lure of oriental trade had created imperialist sentiment. This development, however, was probably due in large measure to Roosevelt's immense popularity, to the death of the silver issue, and to the return of disaffected elements to the party fold. Bryan carried Kentucky, which he had lost in 1896; but here the paramount issue was Goebelism, an outgrowth of factional politics.

*The author's interest in Theodore Roosevelt and his Big Stick brandishings is of long standing. As one of the earliest scholars to be permitted access to the Roosevelt papers (1932), he wrote his first book on the Rough Rider's relations with Japan. In contrast with a velvet-glove treatment of the Japanese, Roosevelt arranged for a pseudo-arbitration of the Canadian boundary, and then browbeat the British into compliance with thinly veiled threats of force. This was not one of America's finest hours.*

# 8.

# THEODORE ROOSEVELT AND THE ALASKA BOUNDARY SETTLEMENT

"It would be not merely foolish but wicked for us as a nation to agree to arbitrate any dispute that affects our vital interest or our independence or our honor. . . ."

—Theodore Roosevelt, 1911

I

The background of the story may be briefly sketched. The Alaska boundary, which had been ambiguously defined in the Anglo-Russian treaty of 1825, seems to have been the object of no particular concern until 1896, when gold was discovered in the Klondike. Desirous of securing a deep-water route through the Alaska panhandle to the goldfields, the Canadians advanced the claim that the boundary did not follow the sinuosities of the coast but cut through the most important inlets in such a way as to leave their heads in the possession of Canada.

*The Canadian Historical Review*, XVIII (June, 1937), 123–30. Reprinted by permission.

The dispute was temporarily adjusted by a *modus vivendi* arranged by Secretary of State John Hay in 1899. When both British and Canadian high officials evinced an increasing willingness to make a permanent settlement, a convention was signed in 1903 which provided for a tribunal of "six impartial jurists of repute," three to be appointed by the President of the United States and three by His Britannic Majesty. Two prominent Canadians, one of whom had had judicial experience, and Lord Alverstone, Lord Chief Justice of England, were chosen to represent Great Britain. Roosevelt appointed Secretary of War Root, Senator Henry Cabot Lodge of Massachusetts, and ex-Senator George Turner of Washington. None of these three men had acquired any considerable "repute" in a judicial capacity, and there were grave doubts as to the impartiality of each one on the Alaska question, particularly so in the case of Senator Lodge. He was not only one of the leading professional Anglophobes in America but had already publicly committed himself against the Canadian claim.

The tribunal met in London late in 1903, and by a vote of four to two, Lord Alverstone siding with the Americans, sustained the main contention of the United States, that regarding the inlets. The equal division of four small islands in dispute, as well as the adjustment of the boundary from the 56th parallel to the 141st meridian, strongly suggests that the division was a compromise rather than a purely judicial award.

Throughout the controversy Roosevelt was unshaken in his conviction that the Canadian allegations did not "have a leg to stand on" and that they were "dangerously near blackmail." [1] In support of his view he asserted in

[1] *Roosevelt Papers:* Roosevelt to Strachey, July 18, 1902; Roosevelt to Hay, July 10, 1902. Unless otherwise indicated, all correspondence hereafter cited may be found in the Roosevelt collection in the Library of Congress, Washington, D.C.

numerous letters that the official British maps, even those presented to the tribunal, upheld the American line. He believed that the Canadians had advanced an extravagant claim to extort some substantial concession from the United States by a compromise settlement, and that they were trading upon their loyalty during the recent Boer War to enlist the support of a somewhat unwilling mother country.[2] Roosevelt felt that by consenting to the treaty of 1903 he was giving the Canadians their last chance to emerge gracefully from the bad hole into which they had worked themselves by insistence upon an indefensible claim. He also believed that it would be wise to settle the dispute before the turbulent mining element got out of control and precipitated a crisis.[3]

## II

The joint commission which met at London was not an arbitral tribunal in the generally accepted sense of the term, for the Americans could expect nothing worse than a deadlock and they had an excellent chance of winning. It is clear from Roosevelt's letters that he had no intention of submitting the dispute to arbitration, and that he did not regard the Alaska tribunal as an arbitral body at all.[4] He explained his attitude fully to F. W. Holls:

An arbitration is where some outside body decides the question at issue between two parties. To call a meeting between representatives of two parties in the endeavor to come to an agreement an "arbitration" is in my idea a foolish mis-

[2] Roosevelt to Strachey, July 18, 1902; Roosevelt to Root, August 8, 1903.

[3] Roosevelt to Morley, December 12, 1903.

[4] Roosevelt wrote to Hay, "I have not regarded the question as one open to reasonable doubt, and for that reason have refused to permit any arbitration upon it . . ." (Roosevelt to Hay, January 14, 1903); see also Roosevelt to Ted (Theodore, Jr.), October 20, 1903.

use of words. . . . There is no "proposition for an arbitration," with an uneven or an even number of judges, or under any name, or upon any condition, which ever has received or ever will receive my sanction; and to call the proposed tribunal an "arbitration" is as absurd as to speak of the correspondence that has gone on between the foreign office and the State Department for the last year and a half on the subject by the same name.[5]

But with regard to the four tiny islands in the Portland Canal, Roosevelt was willing to admit that the Canadians had a case, and he was even prepared to submit this phase of the question to arbitration.[6]

Lest there be any mistake and the American commissioners regard themselves as judicially minded arbiters, Roosevelt wrote all three, shortly after their appointment, positive but somewhat contradictory instructions. "You will," he said, "impartially judge the questions that come before you for decision," but "in the principle involved there will of course be no compromise." He declared that he was issuing such instructions because Sir Wilfrid Laurier, the Canadian premier, had recently made a speech in which he had virtually given the two Canadian commissioners a mandate to uphold the Canadian view.[7] It is interesting to observe that nearly a year before, when the question of the joint commission was under discussion, Roosevelt had informed Hay: "I will appoint three commissioners to meet three of their commissioners, if they so desire, but I think I shall instruct our three commissioners when appointed that they are in no case to yield any of our claim." [8]

5 Roosevelt to F. W. Holls, February 3, 1903.
6 Roosevelt to Hay, September 15, 1903.
7 Roosevelt to Lodge, Turner, and Root, March 25, 1903.
8 Roosevelt to Hay, July 16, 1902; also Roosevelt to Hay, July 10, 1902.

III

The British and the Canadians appear to have consented to the treaty of 1903 with the understanding that the three American jurists would be judicially minded men taken directly from the Supreme Court or perhaps some lesser tribunal. In view of the fact that Roosevelt was accused of having hoodwinked the British and the Canadians by his appointments, it is only fair to say that he offered, or said that he offered, a place on the tribunal to two of the Supreme Court justices, presumably Holmes and White, both of whom declined.[9] But even granting that the Supreme Bench was closed to him, Roosevelt could certainly have found capable and unobjectionable men elsewhere among the federal courts had he intended in good faith to appoint "impartial jurists of repute."

Roosevelt explained his extraordinary choices by writing to Mr. Justice Holmes that "No man in public life in any position of prominence could have possibly avoided committing himself on the proposition" [10]—which was patently not true. The questions at issue were unusually complicated; and it would probably be fair to say that relatively few men in public life, judicial or political, had either formed any opinion on the controversy or had committed themselves on it. Even granting that Roosevelt finally decided to appoint commissioners with closed minds who would staunchly defend the American view, he certainly could have chosen men less offensive to the British and

[9] Roosevelt to Arthur Lee, December 7, 1903. Although it cannot be definitely determined that Holmes and White were the two justices, the internal evidence indicates that they were, strongly so in the case of Holmes.

[10] Roosevelt to Holmes, July 25, 1903.

the Canadians than Senator Lodge and ex-Senator Turner.

A number of years after the event, Senator Lodge wrote that when the Alaska convention came before the Senate it encountered strong opposition from those, particularly from the Northwest states, who feared that the President might appoint commissioners who would not stand fast on the American contention. Lodge then went to the President and secured from him in confidence the names of the men whom he would choose, whereupon the opposition collapsed and the convention was approved.[11]

Assuming that Roosevelt approached the two Supreme Court justices before this arrangement with Lodge, the story hangs together remarkably well, and has the added merit of providing what is perhaps the only rational explanation of why Roosevelt could have made such incredibly improper choices. We do know that the convention encountered enough difficulty in the Senate to cause Hay considerable worry; and that the opposition suddenly ceased and the agreement was approved almost unanimously.[12] We also know that Hay, in explaining the appointments to Henry White, wrote, "the President thought it was impossible to get the treaty through the Senate without the earnest and devoted assistance of Lodge and Turner and of the groups which they represented."[13] Probably this is what Hay had reference to when he wrote to Roosevelt, "The Alaska treaty went through beautifully—thanks to your engineering."[14]

[11] C. G. Washburn, "Memoir of Henry Cabot Lodge," *Massachusetts Historical Society Proceedings*, LVIII (1924–25), 340.

[12] Tyler Dennett, *John Hay* (New York, 1934), p. 362; New York *Times*, February 6, 1903, 8.

[13] Allan Nevins, *Henry White* (New York, 1930), p. 195.

[14] Hay to Roosevelt, February 11, 1903.

## IV

As a matter of pure speculation, it is interesting to consider what would have happened had the two Supreme Court justices consented to serve. The day after the decision of the London tribunal, Mr. Justice Holmes wrote to Roosevelt: "[Mr. Justice] White, the only person with whom I have talked here except my wife, was saying yesterday that with our judicial scepticism neither of us could have taken so convinced an attitude [as the tribunal?] and we agreed that it was a personal triumph of yours." [15] This interesting statement suggests that if Holmes and White had represented the United States, the Canadians probably would have secured a good deal more. But Roosevelt appears to have thought differently, for six weeks later he wrote to Arthur Lee that if the two Supreme Court justices had served, Canada probably would have got nothing.

You speak of your regret that the Commission was not composed exclusively of judges. I asked two judges of our Supreme Court, whom I thought most fit for the positions, to serve. They both declined; and as I now think, wisely. On this Commission we needed to have jurists who were statesmen. If the decision had been rendered purely judicially, *the Canadians would not have received the two islands which they did receive at the mouth of the Portland Canal;* and one of the judges to whom I offered the appointment has told me that on that account he would have been unable to sign the award. He would have felt that he was sitting purely as a judge, and that judicially the case did not admit of a compromise. Personally, while I think the American case even as regards these islands was the stronger, I yet attach so great importance to having the case settled that I am glad that our commissioners yielded to Lord Alverstone and thus rendered

15 Holmes to Roosevelt, October 21, 1903.

it possible for a decision to be made. But my belief is that if you had had two of our Supreme Court judges on the American Commission, they would have stood out steadily for a decision on every point in favor of the American view—a determination which I think would have been technically proper, but in its results most unfortunate.[16]

Assuming that the President was referring to the above-quoted letter of Mr. Justice Holmes, which seems probable, it would appear that his memory was not altogether reliable.

In certain respects the Alaska dispute is an outstanding example of Roosevelt's big-stick technique. He was determined to secure a settlement in his own way or no settlement at all. In March, 1902, he dispatched orders to the Secretary of War to have "additional troops sent as quietly and unostentatiously as possible to Southern Alaska." [17] He wrote numerous letters to Root, Lodge, Hay, and Henry White in which he expressed his determination, if the commission failed, to occupy the disputed area by force, if necessary. Roosevelt's repetition of this theme was so frequent [18] as to suggest that he wanted his views to percolate to British officialdom through these intermediaries. He used a somewhat cruder approach in a remarkable letter to Mr. Justice Holmes, who was then in England. At the outset Roosevelt informed him that he was "entirely at liberty" to tell Joseph Chamberlain, British colonial secretary, "what I say, although of course it must be privately and unofficially." This is the passage that Roosevelt undoubtedly had in mind:

---

[16] Roosevelt to Lee, December 7, 1903; italics Roosevelt's.

[17] Henry Pringle, *Theodore Roosevelt* (New York, 1931), p. 290.

[18] In February, 1903, Roosevelt told the German ambassador substantially the same thing (*Die Grosse Politik*, XVII, 292).

. . . If there is a disagreement I wish it distinctly understood, not only that there will be no arbitration of the matter, but that in my message to Congress I shall take a position which will prevent any possibility of arbitration hereafter; a position, I am inclined to believe, which will render it necessary for Congress to give me the authority to run the line as we claim it, by our own people, without any further regard to the attitude of England and Canada.[19]

Mr. Justice Holmes showed this letter in confidence to two prominent men whom he met in England, including the chairman of the Canadian Grand Trunk Railroad, and then he had an interview with Chamberlain in a purely unofficial capacity. Holmes's report to Roosevelt is both interesting and significant:

He [Chamberlain] expressed regret at the attitude and said that so far as he had examined there seemed to him to be a reasonable case on the other side. I said that I knew nothing about the question although experience had led me to regard most things as open to argument. He thought it would have been a step forward for this world [?] if men with wholly open minds had been appointed. As to this particular controversy he did not care much but England had to back up Canada. . . . He was amiable, but considered the implications of your letter as exceedingly grave and to be regretted.[20]

Other attempts to browbeat the British were more subtle. Late in September, 1903, Roosevelt wrote a letter to Henry White, secretary of the American Embassy in London, in which he expressed his determination to use strong measures.[21] The President evidently expected White to convey this information to high British officials, which

19 Roosevelt to Holmes, July 25, 1903.
20 Holmes to Roosevelt, October 11, 1903.
21 Roosevelt to White, September 26, 1903.

White later testified he did.[22] About the same time Secretary Hay, who had become somewhat alarmed by Roosevelt's bellicose talk, advised White to see that the President's views were conveyed to Prime Minister Balfour. White, presuming on his friendship, obtained an interview with the Prime Minister early in October, 1903, and reported that he had "left no doubt upon his [Balfour's] mind as to the importance of the settlement nor as to the result of a failure to agree." [23]

Two days after his conversation with White, Balfour was closeted twice with Lord Alverstone, who undoubtedly was informed of the seriousness of the situation. About the same time, Lodge, who knew of Roosevelt's views, also discussed the matter at some length with Balfour.[24] A few days earlier, Ambassador Choate reported that he had secured an interview with Lord Lansdowne, British foreign secretary, "in which I pressed upon him very urgently the views of the President as expressed by him in our interview in June. . . ." [25]

## V

Roosevelt evidently believed that his big-stick methods contributed materially to the final result. Shortly after receiving word of the decision he reminded Mr. Justice Holmes: "If you will turn back to the letter I wrote you in July last, and which you showed to Chamberlain, you

[22] Nevins, *White*, p. 199.

[23] *Ibid.*, p. 200. Probably White read Roosevelt's letter of September 26 to Balfour.

[24] *Ibid.*, p. 200.

[25] A. L. P. Dennis, *Adventures in American Diplomacy* (New York, 1928), p. 154; Choate to Hay, October 20, 1903; also Roosevelt to Hay, June 29, 1903.

will notice how exactly the Alaska boundary decision went
along the lines I there indicated. I cannot help having a
certain feeling that your showing that letter to Chamberlain and others was not without its indirect effect on the
decision." [26] But Holmes was not so sure. He replied:
"What you say strikes me as extremely probable, although
the circumstance will remain among the arcana of history.
The English are very touchy about any suggestion of a
threat and I said to Mr. C.[hamberlain] that I did not for
a moment suppose that it was intended in that sense—although he said and fully realized that the intimation was
grave." [27]

Roosevelt undoubtedly overestimated the effect of the
Holmes letter. But his combined efforts, direct and indirect,
to bring pressure on high British officials probably were not
without fruit. It is unthinkable that the colonial secretary,
the foreign secretary, or the Prime Minister could have
failed to convey this information to Lord Alverstone. Faced
with the Canadian clamor on the one hand and with the
knowledge that an adverse decision might cause Roosevelt
to take steps that would lead to war on the other, he was
in an unenviable position. It is also difficult to believe that
Lord Alverstone, who had long known the seamy side of
politics before ascending the bench, was entirely immune
from such pressure, though he may not consciously have
yielded to it.[28] This may in part explain why he signed the
final compromise decision, which was unpalatable to a

[26] Roosevelt to Holmes, October 20, 1903; also Roosevelt to Ted,
October 20, 1903.

[27] Holmes to Roosevelt, October 21, 1903.

[28] The testimony of the two Canadian commissioners supports the
presumption that Lord Alverstone yielded to a compromise settlement.
James White, "Henry Cabot Lodge and the Alaska Boundary Award,"
*Canadian Historical Review*, VI (December, 1925), 345.

purely judicial mind, and gave way on the southern extremity, where even Roosevelt admitted that the Canadians had a case.

Dr. Tyler Dennett is of the opinion that Roosevelt's handling of the dispute suggests that he was looking for an issue in the campaign of 1904.[29] But Roosevelt's own professions, if they mean anything, indicate that he consented to the final arrangements somewhat reluctantly, and that he did not want this problem unnecessarily aroused on the eve of a Presidential election.[30] Nevertheless he was pleased with the advantageous settlement, writing to White: "The Alaska and Panama settlements coming in one year make a very good showing, do they not? I shall get Cuban reciprocity through, too." [31]

VI

As in the case of Panama, Roosevelt got what he wanted by questionable tactics—and at the cost of a neighbor's ill will.[32] Had he been willing to make haste more slowly, he probably would have secured substantially what he desired in both cases without the accompanying heritage of distrust. And one of the most curious things about the whole Alaska episode is that Roosevelt seems never to have

[29] Dennett, *Hay*, p. 359.

[30] Roosevelt to Lodge, July 8, 1903; Roosevelt to Hay, June 29, 1903; Roosevelt to Lodge, June 29, 1903.

[31] Roosevelt to White, November 26, 1903.

[32] Perhaps the intemperance of Roosevelt's language regarding the Canadians is explainable in part by the fact that when the Alaska matter was coming to a head Roosevelt was in a fever over the unwillingness of the "blackmailers of Bogotá" to ratify the Panama Canal treaty. He even used some of the same vituperative expressions in referring both to the Canadians and to the Columbians. See particularly Roosevelt to Hay, September 21, 1903.

realized how deeply his clumsy tactics hurt the Canadians. As he wrote to Mr. Justice White shortly after the news of the decision, "Our case was ironclad, and the chief need was a mixture of unyielding firmness in essentials and a good-humored courtesy in *everything!*" [33] The result, Roosevelt asserted with perhaps unconscious irony, "furnished a signal proof of the fairness and good will with which two friendly nations can approach and determine issues." [34]

Such is not the verdict of the objective historian.

[33] Roosevelt to White, October 19, 1903; italics Roosevelt's.
[34] Annual message to Congress, December 7, 1903 (*Cong. Record,* 58 Cong., 2 sess., 5).

*The significance of the seal-saving, four-power Pacific pact of 1911 has been underrated. The outcome proved to be a major victory for the conservation of natural resources, a signal triumph for diplomacy (with one of the earliest appeals in American experience to a head of state), and a landmark in the history of international cooperation. The pact, in reconstituted form, is still operating with gratifying success (see postscript to this essay).*

# 9.

## THE NORTH PACIFIC SEALING CONVENTION OF 1911

> "Amphibious is the fur seal, ubiquitous and carnivorous, uniparous, gregarious and withal polygamous."
>
> —Dr. Samuel Flagg Bemis, 1936

### I

By the year 1911 the North Pacific fur seal was little more than a reminder of the greed and rapacity of man.[1] The magnificent American herd on the Pribilof Islands had been reduced in numbers from approximately 4,000,000 in 1867 to a rapidly dwindling 100,000.[2] Within a few

*Pacific Historical Review,* IV (March, 1935), 1–14. Reprinted by permission.

[1] The manuscript materials which were used for the diplomatic aspects of this study were found in the Division of Communications and Records, Department of State, file 1797; file 711.417; and Series 99, vol. 22.

[2] A parallel decimation had occurred on Russia's Commander Islands, the only other important seal rookeries in the North Pacific.

years the fur seal, one of the most beautiful of wild creatures, would become practically extinct. The story of how the herd was saved and rehabilitated, in spite of seemingly insuperable obstacles, should be one of absorbing interest.

At the outset something must be said about the private life of the fur seal. This animal is highly polygamous, and the most powerful males, known as beachmasters, gather about them a harem of females, numbering from about twenty to fifty, and fight off their rivals. Since the beachmaster is usually able to maintain his ascendancy for a considerable period, only about one male in a hundred is necessary for the propagation of the herd. The judicious elimination of a large number of bachelor seals is therefore biologically unobjectionable and at the same time commercially desirable.[3]

Sealing operations are ordinarily conducted on land, where the sealers can easily identify and dispose of the superfluous males. But during 1881 or 1882 an entirely new turn was given to the industry through the development on a commercial scale of pelagic sealing—that is, the killing of the seal while swimming or floating in the water.[4] Under these conditions it was impossible to distinguish between the sexes, and, largely because of the feeding habits of the fur seal, approximately eighty percent of those so destroyed were females.[5] To make matters worse, practically every adult female killed in the open sea was not only pregnant but had left at the rookeries a nursing pup, which invari-

---

[3] *House Reports,* 62 Cong., 2 sess., no. 295, p. 10; David Starr Jordan, *The Days of a Man* (Yonkers-on-Hudson, 1922), I, 547–48.

[4] *House Reports,* 62 Cong., 2 sess., no. 295, p. 5.

[5] They ranged farther for food than the males, and because of regulated land killing there were more of them.

ably starved to death when the mother failed to return.[6] Moreover, about half of the seals that were shot from pelagic schooners swam away mortally wounded or sank before the bodies could be recovered.[7] In short, every female skin obtained from the water represented the death of approximately four seals.[8]

## II

The enormously wasteful practice of open-water butchery must not be confused with the land-sealing operations on the Pribilof Islands, which were conducted by the United States under a carefully regulated government monopoly. But the early pelagic sealers, who were exclusively Americans and Canadians, could carry on their work of destruction with impunity just outside the three-mile line. Unwilling to sit quietly by and watch the wiping out of the herd, the United States officials finally took an extreme position. Arguing that since the seals had their breeding grounds on American territory and were therefore American property wherever found, they straightway proceeded to seize American and Canadian pelagic schooners operating on the high seas.

The British Foreign Office naturally protested. The questions at issue were finally referred to a tribunal which

---

[6] In 1896, G. A. Clark counted 16,000 pups starving to death on St. George Island and St. Paul Island. *House Documents,* 62 Cong., 1 sess., no. 93, p. 859.

[7] At times seven out of ten were not recovered; but a conservative figure would be one out of two. *Ibid.,* pp. 255, 278.

[8] An authority on the fur seal estimated that during the thirty years during which pelagic sealing continued 1,000,000 adult breeding females were killed. G. A. Clark, "Conservation of Fur Seals," in *North American Review,* CXCVII (May, 1913), 641.

sat in Paris in 1893; but on every major count the United States lost. This body did, however, lay down certain rules which were calculated to prevent the extermination of the seal. A closed season of three months during which there could be no pelagic sealing was established; the use of firearms was forbidden; and pelagic schooners were prohibited from approaching within sixty miles of the seal rookeries. But the creation of the sixty-mile zone had little practical effect, inasmuch as the female seals usually ranged out to sea from two to three times that distance. The prohibition on firearms led to the substitution of the spear, which was silent and consequently more deadly. And the closed season proved to be the wrong time of the year.[9]

Convinced of the futility of these regulations, the United States, in 1897, again took up the matter of pelagic sealing with Great Britain. As a token of good faith Congress passed a law forbidding its own citizens to engage in that practice.[10] But since nothing came of these negotiations, the net result was to give the Canadians a virtual monopoly of pelagic sealing.

Shortly after the turn of the century a new and highly significant development occurred. Japanese pelagic sealers, operating under a government bounty, began to appear in increasing numbers off the Pribilof Islands. They were in no way affected by the Paris Award, which was binding only upon the United States and Great Britain, and they were consequently at liberty to use firearms, operate in disregard of the closed season, and penetrate the sixty-mile zone up to the three-mile line. Here they would form cor-

[9] *House Documents,* 62 Cong., 1 sess., no. 93, pp. 273, 276, 379, 537, 863; *House Reports,* 62 Cong., 2 sess., no. 295, p. 6; *Cong. Record,* 59 Cong., 2 sess., 34; H. W. Elliott, "The Loot and Ruin of the Fur-Seal Herd of Alaska," in *North American Review,* CLXXXV (1907), 433, 434.

[10] *House Reports,* 62 Cong., 2 sess., no. 295, p. 6.

dons of small boats several miles long, through which practically every seal leaving or approaching the rookeries would have to pass. During 1910, for example, the twenty-five Japanese pelagic schooners employed 816 men and operated 210 small boats. With this wholesale butchery being lawfully carried on just outside the three-mile line, and often illegally within that line, the herd appeared to be doomed.[11]

III

In the light of the facts just presented it is obvious that the pelagic sealing industry was self-destructive. First to feel the pinch were the Canadians. Forced to operate under the restrictions of the Paris Award, they found it difficult if not impossible to compete with the Japanese as the seals became increasingly scarce. A number of the Canadian hunters consequently joined the crews of Japanese ships, and the Canadian owners gave serious thought to the possibility of transferring their vessels to Japanese registry.[12] In its heyday the Canadian fleet numbered about thirty-five schooners, but by 1908 it had dwindled to about eight.[13]

[11] The Japanese operated 31 schooners off the Pribilofs in 1906; 35 in 1907; 38 in 1908; 23 in 1909; and 25 in 1910. *House Documents*, 62 Cong., 1 sess., no. 93, pp. 276, 280, 503, 539, 605, 607, 691, 783, 858, 1083; *Report of the Secretary of Commerce and Labor*, 1905, p. 43; *ibid.*, 1908, p. 78; *ibid.*, 1909, p. 742. President Roosevelt went so far as to suggest to Congress, in 1906, that the government might resort to the desperate expedient of ending pelagic sealing operations by exterminating the Pribilof herd at the rookeries. Under such a procedure the seals would be disposed of in a more humane way than that being employed, and the profits from the skins would go to the United States Treasury and not to aliens. *Cong. Record*, 59 Cong., 2 sess., 34.

[12] There is evidence indicating that at least one ship was so transferred. *House Documents*, 62 Cong., 1 sess., no. 93, pp. 537, 605; Joseph Boscowitz to Bacon, October 21, 1907, Series 99, vol. 22, Department of State; *Japan Times*, August 9, 1908.

[13] *House Documents*, 62 Cong., 1 sess., no. 93, p. 611.

In 1909 the Canadians operated only five ships and in 1910 six. The following year they sent out none at all, as compared with about thirty for the Japanese.[14] The Paris Award regulations, the competition of the Japanese, and the decimation of the seal herd had at last completely ruined the Canadian pelagic sealing industry.

Pelagic sealing was not only frightfully destructive of wild life but it was also a danger spot in the relations of the United States with both Great Britain and Japan. For more than twenty-five years it had vexed Anglo-American affairs, and at times, particularly during the 1880's, had caused international friction of a critical nature. With the decline of the Canadian fleet and the increase in the number of the Japanese pelagic sealers, the danger of serious trouble with Japan became increasingly imminent. Scarcely a season passed without American revenue officers seizing one or more Japanese schooners for poaching inside the three-mile line or otherwise trespassing upon American rights. Warning shots were frequently fired, and occasionally a Japanese schooner eluded pursuit and escaped. An increasing number of lawless white men secured employment on the Japanese vessels, some of which were the terror of the defenseless Indians on the Alaskan islands and coast.[15]

The most serious incident of all occurred on July 16 and 17, 1906, when the crews of four Japanese schooners, acting in concert, penetrated the three-mile line, landed on the Pribilof rookeries, and began butchering the seals. In repelling this piratical raid, the American authorities killed five of the poachers, wounded two others, and took

[14] *Ibid.*, pp. 538, 608, 1072; *House Reports,* 62 Cong., 2 sess., no. 295, p. 6.

[15] *Report of the Secretary of Commerce and Labor,* 1907, p. 52; *ibid.,* 1908, p. 77; *House Documents,* 62 Cong., 1 sess., no. 93, pp. 481, 503, 542, 590, 606, 692, 783, 1005, 1073.

twelve prisoners.[16] Neither the Japanese government nor people were disposed to defend the work of these outlaws, but the incident was distinctly unpleasant. As long as pelagic sealing continued, a repetition of this bloody raid might easily occur, and possibly at such a critical juncture in Japanese–American relations as to lead to disastrous consequences.[17]

IV

Confronted with this situation, Washington made one final effort to solve the problem by international agreement before extermination of the herd further embittered relations with Japan and Great Britain. Passing by the earlier and unsuccessful efforts in this direction,[18] we may observe that the problem was complex. It would be necessary to draw up a self-denying convention which would be acceptable to the United States, Russia, Great Britain, and Japan. The United States was willing to go far, for the alternative to agreement was extermination. Russia was also prepared to cooperate, partly because her herd on the

16 *Report of the Secretary of Commerce and Labor,* 1906, p. 34.

17 The *Japan Daily Mail* observed (August 21, 1909): "Apart . . . from the question of protecting the seals, there is the graver question of protecting international relations. . . ."

18 In 1897 Japan, Russia, and the United States sent representatives to a joint conference in Washington. The three powers agreed to prohibit pelagic sealing for a time if Great Britain would subscribe to the agreement. But the latter, influenced by the protests of the Canadians, refused to do so. The same problem confronted the Joint High Commission which met in Quebec in 1898; but nothing came of the discussions. The question was complicated by the Alaska boundary dispute, for the Canadians attempted to use their right to pelagic sealing as a club to secure concessions in this quarter. In 1905 Secretary Hay worked out a compensation scheme with Canada looking toward the abolition of pelagic sealing. This was on the point of being accepted when Hay died and the plan was abandoned. *House Documents,* 62 Cong., 1 sess., no. 93, pp. 539, 869; *Senate Documents,* 61 Cong., 2 sess., no. 605, p. 11.

Commander Islands, the only other important seal rookery
in the North Pacific, had suffered even more heavily from
the Japanese pelagic sealers than had that of the United
States.[19]
 Japan and Canada, on the other hand, were differently
situated. The former had some thirty pelagic schooners engaged in what was temporarily, at least, a profitable but
self-destructive industry. One could be certain that the
Japanese government would hesitate before signing away
what was indubitably the right of its subjects to kill seals
on the high seas, particularly in view of the fact that this
business represented a large vested interest which had been
built up under the encouragement of a government
bounty.[20] But intelligent Japanese must have realized that
the pelagic sealing industry was suicidal, and that they
would be well advised to secure an indemnity for giving
up a practice which otherwise would have to be abandoned
sooner or later without compensation.[21] Furthermore, one
of the spoils falling to Japan as a result of the Russo-Japa-
nese War was the remnant of a once-important seal herd on
Robben Island, which might be rehabilitated to a point of
commercial importance if the ravages of the pelagic sealers
could be prevented.[22] In other words, the viewpoint of the

[19] *House Documents*, 62 Cong., 1 sess., no. 93, pp. 539, 871; London
*Times*, June 28, 1911.
 [20] The bounty was discontinued in 1909, probably with the preservation of the Robben herd in view. The official explanation was that the
sealing industry had made such progress that it no longer needed
bounties. O'Brien to Knox, March 11, 1911, in file 711.417, Department of
State.
 [21] One Japanese journal noted that the industry, though honest, was
"penny wise and pound foolish." *Japan Times*, August 9, 1908.
 [22] Schuyler to Root, August 11, 1908 (telegram), Series 99, vol. 22, Department of State; Jordan to Roosevelt, October 15, 1907, *ibid.*; *Japan
Mail*, August 18, 1908.

Japanese had changed somewhat since they had come into possession of rookeries of their own. By 1908 the leading Japanese journals were remarking that wise commercial policy, humanitarian considerations, and international comity pointed to the desirability of an international agreement abolishing pelagic sealing.[23]

The position of Great Britain was agonizingly different. The Canadian pelagic sealing industry had come to a standstill; but the Victoria Sealing Company had on hand a number of schooners for which it desired liberal indemnity in return for an agreement to abstain from an industry which it could no longer continue profitably.[24] And this group was able to exert pressure at Ottawa out of all proportion to its numbers and wealth. The British government, which had so often been accused by the Canadians of sacrificing their interests on the altar of Anglo-American amity, was naturally loath to take a step that would be unpopular in western Canada. On the other hand, London was the sealskin dressing and dyeing center of the world, and the destruction of the American herd would naturally put an end to this profitable business.[25]

v

In 1905 and 1906, as a preliminary step, the Department of State attempted to persuade the Canadians to

---

[23] *Japan Mail,* August 18, 20, 21, 1908; Jay (U.S. chargé at Tokyo) to Root, August 23, 1908, Series 99, vol. 22, Department of State; see also Wright to Root, December 11, 1906, in file 1797, Department of State.

[24] *House Documents,* 62 Cong., 1 sess., no. 93, pp. 255–56, 713, 870.

[25] *Ibid.,* p. 539; *Report of the Secretary of Commerce and Labor,* 1911, p. 495.

abandon pelagic sealing in return for an annual share of the land catch on the Pribilof Islands; but these terms were not sufficiently attractive and negotiations were temporarily dropped.[26] A year and a half later, in April, 1908, the Canadians evidenced a desire to reopen the matter, and Secretary of State Root suggested to Ambassador Bryce of Great Britain the desirability of an agreement involving the four powers.[27] A few months later news came to the Department of State that Russia had made overtures to Tokyo looking toward the abolition of pelagic sealing off the Asiatic coast, and that this proposal had met with some favor in Japan.[28]

Upon receipt of these advices, A. A. Adee, Acting Secretary of State, wrote Secretary Root, who was then in New York, that this was an important development and "may open the door to a quadripartite arrangement between the United States, Great Britain, Japan, and Russia." [29] Root appears to have been influenced by this suggestion, for on January 21, 1909, he addressed an identic note to the ambassadors of Japan, Russia, and Great Britain proposing "a conference or a joint commission to consider and endeavor to agree upon some course of action for the protection and preservation of the seals." [30]

26 Extract from Sir Wilfred Laurier's letter of September 25, 1906, to Lord Grey, delivered to Secretary Root by Ambassador Durand of Great Britain, December 6, 1906, Series 99, vol. 22, Department of State; Root to J. Boscowitz, November 4, 1907, in *ibid.*

27 Root to Bryce, April 9, 1908; Memorandum of British Embassy, dated July 27, 1908, both in *ibid.*

28 Schuyler to Root, August 11, 1908 (telegram); Jay to Root, August 23, 1908; Schuyler to Root, September 4, 1908, all in *ibid.*

29 Adee to Root, September 15, 1908, in *ibid.*

30 Root to Takahira, January 21, 1909, in *ibid.* The same note was sent to representatives of the other two powers.

Within two months the governments of both Japan and Russia expressed their willingness to cooperate,[31] but Great Britain held back. Ambassador Reid, representing the United States at the Court of St. James's, presented the proposal to Sir Edward Grey, in November, 1909. He suggested that "Canada's interest in the matter was merely that of the ownership by people at Victoria of a fleet of worn out and unprofitable sealers engaged in the wasteful business of pelagic sealing; and hinted at the shortsightedness of permitting this trivial Canadian interest to prolong a state of affairs which meant for the United States, Japan, and Russia the destruction of the seal herd. . . ." Then the American Ambassador brought in "the one interested motive" on which he could work when he pointed out that the extermination of the herd meant "the destruction of an important industry in London, in dressing and preparing seal skins." As a result of this interview, Reid concluded that the British government "may be induced to exert a little pressure, but they will surely shrink from ever again overruling a self-governing colony on a point to which it attaches importance." [32]

On March 4, 1910, Ambassador Bryce informed Secretary of State Knox, who had succeeded Root, that Canada was "in hearty accord with the desire of your Government to secure the preservation of the seal herd." Without accepting the invitation for a conference, he outlined a proposal which he felt would provide satisfactory compensa-

31 Japan agreed "in principle" provided "the proposal be likewise entertained by the Governments of Great Britain and Russia." Takahira to Bacon, March 1, 1909, in *ibid.* For the Russian acceptance see Rosen to Knox, March 19, 1909, in *ibid.*
32 Reid to Adee, November 5, 1909, in *ibid.*

tion for the Canadians.[33] Knox thereupon drafted a treaty
embodying these suggestions and guaranteeing to Canada
a share in the land catch on the Pribilof Islands in return
for abandoning pelagic sealing. After considerable discussion, this document was signed on February 7, 1911.[34] It
was not to go into effect, however, until an agreement for
the cessation of pelagic sealing had been made by the four
interested powers.[35] In any event, the next logical step was
an international convention, and the British Foreign Office
straightway announced its willingness to participate in the
proposed conference.[36]

VI

In response to an invitation issued by Secretary Knox
on March 3, 1911, delegates representing Great Britain,
Russia, Japan, and the United States began their delibera-
tions at Washington on May 5, 1911.[37] The work of the
conference aroused little public interest, partly because of
the intense fight then being waged over Canadian reci-

[33] Bryce to Knox, March 4, 1910, in file 711.417, Department of
State.

[34] Knox to Bryce, March 25, 1910; Bryce to Knox, May 16, 1910; Bryce
to Hoyt, June 21, 1910; Bryce to Hoyt, June 26, 1910; Innes to Knox,
December 23, 1910; Bryce to Knox, February 27, 1911, all to be found
in *ibid.*

[35] For text, see *Papers Relating to the Foreign Relations of the United
States, 1911*, pp. 256–59. Hereafter cited as *Foreign Relations.*

[36] Bryce to Knox, February 27, 1911, in file 711.417, Department of
State.

[37] Knox to Baron Uchida, March 3, 1911, in *ibid.* The same note was
sent to the representatives of Russia and Great Britain. All three powers
accepted the invitation promptly. Secretary of Commerce and Labor Nagel
presided over the conference. *Report of the Secretary of Commerce and
Labor, 1911*, p. 525.

procity, and the newspapers paid practically no attention to the fate of the seals.[38] Finally, on June 12, 1911, after the delegates had been in session for more than a month, Secretary of Commerce and Labor Nagel issued a statement to the effect that the conference was deadlocked over the amount of compensation that should be paid to Japan for abandoning pelagic sealing.[39]

On that same day President Taft, despairing of an agreement, took the extraordinary and dramatic step of cabling a personal appeal to the Japanese Emperor, urging Japan to meet the United States halfway in settling their differences. The significant portions of this message, the sending of which appears to have been kept a closely guarded secret,[40] are as follows:

> Your Majesty. It has been reported to me . . . that there is no prospect of reaching an agreement unless both the United States and Japan are willing to make some further concessions to each other. It appears that the United States has proposed to give up a twenty-five per cent. gross interest in the American seal herd, which interest Great Britain and Japan would divide equally, the share of each being twelve and one-half per cent. Great Britain seems willing to accept fifteen per cent., but the Japanese Delegation refuses to consider less than seventeen and one-half per cent., which we cannot concede. . . . I am especially desirous that an agreement should be reached not alone because of the importance of preserving the fur seals but also because of the beneficial effect which a settlement of this question would have upon the friendly relations between the Japanese and American nations.

[38] British interest was diverted by the work of the Imperial Conference.

[39] London *Times,* June 13, 1911.

[40] At least it attracted no notice in the press.

Taft then went on to say that an agreement in this case would "open the way for a general international game law for the protection of other mammals of the sea." If, however, the conference should fail the inevitable result would be "the extermination of the fur seals, and owing to the deep interest taken by the people of the United States in this question, such failure would have a most unfavorable effect both upon official and public opinion here." Taft concluded:

> I am therefore prepared, in order if possible to reach a settlement, to instruct the United States Delegation to meet the Japanese Delegation half-way in adjusting the difference between them and if I can be assured of the favorable reception of this offer, the United States Delegation will be authorized to agree to a settlement by which Japan and Great Britain will each be entitled to fifteen per cent. gross interest in the American herd. . . .[41]

Five days later, on June 17, 1911, the Japanese Emperor cabled his reply:

> Being at all times most anxious to strengthen the bonds of friendship and good understanding which unite our two countries and people, I am highly gratified to acquaint you that the last instruction sent to the Japanese delegates to the Conference will enable them to meet the American delegates half-way in adjusting the point at difference between them.[42]

The spirit of mutual accommodation evidenced in this interchange, and particularly the concession on the part of the Japanese, probably saved the conference. From then on it was relatively easy to iron out the remaining differences;

41 Taft to American Embassy (Tokyo), June 12, 1911, in file 711.417, Department of State.
42 Mutsuhito to Taft, June 17, 1911, in *ibid.*

and on July 7, 1911, some two months after the first meeting, the delegates concluded their work.

VII

The North Pacific Sealing Convention of 1911 prohibited pelagic sealing by citizens or subjects of the signatory nations, leaving to the respective governments owning seal rookeries the right to deal independently with land killing. To compensate the pelagic sealing interests thus destroyed, the United States agreed to give Great Britain (Canada) fifteen percent of the sealskins obtained each year on the Pribilof Islands, and a similar share to Japan. Russia bound herself to surrender fifteen percent of all the skins obtained each year from her herd on the Commander Islands to Canada, and fifteen percent to Japan. In turn, Japan assigned ten percent of the sealskins taken from her small herds to each of the other three nations. In other words, each of the four powers now had a vested interest in the preservation of the fur seal. To make possible immediate compensation for the pelagic sealers, the United States agreed to pay $200,000 to Great Britain and a similar sum to Japan, these cash payments to be credited against sealskins due. The convention was to be effective for fifteen years, and as long thereafter as it should remain undenounced by any one or more of the signatory powers.[43]

We have already noted that in 1911 the Canadians sent out no pelagic schooners at all while the Japanese op-

[43] For text, see *Foreign Relations,* 1911, pp. 260–66. The convention was promptly ratified by the four powers. It will be observed that the convention did not and could not prevent the citizens or subjects of other nations from killing seals on the high seas. But since the four signatory powers controlled all the ports that were within striking distance of the North Pacific herd and were bound not to assist pelagic sealers, no real difficulty has been experienced in this quarter. Information provided by Treaty Division of the Department of State, June 1, 1934.

erated about thirty. We must conclude, therefore, that
Canada was treated generously when she received a share
of the land catch equal to that of Japan. This seemingly
illogical division, as well as other features of the convention, naturally caused some discontent among the Japanese.
But they were reconciled to the arrangement by the knowledge that in the long run it would work to their economic
advantage and improve their relations with the United
States.[44] Nor should we overlook the fact that the Russians
were annoyed at having to yield so much to Canada. In
official circles at St. Petersburg the impression prevailed
that the United States had made a number of concessions
to hasten the reciprocity agreement with Canada, on which
President Taft had set his heart, and that Russia had been
sacrificed to this end.[45] All things considered, Canada appears to have driven a hard bargain.[46]

The North Pacific Sealing Convention gave the scientists an opportunity to prove their contention that pelagic
sealing alone had been the curse of the fur seal.[47] Within
one year after the cessation of this practice the Pribilof herd
displayed a noticeable increase, particularly in females.[48] By

[44] Sammons (American consul general at Yokohama) to Knox, June 21,
1911, in file 711.417, Department of State; see also O'Brien to Knox, April
15, 1909, Series 99, vol. 22, Department of State; *Japan Weekly Mail,*
August 20, 1908.

[45] Wheeler to Knox, July 1, 1911, in file 711.417, Department of
State.

[46] In view of the foregoing facts it is difficult to understand why the
American consul at Victoria should have been able to report that the
people there were up in arms at the neglect of the Dominion government
in permitting one of their industries to be wiped out. Smith to Knox,
August 26, 1911, in *ibid.*

[47] The pelagic interests, particularly during the early years of the
controversy, maintained that land killing was chiefly responsible for the
decimation of the herd.

[48] *Senate Documents,* 62 Cong., 3 sess., no. 997, p. 7.

1932, the 100,000 or so of 1911 had increased to 1,219,000. Yet in that same year, under the government monopoly now existing, 49,336 superfluous males were killed and their skins sold, netting a handsome profit. In fact, from 1918 to 1930, after deducting the annual payments to Canada and Japan, the United States government received a total revenue of $4,477,000 from the seal herd.[49] It is not at all improbable that within a few years the average annual catch will be in the neighborhood of 100,000 skins [the figure rose to 76,000 in 1945].

VIII

In conclusion, we may observe that, whatever dissatisfaction may have been felt at the time, all the interested parties have gained from the Convention of 1911. This perhaps best explains why none of the signatory powers has evidenced a disposition to denounce it. First of all, the pelagic sealers, both Japanese and Canadian, were well compensated for discontinuing an industry that would have inevitably passed away within a few years. What is more, the Japanese and Canadian governments received an increasingly large sum of money under the fifteen percent arrangement.[50] Nor can we overlook the fact that the United States government secures a considerable annual revenue from its monopoly, and has been able to cut down the expense of patrolling the Bering Sea. Moreover, the herd has been rehabilitated to such an extent that it now

[49] *Annual Report of the Governor of Alaska*, 1930, p. 53; *ibid.*, 1933, pp. 13–14.

[50] By 1934 Canada and Japan had each received $1,085,971.01 as their total share. Information provided by the United States Commissioner of Fisheries, May 23, 1934.

supports an industry of some importance, which, in all its aspects, employs a large number of men. To mankind in general the preservation and increase of the herd have meant the pleasure and comfort of more abundant and less expensive skins. The nature lover has rejoiced at a conservation measure of the first importance, and has been able to point to the feasibility of an international game law. In its larger aspects the convention removed a perennial source of international ill feeling and laid to rest a problem which for many years seemed incapable of satisfactory solution. More than that, the agreement has proved to be a landmark in the peaceful adjustment of conflicting international interests. The spectacle of the representatives of four great powers gathering together in conference, compromising their differences, and surrendering their national rights in a spirit of mutual accommodation is an infrequent one in the history of nations, and one that can be pointed to in this case as a promising step along the rocky road toward international cooperation.

సౌ

*In 1941, during the tense pre-Pearl Harbor days, Japan terminated the Convention of 1911, after alleging that the seals had become so numerous as to menace fishing resources. In 1957 the four interested powers substantially restored the original scheme, with amendments in 1963. The United States still awards Canada and Japan each 15 percent of the seal catch at its rookeries, while the Soviet Union makes a similar contribution to the Japanese and Canadians. Japan no longer controls the Robben Island rookery, and hence does not render payments to any of the other signatories. Under the existing agreement, sealing is prohibited in the North Pacific, except for scientific purposes. A 1966 estimate, reported by Senator Bartlett of Alaska, placed the American herd at a million and a half seals.*

*The loss of nearly 1,200 civilian lives on the British liner* Lusitania, *sunk by a German submarine on May 7, 1915, must take high rank among the shocking episodes of World War I. It provides a classic study of the difficulty of adapting new weapons—in this case the submarine—to the old rules of international law. One of the ironies is that the United States itself, though profoundly shocked by the sinking of merchantmen and passenger ships without warning, resorted to this inhumane practice in a wholesale fashion in the war against Japan after 1941. The diary of Captain Schwieger, the U-boat captain who sank the* Lusitania, *was edited by the author simultaneously with this article, and may be consulted elsewhere.† The current state of the stricken ship is discussed in a postscript (p. 218).*

† T. A. Bailey, "German Documents Relating to the 'Lusitania,'" *Journal of Modern History,* VIII (1936), 320–37.

# 10.

# THE SINKING
# OF THE LUSITANIA

"This represents not merely piracy, but piracy on a vaster scale of murder than old-time pirates ever practiced."

—Theodore Roosevelt, 1915

I

On November 3, 1914, some three months after the outbreak of the World War, Great Britain proclaimed her intention of mining the North Sea and of transforming it into a military area. The official British statement announced that such "exceptional measures" had been made necessary by Germany's alleged practice of scattering mines in the open sea in violation of international law. The Berlin government, regarding this innovation as both an illegal blockade and an attempt to starve out Germany, concluded that the only effective means of redress lay in retaliation. Accordingly, on February 4, 1915, the German

*The American Historical Review*, XLI (October, 1935), 54–73. Reprinted by permission.

admiralty declared a war zone around the British Isles, effective February 18, 1915, and announced that its submarines would attempt to destroy all enemy merchantmen found within that area.

The war zone had been established for approximately ten weeks and had taken a toll of sixty-six merchant ships, when, on April 30, 1915, the German submarine *U 20* left Emden for a station off Liverpool.[1] The written orders issued to Lieutenant-Commander Schwieger, of the U-boat, instructed him to attack "transport ships, merchant ships [and] warships." There was no mention, at least in writing, of lying in wait for any particular vessel.[2] The voyage of the *U 20* around northern Scotland and western Ireland was comparatively uneventful until the sixth day out, when the submarine destroyed a small British schooner off the southwestern coast of Ireland.[3] On the next day (May 6) the U-boat, although frustrated in an attack on a 14,000 ton White Star passenger liner, succeeded in sinking two

[1] This figure includes several which were sunk by mines. See New York *Times*, May 8, 1915.

[2] The general orders issued jointly to both the *U 27* and the *U 20* are found in the war diary of Fregattenkapitän Bauer and read as follows [tr.]: "The Third Submarine Half-Flotilla accordingly receives wireless orders for *U 20* and *U 27*: 'Large English troop transports expected starting from Liverpool, Bristol Channel, Dartmouth. In order to do considerable damage to transports *U 20* and *U 27* are to be dispatched as soon as possible. Assign stations there. Get to stations on the fastest possible route around Scotland; hold them as long as supplies permit. *U 30* has orders to go to Dartmouth. Submarines are to attack transport ships, merchant ships, warships. Wire time of departure.'" Marine-Archiv, Kriegstagebuch des Führers der U-Boote der Hochseeflotte, Fregattenkapitän Bauer, Band 2, vom 25 (April, 1915). A photostatic copy of these orders was obtained from the German marine archives through the courtesy of Admiral Arno Spindler. If Schwieger had received supplementary oral or wireless orders to sink the *Lusitania* his course would have been altogether different.

[3] *Ibid.*, Kriegstagebuch S.M.U.-Boot U 20, Band 3, vom 30. IV. bis 13. V. 15, Kommandant Kapitänleutnant Schwieger. Unless otherwise noted, the details preceding and including the sinking of the *Lusitania* have been taken from the diary of Schwieger, a photostatic copy of which was also secured through Admiral Spindler.

British freighters. On the same afternoon Schwieger decided, primarily because of an unexpected shortage of oil, to discontinue the trip to Liverpool and to remain south of the entrance to Bristol Channel until the fuel supply made the return trip imperative.[4]

Thus it was that on the early afternoon of May 7, 1915, the *U 20*, having already begun its homeward voyage, sighted a large passenger steamer (later discovered to be the *Lusitania*) about a dozen miles off the Old Head of Kinsale, southern Ireland.[5] In pursuance of his general and specific orders, Schwieger immediately prepared to attack without revealing his presence. His natural impulse probably was

[4] Apropos of this decision the Schwieger diary for May 6 reads [tr.]: "A further advance toward Liverpool, the real field of operations, abandoned for the following reasons: [three have to do with heavy fog as a factor] (4) The voyage to the St. George's Channel had consumed so much of our fuel oil that it would be impossible for us to return [to Germany] around the southern end of Ireland if we had now continued to Liverpool. I intend to return as soon as two fifths of our fuel oil is used up. I intend to avoid, if at all possible, the trip through the North Channel on account of the type of patrol service which the *U 20* encountered there on her last trip. (5) Only three torpedoes are still available, of which I wish to save two, if possible, for the return trip. It is therefore decided to remain south of the entrance into the Bristol Channel and to attack steamers until two fifths of the fuel oil has been used up; especially since chances for favorable attacks are better here and enemy defensive measures less effective, than in the Irish Sea near Liverpool." The entry for 10 A.M. on May 7 reads, "Since the fog does not abate, I now resolve upon the return journey, in order to push out into the North Channel in case of good weather."

[5] The diary reads [tr.]: "Ahead and to starboard four funnels and two masts of a steamer with course perpendicular to us come into sight (coming from SSW it steered toward Galley Head). Ship is made out to be large passenger steamer. [We] submerged to a depth of eleven meters and went ahead at full speed, taking a course converging with the one of the steamer, hoping it might change its course to starboard along the Irish coast. The steamer turns to starboard, takes course to Queenstown thus making possible an approach for a shot. Until 3 P.M. we ran at high speed in order to gain position directly ahead. Clean bow shot at a distance of 700 meters (G-torpedo, three meters depth adjustment); angle 90°, estimated speed twenty-two knots. Torpedo hits starboard side right behind the bridge. An unusually heavy explosion takes place with a very strong explosion cloud (cloud reaches far beyond front funnel). The explosion of the torpedo must have been followed by a second one (boiler

to warn the vessel, in accordance with international law, and give the passengers and crew an opportunity to take to the small boats before he fired a torpedo. But to do so he would have to emerge and expose his frail craft to the risk of being rammed by the swift liner—a danger of which he was fully conscious.[6] Although he may have had no specific knowledge as to the presence or absence of arms on this particular ship, he knew perfectly well (as his diary shows) that many British merchantmen were armed, and that if he attempted to warn this one he would be taking a dangerous chance. Moreover, it was obvious that if the slow-moving *U 20* emerged to warn its victim the swift liner could easily outdistance the submarine and carry its cargo of ammunition (which British passenger ships were known to carry) safely to its destination.[7] From a purely military standpoint it seemed foolhardy to expose the *U 20* to un-

---

or coal or powder?). The superstructure right above the point of impact and the bridge are torn asunder, fire breaks out, and smoke envelops the high bridge. The ship stops immediately and heels over to starboard very quickly, immersing simultaneously at the bow. It appears as if the ship were going to capsize very shortly. Great confusion ensues on board; the boats are made clear and some of them are lowered to the water. In doing so great confusion must have reigned; some boats, full to capacity, are lowered, rushed from above, touch the water with either stem or stern first and founder immediately. On the port side fewer boats are made clear than on the starboard side on account of the ship's list. The ship blows off [steam]; on the bow the name 'Lusitania' becomes visible in golden letters. The funnels were painted black, no flag was set astern. Ship was running twenty knots. Since it seems as if the steamer will keep above water only a short time, we dived to a depth of twenty-four meters and ran out to sea. It would have been impossible for me, anyhow, to fire a second torpedo into this crowd of people struggling to save their lives." Fifty minutes later the *U 20* viewed the scene through her periscope. The *Lusitania* had disappeared. In the distance a number of lifeboats were drifting.

6 Schwieger's diary clearly reveals this.

7 Churchill admitted on the floor of the House of Commons, March 16, 1914, that forty merchantmen were then defensively armed. *Parliamentary Debates*, 5th ser., vol. LIX, col. 1683. The maximum speed of the *U 20* was approximately twelve knots; that of the *Lusitania* between twenty-one and twenty-four knots.

necessary danger and permit the enemy munitions to escape, especially when a sure means of destroying the liner lay at hand. There appeared to be no safe middle ground between attacking without warning and not attacking at all. The speeding submarine would have failed by a wide margin to intercept the *Lusitania* had not the liner suddenly and at precisely the critical moment changed her course to starboard, thus enabling the *U 20* to discharge one torpedo, which struck with terrible effect. This explosion was immediately followed by another, the cause of which is still conjectural. In spite of the smooth seas the liner immediately began to founder, and in the astonishingly short time of eighteen minutes disappeared beneath the waves. Schwieger recorded that just before the vessel sank the name "Lusitania" became visible on the bow; and he expressed surprise at finding this well-known ship plying her regular course, particularly in view of the fact that he had sunk two British steamers near the same place just the day before. He knew perfectly well that the British admiralty was sending out wireless warnings of submarine activity, and had it been his purpose to waylay the *Lusitania* he probably would have taken every precaution to avoid betraying his presence.

II

The appalling destruction of women, children, and other noncombatants on the *Lusitania* [8] shocked the civi-

---

[8] Of the 1,959 passengers and members of the crew, 1,198 perished; of the passengers drowned, 270 were women and 94 children. Of 197 Americans, 128 lost their lives. The general figures may be found in the official report of Lord Mersey, wreck commissioner of the United Kingdom, which appeared in 1915. *Parl. Papers* [Command 8022], 1915, *Reports,* vol. XXVII, hereafter cited as *Mersey Report.* The more accurate figures relating to the Americans may be found in Secretary Hughes's report of March 31, 1922. *Sen. Doc.,* 67 Cong., 2 sess., no. 176.

lized world and caused the United States, as the only power-ful neutral involved and as the one suffering the heaviest losses, to make strong representations to Germany. In de-fending the action of the submarine the German Foreign Office maintained, first of all, that the *Lusitania* was in effect a British warship, and that as such she was subject to destruction without warning. Since international law pro-vided that a man-of-war might be attacked on sight (unlike bona fide merchantmen, which must always be warned) this charge should be examined.

It was general knowledge that both the *Lusitania* and her sister ship, the *Mauretania,* in line with a policy com-mon among nations with a large merchant marine, had been built with money lent by the British government at a low rate of interest, and that the Cunard company re-ceived a large annual subsidy for holding these two liners in readiness for war service. As the plans published in 1907 indicated, the *Lusitania* was constructed with emplacements for twelve six-inch quick-firing guns (from the draw-ings the guns appeared to be mounted), and it was gener-ally known that in the event of hostilities the vessel could be speedily converted into a fighting craft.[9] The *Maure-tania* was, in fact, transferred to the British admiralty early in the war, and was used for some time exclusively for mili-tary purposes, in which capacity she was subject to destruc-tion without warning. The *Lusitania* was also taken over by the admiralty, but because of her heavy consumption of coal was soon returned to the Cunard company.[10] It would seem, however, that this temporary detention by the British

[9] See the British weekly journal, *Engineering* (August 2, 1907), 133.
[10] Sir Julian S. Corbett, *Naval Operations* (London, 1920–21), I, 29–30; II, 391. This account is based on admiralty documents.

authorities could not be construed as materially affecting her status.

It should also be noted that the captain of the *Lusitania* was a commander of the British Royal Naval Reserve.[11] A silhouette of his vessel appeared in Jane's *Fighting Ships* for 1914; and both the *Lusitania* and the *Mauretania* were listed as "armed merchantmen" under "Royal Naval Reserve Merchant Cruisers" in the British *Naval Pocket Book for 1914*.[12] But these details do not alter the fact that technically the *Lusitania* was not a warship. Although operating under the direction of the British admiralty, she was not incorporated in the armed forces of a belligerent, and she was known to be engaged solely in the transportation of passengers, mail, and freight, in pursuance of which she was just completing her fifth round trip across the Atlantic since the beginning of the war.[13] As an enemy merchantman she was fair prize, but under the law of nations she could not be sunk without warning.

### III

If the *Lusitania* had been armed and otherwise prepared for offensive operations, her status would have been that of a warship. The German Foreign Office at first insisted that she was equipped with guns, and the German Ambassador to the United States, Count Bernstorff, presented several affidavits to the Department of State in sup-

---

[11] But she was neither officered nor manned by the regular navy.

[12] Fred T. Jane, *Fighting Ships* (London, 1914), p. 32; Viscount Hythe and John Leyland, eds., *The Naval Annual, 1914* (London, 1914), p. 207; see also a summary by Park Benjamin in the *Independent* (May 17, 1915), 284–87. Von Jagow to Gerard, May 28, 1915, *Foreign Relations, 1915 Supplement*, p. 420. Hereafter cited as *For. Rel., 1915 Suppl.*

[13] If the *Lusitania* had been engaged in warlike service she would not have been cleared by the New York port authorities. Lansing to Gerard (telegram), June 9, 1915, *ibid.*, p. 437.

port of this contention. Such evidence, however, was soon discredited, particularly when one of the witnesses involved, a German reservist, confessed to perjury and was imprisoned.[14] If, in fact, the German authorities had known that the *Lusitania* was offensively armed, it is difficult to understand why they did not take steps to secure her detention.

With regard to the absence of guns we may observe that the *Lusitania* was searched during the week prior to sailing by the special "neutrality squad," and on the morning of her departure by Mr. Dudley Field Malone, collector of the Port of New York. No armament was found.[15] To the official denial of the British government must be added the testimony of the officers of the *Lusitania* to the effect that there were no guns on board. Not a single one of the one hundred and nine witnesses who eventually testified appears to have even glimpsed any armament.[16] The extreme difficulty, to say nothing of impossibility, of con-

---

[14] New York *Times*, June 3, 9, 11, 19, September 10, 1915.

[15] The "neutrality squad" was given detailed instructions to look for guns or evidences of an attempt to mount guns. Since the location of the emplacements was known, and since the planking covering them had to be torn up before the vessel could be armed, it is evident that the concealment of this operation would have been difficult. A good idea of the extreme care exercised by the port officials at this time may be obtained from the copy of Dudley Field Malone's official report on the *Lusitania* which appeared in the New York *World*, December 4, 1922. In August, 1934, Mr. Malone assured the writer that nothing essential was omitted from the printed report. His own copy of the original could not be conveniently located. Neither the Treasury Department, the Department of State, nor former Secretary of the Treasury McAdoo was able to find the original report or a copy of it. [It was later officially published with a summary of the manifest, in Carlton Savage, ed., *Policy of the United States Toward Maritime Commerce in War* (Washington, D.C., 1936), II, 332–340.]

[16] Thirty-six witnesses testified during the Mersey investigation, and the remainder (some repeaters) in connection with the decision of Judge Mayer, of the United States District Court, Southern District of New York, with regard to limiting the liability of the Cunard company. "The 'Lusitania,'" in *International Conciliation* (November, 1918), no. 132, pp. 5–6. For the decision, see 251 *Federal Reporter* 715.

cealing mounted guns from so great a number of observers must be apparent. We may conclude, therefore, that the evidence points strongly, if not overwhelmingly, to the absence of armament on the *Lusitania*.

One other aspect of this same problem must be considered. Early in the war two British merchantmen entered American ports equipped with guns for defense against German cruisers being employed as commerce destroyers. Since the law of nations had long permitted merchant vessels to carry an armament for protection against pirates and privateers, the Department of State ruled, on September 19, 1914, that belligerent merchantmen would be permitted to leave American ports with mounted six-inch guns if it could be demonstrated that these weapons were designed for defensive purposes only.

The German Foreign Office argued that what was defensive armament against cruisers was offensive armament against submarines. No armed merchantman would go out of its way to try conclusions with a German warship, since the best that it could hope for was to escape after a running fight. But one well-placed shot from an armed passenger ship could easily send a submarine to the bottom; and consciousness of this superiority in strength might easily tempt the merchantman to assume the offensive. In these circumstances Berlin maintained that the introduction of the submarine made the old distinction between offensive and defensive armament illusory. Early in 1916, the Department of State, although later reversing itself, evidenced a disposition to accept this interpretation.[17] In any event, even if the *Lusitania* had left New York with a defensive armament of six-inch guns, it does not appear that international law, at least as it was interpreted at that time by the United

[17] For the correspondence on this subject, see *For. Rel., 1914 Suppl.,* pp. 593–615; *1916 Suppl.,* pp. 146–47.

States, would have sanctioned her destruction without warning.

### IV

The question of ramming, as well as that of armament, has an important bearing on the *Lusitania* case. On February 10, 1915, the British admiralty issued secret orders in which the masters of British merchantmen were instructed as follows: "If a submarine comes up suddenly close ahead of you with obvious hostile intention, steer straight for her at your utmost speed, altering course as necessary to keep her ahead." [18] In other words, orders were given to attack before the enemy craft could possibly give the warning prescribed by international law. Captain Turner of the *Lusitania* later admitted under oath that he was in possession of these instructions; presumably he was cognizant of their import.[19] The Berlin government soon learned of the secret orders (from time to time copies of them were secured from captured vessels), and on February 15, 1915, presented its grievance to the Department of State, including the charge that the British had offered a large sum of money for the destruction of the first German submarine by a British merchantman.[20] This reward, in fact, was soon claimed by three different ships, and during the ensuing months several British captains were decorated or otherwise rewarded for ramming or attempting to ram submarines.[21]

---

18 Other orders were given to facilitate escape from submarine attack, photographic copies of which were sent by Ambassador Gerard to the Department of State. *Ibid., 1915 Suppl.,* pp. 653–54.

19 See hearings, *in camera,* before Lord Mersey. *Parl. Papers* [Command 381], *Reports, 1919,* vol. XXV, pp. 2–3; hereafter cited as *Mersey Hearings.*

20 *For. Rel., 1915 Suppl.,* pp. 104–05.

21 New York *Times,* March 6, 1915; *For. Rel., 1915 Suppl.,* p. 442.

The German Foreign Office maintained, not without reason, that in view of the British secret orders it was suicidal for Germany to conform to international law in its submarine warfare; that these orders converted British merchantmen into offensively armed vessels; and that as such they were warships subject to destruction without warning.[22] Just a few weeks after the *Lusitania* disaster, a British liner, the *Cameronia*, almost rammed a German submarine, and then outdistanced it.[23] Captain Turner probably would have resorted to similar measures, and perhaps with more success, had an opportunity presented itself. A merchantman, of course, is privileged to resist attack, but the law of nations held that in so doing it assumed the status of a man-of-war. In other words, Captain Turner was sailing under orders, which, if he had attempted without success to carry out, would have made it lawful for the submarine ruthlessly to destroy his vessel with everyone on board.

There appears to have been considerable justice in the contention of Berlin that the giant Cunarder, whatever its technical status, was not just an "ordinary unarmed merchant vessel." Even the American ambassador to Germany, James W. Gerard, who was by no means pro-German in his sympathies, wired that "English passenger ships sailing with orders to ram submarines and often armed" could not "be put quite in the category of altogether peaceful merchantmen." [24]

---

[22] Von Jagow to Gerard, July 8, 1915, *ibid.*, p. 465. The British view was that such secret orders had become necessary because of the German practice of sinking without warning.

[23] New York *Times*, June 22, 1915.

[24] Von Jagow to Gerard, May 28, 1915, *For. Rel., 1915 Suppl.*, p. 420; Gerard to Lansing (telegram), July 5, 1915, *ibid.*, p. 461.

v

In attempting to justify the action of the *U 20,* the German Foreign Office made much of the fact that the *Lusitania* was carrying a considerable quantity of munitions. This is true but, from the standpoint of international law, entirely irrelevant. Whatever the moral implications, the nature of the cargo had no legal bearing upon the time-honored rule that no merchantman should be sunk without warning. But since the death of so many unoffending noncombatants profoundly aroused world opinion, and since Berlin claimed that the passengers probably would have been saved had not the sinking of the vessel been greatly accelerated by exploding munitions, this charge must be examined.[25] The question assumes an even more serious aspect when we bear in mind that one of the few points upon which the survivors almost unanimously agreed was that a second explosion of some kind immediately followed the detonation of the torpedo.

In monetary value approximately one half of the *Lusitania's* cargo was composed of materials being shipped for the use of the Allied forces. The manifest listed such items as brass, copper, 4,200 cases of cartridges for rifles, and "1,250 cases Shrapnel." [26] Mr. Malone stated in his official report, however, that the shrapnel cases were empty and "contained no fuses and no explosives of any description whatsoever." But with regard to the cartridges Berlin pointed out that the statutes of the United States forbade the transportation of explosives on passenger vessels, and

[25] See the three German *Lusitania* notes. *Ibid.,* pp. 389, 420, 465; Von Jagow to Gerard, May 28, 1915, *ibid.,* p. 420.

[26] The writer was privileged to examine a photostatic reproduction of the original manifest in Washington, D.C. He was requested, however, not to state where this document is filed. An abbreviated copy may be found in the New York *Times,* May 8, 1915.

that as a consequence the *Lusitania* had placed herself outside the pale by violating the law. Mr. Malone's answer was that in President Taft's Administration ordnance experts had concluded that such small arms ammunition could not be exploded *en masse* by fire or concussion, and that the Department of Commerce and Labor had consequently ruled that munitions of this kind could be legally carried on passenger ships.[27] It is conceivable, however, that the experts were mistaken, and that the intense heat generated by the torpedo explosion ignited the ten to eleven tons of powder in the cartridges. Mr. Malone himself thought that this possibility was not to be dismissed lightly. He even conceded that considerable quantities of high explosives may have been smuggled on board.[28]

The exploding-munitions theory gains further support when we note that the giant Cunarder, which was equipped with devices to render her "unsinkable," went to the bottom within eighteen minutes after being torpedoed. By way of contrast it should be observed that there were many instances, as Schwieger had had occasion to observe on the previous day, when vessels not even one fifth the size of the *Lusitania* did not sink at all after being torpedoed only once, or sank slowly, or required a second torpedo or gunfire to complete their destruction. In any event, since we can definitely eliminate a second torpedo, the odds in

[27] Ruling of May 2, 1911, in interpretation and limitation of section 4472 of the *Revised Statutes of the United States*. See Malone Report, New York *World*, December 4, 1922; also Mr. Malone's letter to the New York *Nation* (January 3, 1923), 15–16.

[28] Conversation with the writer in August, 1934. Mr. Malone had previously stated that it was a "physical impossibility" to examine every package going on board every ship, and that he relied upon the sworn manifest unless suspicious circumstances seemed to warrant an exhaustive search. Letter to the *Nation* (January 3, 1923), 15–16. The *Mersey Report* (p. 6) states that the ammunition was stored well forward, about 150 feet from the spot where the torpedo struck. This, however, is not an unbiased source.

favor of the exploding-munitions theory are considerably increased, although the possibility of an explosion from the boilers or from some other source must not be disregarded. The German Foreign Office further charged, at first, that the *Lusitania* was carrying Canadian troops, the implication being that as a transport in the service of the enemy she was liable to destruction without warning. It would seem, however, that the *Lusitania* could not be regarded as a transport unless she was carrying an organized body of troops; and of their existence there is no evidence. Assuming that the Canadian authorities resorted to the clumsy and highly irregular practice of embarking their troops at American ports, it is difficult to see how such a body of soldiers, even without uniforms, could have escaped the vigilance of the port authorities or the observation of the officers on the vessel.[29] If the German officials, as they stated, knew that the *Lusitania* was a troop ship, they could easily have secured her detention by placing the necessary evidence in the hands of the American authorities.

### VI

We have repeatedly observed that the *Lusitania* was torpedoed without warning. The Berlin officials admitted that she was not destroyed in the orthodox fashion, but they contended that she had been adequately warned and that

---

[29] Von Jagow to Gerard, May 28, 1915, *For. Rel., 1915 Suppl.*, p. 420. Secretary Lansing invited the German government to present any evidence it possessed to the effect that the port authorities had been derelict in their duty. Lansing to Gerard (telegram), June 9, 1915, *ibid.*, p. 437. The *Lusitania's* officers testified that the steamer was transporting no troops. *Mersey Report*, p. 6. There were a number of Canadians on board, some of them the families of officers abroad. It was possible, as Mr. Malone suggested, that a few reservists may have sailed as ordinary civilians. See Malone Report, New York *World*, December 4, 1922. See also New York *Times*, May 9, 11, 1915; New York *Evening Journal*, May 1, 1915.

as a consequence her sinking was in conformity with international law. They pointed out that the first warning had been given in February, 1915, some three months before the *Lusitania* disaster, when Germany announced that she would destroy all enemy ships found within the zone established around the British Isles. The second warning came, indirectly yet forcefully, when the Germans demonstrated their seriousness of purpose by sinking dozens of merchantmen within that zone. Indeed, ninety merchantmen were so destroyed during the eleven weeks before the *Lusitania* went down, twenty-two of them while the giant Cunarder was actually making her last voyage.[30] The third warning appeared as a newspaper advertisement, and to this we must now turn.

On the morning of May 1, 1915, the day the *Lusitania* departed, the following advertisement, placed conspicuously near the sailing notices of the Cunard company, appeared in the leading New York newspapers:

NOTICE!

TRAVELLERS intending to embark on the Atlantic voyage are reminded that a state of war exists between Germany and her allies and Great Britain and her allies; that the zone of war includes the waters adjacent to the British Isles; that, in accordance with formal notice given by the Imperial German Government, vessels flying the flag of Great Britain, or of any of her allies, are liable to destruction in those waters and that travellers sailing in the war zone on ships of Great Britain or her allies do so at their own risk.

IMPERIAL GERMAN EMBASSY
Washington, D.C., April 22, 1915 [31]

In the light of what subsequently happened, the appearance of the warning on the sailing day and its proxim-

---

[30] For the list, see New York *Times,* May 8, 1915.
[31] *Ibid.,* May 1, 1915.

ity to the Cunard advertisement were regarded as conclusive proof of German premeditation. Yet it should be observed that the statement contained no specific mention of the *Lusitania;* and this fact would tend to support the statement of Ambassador Bernstorff, made shortly before the sinking, that the notice was intended merely as a general friendly warning.[32] Several days later the German Embassy added that such action had been necessary because the Department of State, in spite of German representations, had refused to apprise Americans of the grave risks they ran in traveling on Allied ships.[33] Ambassador Bernstorff's own explanation of the date of insertion, which is supported by circumstantial evidence, further weakens the premeditation theory.[34] Finally, Schwieger's orders and his diary, which we have already considered, reveal clearly that the meeting of the *U 20* with the *Lusitania* was purely fortuitous.[35]

In this connection we may further observe that the Manchester *Guardian* attached particular significance to

[32] *Ibid.,* May 2, 1915. Other New York newspapers printed similar accounts.

[33] *Ibid.,* May 10, 1915; Count Bernstorff, *My Three Years in America* (New York, 1920), pp. 131, 139.

[34] Count Bernstorff states that it had been decided to insert the notice for three successive Saturdays (the day on which the Cunarders sailed), but because of certain technical difficulties the advertisement appeared for the first time on May 1 instead of April 24. In support of this statement we find that the warning was dated Washington, D.C., April 22, thus allowing only two days for insertion, and that it appeared again in the New York newspapers on Saturday, May 8, the day after the disaster and at a time when deference to outraged American opinion would have dictated its omission. The German Embassy sensed the situation, and on May 12 notified the newspapers to discontinue the notice, which was scheduled to be printed again on the following Saturday. New York *Times,* May 1, 8, 10, 1915; *Current History,* II (June, 1915), 413; Bernstorff, pp. 135ff.; George Sylvester Viereck, *Spreading Germs of Hate* (New York, 1930), pp. 59ff.

[35] The futility of ordering a slow-moving submarine to waylay a swift liner in what was virtually the open seas must be evident.

the fact that the *Lusitania* was the first transatlantic liner out of ninety-one vessels to be sunk in the submarine zone, and concluded that the Germans had suddenly decided to inaugurate a new campaign of frightfulness by attacking passenger ships, and that they had deliberately begun with the queen of Britain's merchant fleet.[36] But the fate of the *Falaba*,[37] to say nothing of earlier victims, suggests that Germany would not hesitate to sink a passenger liner if an opportunity presented itself; and it appears that the superior speed of the transatlantic vessels was chiefly responsible for preventing an earlier disaster of this kind. Late in March, 1915, a White Star liner, the *Arabic,* and a French Line passenger ship, the *Niagara,* both outran attacking submarines.[38] The day before Schwieger torpedoed the *Lusitania* he attempted to sink a White Star passenger liner but was frustrated by the superior speed of his intended victim.[39] There seems to be no good reason for supposing that the Germans would not have sunk the giant Cunarder earlier if they had been able to do so.

## VII

The misconception is prevalent that the newspaper warning was not printed in time to be effective, or that it

[36] Manchester *Guardian,* May 8, 1915; New York *Sun,* May 9, 1915.

[37] On March 28, 1915, an unarmed British passenger ship bound for West Africa, the *Falaba,* was destroyed with a loss of 104 lives, one of them an American. The British claimed that the vessel had not been properly warned. This was the first passenger ship, although the thirty-sixth merchantman, to be sunk after the war zone became effective.

[38] Alfred Booth, an official of the Cunard company, stated that up to May 7, 1915, the Germans had never torpedoed a ship that was traveling faster than fourteen knots. New York *Times,* March 28, June 17, 1915.

[39] Schwieger diary, entry of May 6, 1915.

did not impress upon the passengers the danger into which they were venturing. As a matter of fact, the advertisement created a sensation, which was abundantly reflected in leave-takings at the pier and in anxious conversations during the voyage.[40] A number of the English voyagers even wrote farewell letters to their home folks to follow later that day on an American vessel. It would, of course, have been awkward at that late hour to change to other ships, but in most cases this could have been done. Nevertheless, practically no bookings were canceled, and the *Lusitania* sailed with her largest eastbound passenger list of the year.[41]

We may assume that the passengers weighed the inconvenience of changing to another and slower vessel against the possibilities of being sunk, and decided to stay with the *Lusitania*. It was widely believed that the Germans were bluffing and that they would not dare to outrage world opinion by sinking an unarmed passenger ship laden with women and children. A number of the more prominent passengers were even quoted as having spoken flippantly of their danger. Moreover, there was great confidence in the remarkable speed of the vessel, and a general feeling, approaching boastfulness among the ship's officers, Cunard officials, and others, that the *Lusitania* could run away from any possible assailant. It was also assumed, even among naval experts, that the great size and special construction of the liner rendered her unsinkable, or at least capable of remaining afloat until all the lifeboats could be lowered. Finally, a number of passengers appear to have been led to

[40] New York *Times,* May 8, 9, 10, 1915. The rumor that prominent passengers were personally warned at the pier by German agents appears to have been without foundation. New York *American,* May 2, 1915; New York *Evening Journal,* May 1, 1915; New York *Tribune,* May 2, 1915; New York *Times,* May 2, 8, 1915.
[41] Lady Rhondda, "May 7th, 1915," *Spectator* (May 5, 1923), 747–48. *Der Lusitania-Fall im Urteile von deutschen Gelehrten* (Breslau, 1915), p. 9.

believe that the British admiralty would send out an armed escort when the ship neared home waters [42]—a delusion which will be examined later.

The appalling loss of American life, which apparently blinded public opinion in the United States to the fact that several Americans had already been killed under similar circumstances in the war zone,[43] was the feature of the disaster which caused the most serious international complications. As a consequence, the question was frequently asked why these unfortunate voyagers should have taken passage on a munitions-laden British ship, particularly after they had been generally and specifically warned of their danger.

It is true that American citizens had an indisputable legal right to travel on an unarmed belligerent merchantman. At the same time it was perfectly evident that British merchant ships, as well as those of neutrals,[44] were then being sunk without adequate provision for the safety of those on board, and that, regardless of neutral rights, the Germans would probably deal with the *Luistania* in the

---

[42] New York *Times,* May 2, 8, 9, 10, 16, 1915; New York *Tribune,* May 2, 1915; Wesley Frost, *German Submarine Warfare* (New York, 1918), pp. 186–87, 195; Charles Seymour, *The Intimate Papers of Colonel House* (Boston, 1926), I, 361; Charles E. Lauriat, Jr., *The Lusitania's Last Voyage* (Boston, 1915), p. 6.

[43] An American had lost his life on the British passenger ship, the *Falaba* (March 28, 1915); and at least two Americans had been killed when an American steamer, the *Gulflight,* was torpedoed on May 1, 1915. Technically the first case was as great a violation of American rights as the sinking of the *Lusitania;* and the torpedoing of a ship flying the United States flag was certainly a more flagrant violation of American rights than the destruction of a British vessel with the incidental loss of neutral lives.

[44] Of the ninety merchantmen destroyed in the submarine zone before the *Lusitania* sank, twenty-one were neutral. In issuing the war zone proclamation the German admiralty had announced that because of the flying of neutral flags by the belligerents and the contingencies of maritime warfare, it would not always be possible to avoid sinking neutral ships.

same way if they had a chance. Nevertheless, 197 Americans went—"committed suicide," as one German sympathizer put it.[45] Some were in haste to transact legitimate business, and to gain a day or so they risked and lost their lives. Others were pleasure-bound; and their sporting instinct prompted them to take a chance—a well-recognized American trait.[46] If these misguided people saw fit to court death in this fashion, that, many argued, was their business. But the disaster came uncomfortably close to plunging 100,000,000 Americans into the war as early as May, 1915; and a number of observers agreed with Secretary Bryan that it was hardly fair for irresponsible or selfish persons to be allowed to exercise such tremendous power for ill.[47] Those Americans who sailed on the *Lusitania* were well within their rights but they were not prudent.

### VIII

We may further observe that Secretary Bryan had considerable support when he argued that, regardless of technical rights, the United States could avoid a great deal of trouble by prohibiting its citizens from traveling on munitions-laden British merchantmen. But President Wilson insisted upon the full letter of the law.[48] The Germans were quick to note an inconsistency here. In 1913 and 1914, following outbursts in Mexico during which scores of Americans lost their lives, the United States government warned its citizens to leave that distraught country or re-

45 New York *Times*, May 10, 1915.
46 *Ibid.*, May 2, 1915.
47 *The Memoirs of William Jennings Bryan*, by himself and his wife, Mary Baird Bryan (Chicago, 1925), pp. 396, 397. See similar statements of Senator Stone of Missouri, Senator Jones of Washington, Vice-President Marshall, and A. Mitchell Palmer. New York *Times*, May 9, 11, 1915.
48 Bryan, *Memoirs*, p. 403; New York *Times*, June 10, 1915.

main there at their own risk. This precaution was taken, even though it meant that a number of investors would lose everything, to prevent a few Americans from involving the entire nation in war. If, argued the Germans, the American government had informed its citizens that they could enter the Mexican war zone only at their own risk, why could it not issue a similar warning regarding the German war zone? [49]

It is not true, as has been alleged, that if the Americans on the *Lusitania* had canceled their passages they would have been forced to wait an inconveniently long period for a neutral ship. The American Line was operating vessels practically every week from New York. They did not carry munitions during the neutrality period and they were conspicuously advertised as flying the American flag. One of these liners, the *New York,* was scheduled to sail only two hours after the departure of the *Lusitania,* and for the same port, Liverpool. Furthermore, the records of the company show that the *New York* had room for 300 more passengers, or all of the 197 Americans who departed on the *Lusitania.* The accommodations on the American liner were not so luxurious as those on the Cunarder, for the *Lusitania* was the largest and swiftest vessel then on the transatlantic run, but they were comfortable and respectable.[50] In other

---

[49] Gerard to Bryan (telegram), May 19, 1915, *For. Rel., 1915 Suppl.,* p. 402; New York *Times,* May 9, 1915. Ambassador Gerard was but one of a number of men in public life who expressed the following thought: "Anyway, when Americans have reasonable opportunity to cross the ocean why should we enter a great war because some American wants to cross on a ship where he can have a private bathroom. . . ." Gerard to Lansing (telegram), July 5, 1915, *For. Rel., 1915 Suppl.,* p. 461.

[50] See the advertisement which appeared below that of the Cunard company in the New York *Times,* May 1, 1915. The information regarding munitions and passengers was provided by the General Passenger Traffic Manager of the International Mercantile Marine Company, which managed the American Line, in letters of September 20 and November 17, 1933.

words, for the sake of a little more luxury and the saving of a few hours of time, to say nothing of such trivial reasons as desiring to be with friends, the American passengers disregarded pointed warnings and ventured into the danger zone.[51]

After the disaster several of the survivors stated that they had sailed on the Lusitania because they were convinced that the Germans would sink an American as readily as a British liner. Yet on February 20, 1915, shortly after the war zone proclamation, Ambassador Gerard wired the State Department that the German admiralty had asked him for silhouettes and other descriptive data regarding the American liners entering the war zone so as to ensure against their being destroyed by mistake. Such a step had doubtless been prompted to some extent by the fact that British merchantmen, including the Lusitania, had been making a practice of flying the American flag.[52] Gerard reported that he had supplied information concerning the arrival and departure of ships of the American Line, as well as silhouettes, among which he included the New York.[53] It would seem as if the State Department might well have given effective publicity to this evidence of a willingness

[51] Following the tragedy several persons reported that for this voyage, as well as for a previous voyage, they had become sufficiently alarmed to transfer from the Lusitania to the New York. New York Times, May 8, 9, 11, 1915.

[52] Early in February, 1915, the Lusitania had raised the American flag when she approached the submarine zone. This incident caused a considerable amount of comment in both England and America, and great indignation in Germany, where it was felt that the Cunarder had resorted to an illegal device to avoid destruction. But since international law has long sanctioned the display of false colors by merchantmen seeking to elude the enemy, the use of the American flag on an earlier voyage could scarcely be construed as giving Germany legal grounds for sinking the Lusitania without warning.

[53] Gerard to Lansing (telegram), February 20, 1915, For. Rel., 1915 Suppl., p. 121.

on the part of the German government to avoid sinking American vessels.

## IX

There were many complaints to the effect that if the Cunard company had taken reasonable precautions the disaster would not have occurred. It appears that neither the *Lusitania*'s officers nor the shipping circles in Liverpool were particularly alarmed by the published warning, which was regarded as both a bluff and as one more attempt to injure British shipping.[54] After the loss of his vessel, Captain Turner was summoned before the wreck commissioner, and it was revealed that he had been instructed by the admiralty to steer a mid-channel course and to avoid headlands (near which submarines usually lurked); to proceed at a high speed; and to zigzag. In all these particulars he had disregarded his orders. When torpedoed, he was steaming along the usual course, about a dozen miles off the Old Head of Kinsale. He explained this by saying that it was necessary to approach land and take bearings before proceeding any further up St. George's Channel. He had reduced his speed from twenty-one to eighteen knots, in order, so he claimed, not to arrive off Liverpool too soon and be forced to wait outside the bar for the tide while exposed to submarine attack. It was pointed out at the hearings, however, that he could have accomplished the same result by proceeding at high speed on a roundabout course.

[54] London *Times*, May 3, 1915; New York *Times*, May 8, 1915; New York *Sun*, May 9, 1915; 251 *Fed. Reporter* 721; Viereck, p. 64; Frost, pp. 186–87. A Cunard official in New York reported that the line had already been threatened with advertisements that would hurt its business if it did not pay blackmail. New York *Times*, May 1, 1915.

Finally, Captain Turner confessed that he had misread his orders, despite their explicitness, to mean that he was to zigzag only when he sighted an enemy submarine.[55] This was both a stupid and a fatal error.

A number of American survivors attributed much of the loss of life to the incompetence of officers and crew after the torpedo had struck. There was, of course, a great deal of confusion, some of which was perhaps due to the fact that there had been only one boat drill on the voyage, despite requests from the passengers for special training.[56] The crew was admittedly below prewar standards because many of the younger men had heeded the call to the colors. Other charges involved open portholes, inadequate equipment, and unwise orders. These matters were all examined at length by the Mersey Commission, which sat in 1915, and by the United States District Court of the Southern District of New York, which, in 1918, passed upon the sixty-seven consolidated damage actions brought against the Cunard line. Both of these tribunals, which abundantly reflected the prevailing war spirit, absolved the company of negligence in handling the ship. As for Captain Turner's disregard of orders, the time-honored dictum was invoked that the commander's judgment regarding a given situation must take precedence over blanket instructions. The report of the Mersey Commission, however, was indignantly received by a number of the American survivors, who branded it a "whitewash." [57]

---

[55] *Mersey Hearings*, pp. 2ff.

[56] New York *Times*, May 10, June 17, 1915. The stricken vessel listed so far to one side as to make difficult or impossible the proper lowering of lifeboats.

[57] 251 *Fed. Reporter* 728; New York *Times*, July 18, 1915.

## X

It was widely felt, both in England and in America, that the British authorities were guilty of criminal negligence in permitting the tragedy to occur. The First Lord of the Admiralty, Winston Churchill, later admitted that the warning advertisement was a matter of "general knowledge" before the disaster.[58] Yet no precautions were taken except to send almost a dozen wireless messages of direction and warning (including general reports of the sinkings of the *U 20*) to the approaching *Lusitania* on May 6 and 7.[59] These communications led to the German charge that the vessel was not being operated by the Cunard company at all but by the British admiralty.[60]

A number of passengers appear to have embarked on the *Lusitania* with the expectation, and even with assurances, that an armed escort would be provided when the danger zone was reached. But despite the fact that there were several available destroyers at nearby Queenstown, no such protection was forthcoming.[61] When Churchill was charged with remissness, he replied that since it was impossible to provide protection for all British merchantmen, the admiralty had adopted the general policy of escorting none. Concentration of energy for war purposes and the avoidance of charges of discrimination obviously dictated such

---

[58] *Parl. Debates* (Commons), 5th scr., vol. LXXI, col. 1361.

[59] 251 *Fed. Reporter* 722; Winston S. Churchill, *The World Crisis, 1915* (New York, 1923), II, 347.

[60] See Viereck's statement in the New York *Times*, May 9, 1915.

[61] Lauriat, p. 6; New York *Times*, May 10, June 15, 1915. See the ambiguous assurances of a Cunard official in *ibid.*, May 1, 1915. Corbett, II, 393.

a policy. Yet there were many who felt with the London *Morning Post* that since the Germans had apparently announced their intention through a published notice of "getting" the pride of Britain's merchant fleet, the admiralty would have been justified in making an exception in this one instance. In support of such a contention it may be observed that Churchill, under persistent questioning, admitted on the floor of the House of Commons that the admiralty had sent out escorts on two different occasions to bring in British freighters laden with American horses.[62]

Whatever the basis for the charges against both the Cunard company and the admiralty, the fact remains that the *Lusitania* was doing almost everything possible to make easier her destruction. On a clear day she was steaming at reduced speed; she was following her usual course; she was near what was known to be a submarine-infested headland; she was not in mid-channel; she was not zigzagging; and she was without armed escort. The admiralty probably reasoned that the Germans were incapable of sinking so swift a vessel, or that they had neither the effrontery nor the stupidity to outrage world opinion by destroying so many innocent noncombatants. In fact, Berlin accused the Cunard company of deliberately carrying American passengers so that they might serve as living shields for cargoes of munitions, and the German view was that Americans could not legitimately expect immunity while lending themselves to such a scheme.[63] A more serious charge was that the

---

[62] *Parl. Debates* (Commons), 5th ser., vol. LXXI, cols. 1361–62. *Morning Post,* quoted in the *Outlook* (May 19, 1915), 112.

[63] Von Jagow to Gerard, May 28, July 8, 1915, *For. Rel., 1915 Suppl.,* pp. 420, 465. This charge, repeatedly made, cannot be proved. It is clear, however, that the British were not displeased that Americans should want to travel on their ships, and no effort appears to have been made to discourage them from doing so.

British government made no effort to protect the *Lusitania* because it hoped that her destruction would force the United States into the war. This view was widely held by the Germans, and was even communicated to Ambassador Gerard by the Kaiser.[64] No credible evidence has yet been presented to support the theory.[65]

XI

In the light of the facts herein presented, it becomes less difficult to understand why the German government believed that it was acting "in just self-defense" when it sought "to protect the lives of its soldiers by destroying ammunition destined for the enemy with the means of war at its command." [66] The Germans felt that if international law did not justify them in what they did, in spite of the living screen of noncombatants and neutrals who had been warned, something was wrong with international law, and that the alternative was to modify it just as the Allies were doing. But Great Britain, although admitting that the "peculiar" or "novel" conditions of the war made it necessary for her blockade to employ "exceptional measures," was unwilling to accord the same privilege to the Germans in their submarine warfare on merchantmen, insisting that the enemy modifications of international law, strikingly demonstrated in the case of the *Lusitania*, were so ruthless

[64] Gerard to Lansing (telegram), May 6, 1916, *For. Rel., 1916 Suppl.,* p. 260. See also New York *Times,* May 11, 1915.

[65] Some scholars have made too much of the fact that while the *Lusitania* was en route, King George speculated to Colonel House about what would happen if the Germans should sink her with Americans aboard. It is unlikely that the King was privy to secret discussions, and the warning advertisement was a common topic of conversation.

[66] Von Jagow to Gerard, May 28, 1915, *For. Rel., 1915 Suppl.,* p. 420.

and inhuman as to be inadmissible. This was the view of millions, perhaps the majority, of Americans, to say nothing of other neutrals. They believed that, whatever technical grounds might be advanced by way of justification, the torpedoing of the *Luistania* was the cold-blooded mass murder of 1,198 unoffending and helpless men, women, children, and babies. They were convinced that no interpretation or modification of international law should ever permit the sinking of passenger ships without warning because such an act was a violation of the rights of humanity.

The present discussion is concerned with the actual facts of the disaster rather than with the intricacies of diplomacy or international law. This much, however, may be said. If we leave out of consideration the question of reprisals and assume that the *Lusitania* was not a warship, her sinking appears to have been a clear violation of the law of nations. But whether or not her destruction was a justified reprisal for the Allied attempt to starve out Germany is a matter over which the authorities are divided, depending to a considerable extent upon their nationality and their sympathy or lack of sympathy with the cause of the Central Powers.[67] And whether or not the *Lusitania* was essentially

[67] The attempt to starve a belligerent population by means of a legal blockade is not a violation of international law. But the Germans maintained that the so-called British blockade was illegal; and they later argued that the sinking of the *Lusitania* was a legitimate reprisal for the prior British violation of international law. A number of the best authorities (American and British) are agreed that a reprisal, to be permissible, must be a retortion in kind and that it must not involve neutrals. The *Lusitania* disaster did affect neutrals, and (the Allies claimed) was so ruthless and undiscriminating a slaughter of noncombatants as not to constitute a legitimate reprisal for the slow starvation of a civilian population— a process which would cease whenever the Germans were disposed to surrender. The German Foreign Office finally admitted (February 4, 1916) that "retaliation must not aim at other than enemy subjects" and agreed to make pecuniary reparation for the loss of American citizens on the *Lusitania. Ibid., 1916 Suppl.,* p. 157. This concession, however, was to some extent dictated by the necessity of mollifying the United States and probably did not represent the convictions of the Germans. In a report of

a warship will depend largely on how one is disposed to interpret the facts here presented, particularly the secret orders to ram. This interpretation, in turn, will be influenced by the subjective factors just mentioned. Since there is no international tribunal for passing upon such questions, and since the authorities are in disagreement and doubtless always will be, the legal aspects of the case probably will never be settled to the satisfaction of everyone concerned.

But the discussion of legal justification is largely academic. The supreme objective in war is victory; and the acid test of any measure is its contribution to that end. It is true that the 4,200 cases of ammunition never reached England. But the terrible inhumanity of the *Lusitania* disaster shocked the civilized world; it added immeasurably to the moral fervor of the Allied cause; it alienated a vast amount of sympathy for the Central Powers, particularly in America; it caused the almost complete collapse of the German propaganda campaign in the United States; it gave a strong impetus to the American preparedness movement; and, though not directly responsible for the entrance of the United States into the war, it contributed powerfully to the inflamed state of mind which made possible the final break nearly two years later. Even military necessity could hardly justify the results.

---

Privy Councilor Kriege, which contains what is probably the best case that can be made out for Germany on the grounds of reprisal, it is argued that neutrals, by acquiescing in British violations of international law, could properly be included in German measures of reprisal. See *Völkerrecht im Weltkrieg* (Berlin, 1927), vol. IV, ser. III, sec. 3. There is, in fact, something to be said for the German contention that the Americans were at fault in passively submitting to the restrictions established by the British war zone while ignoring or trying to force their way through the German submarine zone. Of the numerous monographs written by German investigators that by Friedrich Lützow, *Der Lusitania-Fall* (Leipzig, 1921) is the most useful. An able presentation of the German point of view by a recognized authority is Arno Spindler, "The 'Lusitania' Case," in the *Berliner Monatshefte* (May, 1935), 402–10.

❧

*The wreck of the* Lusitania *was located with difficulty in about 300 feet of water, and various salvage attempts at this dangerous depth were begun in 1935, without much result. The most recent efforts have been those of John Light, a former U.S. Navy diver and a free-lance movie photographer, who made a series of dives between 1960 and 1962. Some of his underwater photographs were shown on British television. At various times he encountered harassment by British naval officials, and some of his experiences are recounted in a popular magazine.†* *Among other revelations, he declared that the wreck had been tampered with, either by using depth bombs or cutting devices. He and a companion reportedly discovered that a deep hole had been cut in the deck where a gun could have been emplaced, and within it they glimpsed a shadowy object which may have been a gun—possibly a pipe or a spar. Assuming that the tampering was done by British officials, one is hard put to explain why they should have gone to this trouble, particularly since passenger liners could legitimately carry guns for defensive purposes.*

The Observer, *a London weekly, reported in 1967 that the same diver, John Light, had purchased the wreck for £1,000 and was continuing highly secret dives. Supposedly he was endeavoring to salvage valuables and at the same time produce a highly salable book.††* *The present*

---

† *Sports Illustrated,* XVII (December 24, 1962), 37–47; shorter and earlier versions of Light's activities appeared in the New York *Times,* May 10, 1962, 27.

†† *The Observer* (August 20, 1967), 3.

author has been in correspondence with Mr. Light, but does not feel at liberty to reveal more than has appeared in the press. The intrepid diver promises further sensational revelations.

In 1956 Adolph A. and Mary Hoehling published their book, The Last Voyage of the Lusitania. No essential new facts were revealed. The emphasis is on the breathless drama and the human interest, including imagined thoughts and conversations.

*Remembering the tragic fruits of isolationism in the 1920's and 1930's, the author greatly feared during World War II that the United States would repeat the same blunders. He therefore felt the call to examine critically the mistakes of the peacemakers of 1919–20 with the hope of educating American public opinion to its responsibilities in shaping an enduring peace. The result was two books, published in 1944 and 1945, on Wilson's efforts as a peacemaker. The following is in essence a summary of his findings, prepared later at the invitation of a leading popularizer of historical writing.*

# 11.

## WOODROW WILSON WOULDN'T YIELD

"As a friend of the President . . . I solemnly declare to him this morning: If you want to kill your own child [League of Nations] because the Senate straightens out its crooked limbs, you must take the responsibility and accept the verdict of history."
—Senator Henry F. Ashurst, in Senate, 1920

I

The story of America's rejection of the League of Nations revolves largely around the personality and character of Thomas Woodrow Wilson.

Born in Virginia and reared in Yankee-gutted Georgia and the Carolinas, Wilson early developed a burning hatred of war and a passionate attachment to the Confederate-embraced principle of self-determination for minority peoples. From the writings of Thomas Jefferson he derived much of his democratic idealism and his invincible faith

*American Heritage*, VIII (June, 1957), 20–25, 105–06. Reprinted by permission.

in the judgment of the masses, if properly informed. From his stiff-backed Scotch-Presbyterian forebears, he inherited a high degree of inflexibility; from his father, a dedicated Presbyterian minister, he learned a stern moral code that would tolerate no compromise with wrong—as defined by Woodrow Wilson.

As a leading academician who had first failed at law, he betrayed a contempt for "money-grubbing" lawyers, many of whom sat in the Senate, and an arrogance toward lesser intellects, including those of the "pygmy-minded" senators. As a devout Christian keenly aware of the wickedness of this world, he emerged as a fighting reformer, whether as president of Princeton, governor of New Jersey, or President of the United States.

As a war leader, Wilson was superb. Holding aloft the torch of idealism in one hand and the flaming sword of righteousness in the other, he aroused the masses to a holy crusade. We would fight a war to end wars; we would make the world safe for democracy. The phrase was not a mockery then. The American people, with an amazing display of self-sacrifice, supported the war effort unswervingly.

The noblest expression of Wilson's idealism was his Fourteen Points address to Congress in January, 1918. It compressed his war aims into punchy, placard-like paragraphs, expressly designed for propaganda purposes. It appealed tremendously to oppressed peoples everywhere by promising such goals as the end of secret treaties, freedom of the seas, the removal of economic barriers, a reduction of arms burdens, a fair adjustment of colonial claims, and self-determination for oppressed minorities. In Poland, university men would meet on the streets of Warsaw, clasp hands, and soulfully utter one word, "Wilson." In remote regions of Italy peasants burned candles before poster portraits of the mighty new prophet arisen in the West.

The fourteenth and capstone point was a league of nations, designed to avert future wars. The basic idea was not original with Wilson; numerous thinkers, including Frenchmen and Britons, had been working on the concept long before he embraced it. Even Henry Cabot Lodge, the Republican senator from Massachusetts, had already spoken publicly in favor of *a* league of nations. But the more he heard about the Wilsonian League of Nations, the more critical of it he became.

A knowledge of the Wilson–Lodge feud is basic to an understanding of the tragedy that unfolded. Tall, slender, aristocratically bewhiskered, Dr. Henry Cabot Lodge (Ph.D., Harvard), had published a number of books and had been known as "the scholar in politics" before the appearance of Dr. Woodrow Wilson (Ph.D., Johns Hopkins). The Presbyterian professor had gone further in both scholarship and politics than the Boston Brahmin, whose mind was once described as resembling the soil of his native New England: "naturally barren but highly cultivated." Wilson and Lodge, two stubborn men, developed a mutual antipathy which soon turned into freezing hatred.

II

The German armies, reeling under the blows of the Allies, were ready to surrender by November, 1918. The formal armistice terms stipulated that Germany was to be guaranteed a peace based on the Fourteen Points, with two reservations concerning freedom of the seas and reparations.

Meanwhile the American people had keyed themselves up for the long-awaited march on Berlin; eager voices clamored to hang the Kaiser. Thus the sudden end of the shooting left inflamed patriots with a sense of frustration and letdown that boded ill for Wilson's policies. The red-faced Theodore Roosevelt, Lodge's intimate of long standing, cried that peace should be dictated by the chatter of machine guns and not "the clicking of typewriters."

Wilson now towered at the dizzy pinnacle of his popularity and power. He had emerged as the moral arbiter of the world and the hope of all peoples for a better tomorrow. But regrettably his wartime sureness of touch began to desert him, and he made a series of costly fumbles. He was so preoccupied with reordering the world, someone has said, that he reminded one of the baseball player who knocks the ball into the bleachers and then forgets to touch home plate.

First came his tactlessly direct appeal for a Democratic Congress in October, 1918. The voters trooped to the polls the next month and, by a narrow margin, returned a Republican Congress. Wilson had not only goaded his partisan foes to fresh outbursts of fury, but he had unnecessarily staked his prestige on the outcome—and lost. When the Allied leaders met at the Paris peace table, he was the only one not entitled to be there—on the European basis of a parliamentary majority.

Wilson next announced that he was sailing for France, presumably to use his still enormous prestige to fashion an enduring peace. At that time no President had ever gone abroad, and Republicans condemned the decision as evidence of a dangerous Messiah complex—of a desire, as former President Taft put it, "to hog the whole show."

The naming of the remaining four men to the peace delegation caused partisans further anguish. Only one, Henry White, was a Republican, and he was a minor figure at that. The Republicans, now the majority party, complained that they had been good enough to die on the battlefield; they ought to have at least an equal voice at the peace table. Nor were any United States senators included, even though they would have a final whack at the treaty. Wilson did not have much respect for the "bungalow-minded" senators, and if he took one, the logical choice would be Henry Cabot Lodge. There were already enough feuds brewing at Paris without taking one along.

Doubtless some of the Big Business Republicans were out to "get" the President who had been responsible for the hated reformist legislation of 1913–14. If he managed to put over the League of Nations, his prestige would soar to new heights. He might even arrange—unspeakable thought!—to be elected again and again and again. Much of the partisan smog that finally suffocated the League would have been cleared away if Wilson had publicly declared, as he was urged to do, that in no circumstances would he run again. But he spurned such counsel, partly because he was actually receptive to the idea of a third term.

III

The American President, hysterically hailed by European crowds as "Voovro Veelson," came to the Paris peace table in January, 1919, to meet with Lloyd George of Britain, Clemenceau of France, and Orlando of Italy. To his dismay, he soon discovered that they were far more interested in imperialism than in idealism. When they sought to carve up the territorial booty without regard for the colonials, contrary to the Fourteen Points, the stern-jawed Presbyterian moralist interposed a ringing veto. The end result was the mandate system—a compromise between idealism and imperialism that turned out to be more imperialistic than idealistic.

Wilson's overriding concern was the League of Nations. He feared that if he did not get it completed and embedded in the treaty, the imperialistic powers might side-track it. Working at an incredible pace after hours, Wilson headed the commission that drafted the League Covenant in ten meetings and some thirty hours. He then persuaded the conference not only to approve the hastily constructed Covenant but to incorporate it bodily in the peace treaty. In support of his adopted brain child he spoke so movingly on one occasion that even the hard-boiled reporters forgot to take notes.

Wilson now had to return hurriedly to the United States to sign bills and take care of other pressing business. Shortly after his arrival the mounting Republican opposition in the Senate flared up angrily. On March 4, 1919, 39 senators or senators-elect—more than enough to defeat the treaty—published a round robin to the effect that they would not approve the League in its existing form. This meant that Wilson had to return to Paris, hat in hand, and there weaken his position by having to seek modifications.

Stung to the quick, he struck back at his senatorial foes in an indiscreet speech in New York just before his departure. He boasted that when he brought the treaty back from Paris, the League Covenant would not only be tied in but so thoroughly tied in that it could not be cut out without killing the entire pact. The Senate, he assumed, would not dare to kill the treaty of peace outright.

## IV

At Paris the battle was now joined in deadly earnest. Clemenceau, the French realist, had little use for Wilson, the American idealist. "God gave us the ten commandments and we broke them," he reportedly sneered. "Wilson gave us the Fourteen Points—we shall see." Clemenceau's most disruptive demand was for the German Rhineland; but

Wilson, the champion of self-determination, would never consent to handing several million Germans over to the tender mercies of the French. After a furious struggle, during which Wilson was stricken with influenza, Clemenceau was finally persuaded to yield the Rhineland and other demands in return for a security treaty. Under it, Britain and America agreed to come to the aid of France in the event of another unprovoked aggression. The United States Senate shortsightedly pigeonholed the pact, and France was left with neither the Rhineland nor security.

Two other deadlocks almost broke up the conference. Italy claimed the Adriatic port of Fiume, an area inhabited chiefly by Yugoslavs. In his battle for self-determination, Wilson dramatically appealed over the head of the Italian delegation to the Italian people, whereupon the delegates went home in a huff to receive popular endorsement. The final adjustment was a hollow victory for self-determination.

The politely bowing Japanese now stepped forward to press their economic claims to China's Shantung, which they had captured from the Germans early in the war. But to submit 30,000,000 Chinese to the influence of the Japanese would be another glaring violation of self-determination. The Japanese threatened to bolt the conference, as the Italians had already done, with consequent jeopardy to the League. In the end, Wilson reluctantly consented to a compromise that left the Japanese temporarily in possession of Shantung.

The Treaty of Versailles, as finally signed in June, 1919, included only about four of the Fourteen Points essentially intact. The Germans, with considerable justification, gave vent to loud cries of betrayal. But the iron hand of circumstance had forced Wilson to compromise away many of his points in order to salvage his fourteenth point, the League of Nations, which he hoped would iron out the injustices that had crept into the treaty. He was like the mother who throws her younger children to the pursuing wolves in order to save her sturdy firstborn son.

v

Bitter opposition to the completed treaty had already begun to form in America. Tens of thousands of homesick and disillusioned soldiers were pouring home, determined to let Europe "stew in its own juice." The wartime idealism, inevitably doomed to slump, was now plunging to alarming depths. The beloved Allies had apparently turned out to be greedy imperialists. The war to make the world safe for democracy had obviously fallen dismally short of the goal. And at the end of the war to end wars there were about twenty conflicts of varying intensity being waged all over the globe.

The critics increased their clamor. Various foreign groups, including the Irish-Americans and the Italian-Americans, were complaining that the interests of the "old country" had been neglected. Professional liberals, notably the editors of the *New Republic,* were denouncing the treaty as too harsh. The illiberals, far more numerous, were denouncing it as not harsh enough. The Britain-haters, like the buzz-saw Senator James Reed of Missouri and the acid-penned William R. Hearst, were proclaiming that the British had emerged with undue influence. Such ultra-nationalists as the isolationist Senator William E. Borah of Idaho were insisting that the flag of no superstate should be hoisted above the glorious Stars and Stripes.

When the treaty came back from Paris, with the League firmly riveted in, Senator Lodge despaired of stopping it. "What are you going to do? It's hopeless," he complained to Borah. "All the newspapers in my state are for it." The best that he could hope for was to add a few reservations. The Republicans had been given little opportunity to help write the treaty in Paris; they now felt that they were entitled to do a little rewriting in Washington.

Lodge deliberately adopted the technique of delay. As chairman of the powerful Senate Committee on Foreign Relations, he consumed two weeks by reading aloud the entire pact of 264 pages, even though it had already been printed. He then held time-consuming public hearings, during which persons with unpronounceable foreign names aired their grievances against the pact.

Lodge finally adopted the strategy of tacking reservations onto the treaty, and he was able to achieve his goal because of the peculiar composition of the Senate. There were 49 Republicans and 47 Democrats. The Republicans consisted of about twenty "strong reservationists" like Lodge, about twelve "mild reservationists" like future Secretary of State Kellogg, and about a dozen "irreconcilables." This last group was headed by Senator Borah and the no less isolationist Senator Hiram Johnson of California, a fiery spellbinder.

The Lodge reservations finally broke the back of the treaty. They were all added by a simple majority vote, even though the entire pact would have to be approved by a two-thirds vote. The dozen or so Republican mild reservationists were not happy over the strong Lodge reservations, and if Wilson had deferred sufficiently to these men, he might have persuaded them to vote with the Democrats. Had they done so, the Lodge reservations could have all been voted down, and a milder version, perhaps acceptable to Wilson, could have been substituted.

## VI

As the hot summer of 1919 wore on, Wilson became increasingly impatient with the deadlock in the Senate. Finally he decided to take his case to the country, as he had so often done in response to his ingrained "appeal habit." He had never been robust, and his friends urged him not to risk breaking himself down in a strenuous barnstorming campaign. But Wilson, having made up his mind, was unyielding. He had sent American boys into battle in a war to end wars; why should he not risk his life in a battle for a League to end wars?

Wilson's spectacular tour met with limited enthusiasm in the Middle West, the home of several million German-Americans. After him, like baying bloodhounds, trailed Senators Borah and Johnson, sometimes speaking in the same halls a day or so later, to the accompaniment of cries of "Impeach him, impeach him!" But on the Pacific Coast and in the Rocky Mountain area the enthusiasm for Wilson and the League was overwhelming. The high point— and the breaking point—of the trip came at Pueblo, Colorado, where Wilson, with tears streaming down his cheeks, pleaded for his beloved League of Nations.

That night Wilson's weary body rebelled. He was whisked back to Washington, where he suffered a stroke that paralyzed the left side of his body. For weeks he lay in bed, a desperately sick man. The Democrats, who had no first-rate leader in the Senate, were left rudderless. With the wisdom of hindsight, we may say that Wilson might better have stayed in Washington, providing the necessary leadership and compromising with the opposition, insofar as compromise was possible. A good deal of compromise had already gone into the treaty, and a little more might have saved it.

Senator Lodge, cold and decisive, was now in the driver's seat. His Fourteen Reservations, a sardonic parallel to Wilson's Fourteen Points, had been whipped into shape. Most of them now seem either irrelevant, inconsequential, or unnecessary; some of them merely reaffirmed principles and policies, including the Monroe Doctrine, already guaranteed by the treaty or by the Constitution.

But Wilson, who hated the sound of Lodge's name, would have no part of the Lodge reservations. They would, he insisted, emasculate the entire treaty. Yet the curious fact is that he had privately worked out his own set of reservations with the Democratic leader in the Senate, Gilbert M. Hitchcock, and these differed only in slight degree from those of Senator Lodge.

VII

As the hour approached for the crucial vote in the Senate, it appeared that public opinion had evidently veered considerably. Although confused by the angry debate, it still favored the treaty—but with some safeguarding reservations. A stubborn Wilson was unwilling to accept this disheartening fact, or perhaps he was not made aware of it. Mrs. Wilson, backed by the President's personal physician, Dr. Cary Grayson, kept vigil at his bedside to warn the few visitors that disagreeable news might shock the invalid into a relapse.

In this highly unfavorable atmosphere, Senator Hitchcock had two conferences with Wilson on the eve of the Senate ballot. He suggested compromise on a certain point, but Wilson shot back, "Let Lodge compromise!" Hitchcock conceded that the Senator would have to give ground but suggested that the White House might also hold out the olive branch. "Let Lodge hold out the olive branch," came the stern reply. On this inflexible note, and with Mrs. Wilson's anxiety mounting, the interview ended.

The Senate was ready for final action on November 19, 1919. At the critical moment Wilson sent a fateful letter to the Democratic minority in the Senate, urging them to vote down the treaty with the hated Lodge reservations so that a true ratification could be achieved. The Democrats, with more than the necessary one-third veto, heeded the voice of their crippled leader and rejected the treaty with reservations. The Republicans, with more than the necessary one-third veto, rejected the treaty without reservations.

The country was shocked by this exhibition of legislative paralysis. About four-fifths of the senators professed to favor the treaty in some form, yet they were unable to agree on anything. An aroused public opinion forced the Senate to reconsider, and Lodge secretly entered into negotiations with the Democrats in an effort to work out acceptable reservations. He was making promising progress when Senator Borah got wind of his maneuvers through an anonymous telephone call. The leading irreconcilables hastily summoned a council of war, hauled Lodge before them, and bluntly accused him of treachery. Deeply disturbed, the Massachusetts Senator said: "Well, I suppose I'll have to resign as majority leader."

"No, by God!" burst out Borah. "You won't have a chance to resign! On Monday, I'll move for the election of a new majority leader and give the reasons for my action." Faced with an upheaval within his party such as had insured Wilson's election in 1912, Lodge agreed to drop his backstage negotiations.

VIII

The second-chance vote in the Senate came on March

19, 1920. Wilson again directed his loyal Democratic following to reject the treaty, disfigured as it was by the Lodge reservations. But by this time there was no other form in which the pact could possibly be ratified. Twenty-one realistic Democrats turned their backs on Wilson and voted Yea; 23 loyal Democrats, mostly from the rock-ribbed South, joined with the irreconcilables to do the bidding of the White House. The treaty, though commanding a simple majority this time of 49 Yeas to 35 Nays, failed of the necessary two-thirds vote.

Wilson, struggling desperately against the Lodge reservation trap, had already called upon the nation, in a "solemn referendum," to give him a vote in favor of the League in the forthcoming Presidential election of 1920. His hope was that he could then get the treaty approved without reservations. But this course was plainly futile. Even if all the anti-League senators up for reelection in 1920 had been replaced by pro-League senators, Wilson would still have lacked the necessary two-thirds majority for an unreserved treaty.

The American people were never given a chance to express their views directly on the League of Nations. All they could do was vote either for the voluble Democratic candidate, Cox, who stood for the League, or the stuffed-shirt Republican candidate, Harding, who wobbled all over the evasive Republican platform. If the electorate had been given an opportunity to express itself, a powerful majority probably would have favored the world organization, with at least some reservations. But wearied of Wilsonism, idealism, and self-denial, and confused by the wordy fight over the treaty, the voters rose up and swept Harding into the White House on a tidal wave of votes. The winner had been more anti-League than pro-League, and his prodigious plurality of 7,000,000 votes condemned the League to death in America.

## IX

What caused this costly failure of American statesmanship?

Wilson's physical collapse intensified his native stubbornness. A judicious compromise here and there no doubt would have secured Senate approval of the treaty, though of course with qualifications. Wilson believed that in any event the Allies would reject the Lodge reservations. The probabilities are that the Allies would have worked out some kind of acceptance, so dire was their need of America's economic support, but Wilson never gave them a chance to act.

Senator Lodge was also inflexible, but prior to the second rejection he was evidently trying to get the treaty through—on his own terms. As majority leader of the Republicans, his primary task was to avoid another fatal split in his party. Wilson's primary task was to get the pact approved. From a narrowly political point of view, the Republicans had little to gain by engineering ratification of a Democratic treaty.

The two-thirds rule in the Senate, often singled out as the culprit, is of little relevance. Wilson almost certainly would have pigeonholed the treaty, as he threatened, if it had passed with the Lodge reservations appended.

Wilson's insistence that the League be wedded to the treaty actually contributed to the final defeat of both. Either would have had a better chance if it had not been burdened by the enemies of the other. The United Nations, one should note, was set up in 1945 independently of any peace treaty.

Finally, the American public in 1919–20 was not yet ready for the onerous new world responsibilities that had suddenly been forced upon it. The isolationist tradition was still potent, and it was fortified by postwar disillusionment. If the sovereign people had cried out for the League with one voice, they almost certainly would have had their way. A treaty without reservations, or with a few reservations acceptable to Wilson, doubtless would have slipped through the Senate. But the American people were one war short of accepting that leadership in a world organization for peace which, as Wilson's vision perceived, had become a necessity for the safety and the welfare of mankind.

The blame for this failure of statesmanship cannot fall solely on the excessive partisanship of both parties, the shortsighted outlook of Lodge, or the rigidity of a sick and ill-informed President. Much of the responsibility must be placed at the door of a provincial population anxious to escape overseas responsibilities while basking in the sunshine of normalcy and prosperity.

*Shortly after the publication of his* Presidential Greatness *(1966), the author was invited by* The New York Times Magazine *to write the following article, which is included here as an example of his less formal style. Subsequent events seem to call for a modification of a few of the judgments, but this is how the picture looked to the author at the time, and his appraisal still has considerable relevance to current foreign policy.*

# 12.

## JOHNSON AND KENNEDY: THE TWO THOUSAND DAYS

"His [Kennedy's] untimely and violent death will
affect the judgment of historians, and the danger is
that it will relegate his greatness to legend. . . .
In my view, the man was greater than the legend.
His life, not his death, created his greatness."
—Theodore C. Sorensen, Kennedy's assistant, 1965

I

To rank Presidents, living or dead, is tricky business.
To compare Presidents, one still superactive and the
other an overnight legend, is risky business. But now that
Lyndon B. Johnson has passed the test of his first thousand
days we may hazard some kind of comparison with his
predecessor of the original thousand days.[1]

*The New York Times Magazine* (November 6, 1966), 30ff. © 1966 by
the New York Times Company. Reprinted by permission.
[1] Kennedy's "thousand days" in the Presidency were actually 1,037
days (January 20, 1961–November 22, 1963). Johnson completed an equal
period in office September 23, 1966.

Kennedy's tragic death gave almost instant birth to a cult which contrives, consciously or unconsciously, to magnify his achievements and minify his shortcomings. He entered the White House pledged to get the country moving again, but it was not moving forward conspicuously when the fatal shots rang out in Dallas.

All we have to do is go back to the newspapers and magazines of the week or so before the end. We find that the nation seemed to be on dead center and that the Congress—a heavily Democratic Congress at that—was in virtual revolt. Kennedy's tax-reduction and tax-reform bill was bogged down in a seniority-strangled Congress, as was his crucial civil-rights legislation. The foreign-aid authorization was being meat-axed. Federal aid to education had fallen far short of expectations, while Medicare for the aged, already rejected by the previous Congress, was neatly shelved. The polls showed that Kennedy's popularity had dropped from 83 percent, following the Bay of Pigs fiasco, to about 57 percent in October, 1963.

Then came the assassination and the deification. Most of the setbacks, as was true of Lincoln, were buried under an outpouring of eulogy and elegy. To intimate that Kennedy was less than a great President verges on blasphemy.

## II

President Johnson now finds himself in an increasingly uncomfortable position. His popularity is slipping badly, as it was bound to slip. No incumbent can possibly sustain for a protracted period the momentum achieved by an unprecedented 61 percent of the popular vote. Vietnam is the dead albatross around Johnson's neck that may pull him down. Except for this seemingly insoluble problem, his achievements have been little short of amazing, not only with his inherited Eighty-eighth Congress but more especially with his landslide Eighty-ninth Congress. But from Vietnam flows a river of woe: inflation, the price–wage pinch, mounting strikes, restrictions on credit, the need for increased taxes, the further drain of gold, pressure for calling up the Reserves, dissatisfaction with the draft, and a drumfire of world criticism, much of it from allies.

But sagging popularity is an old story, and Johnson is worried, perhaps unduly, about it. George Washington and Thomas Jefferson, generally judged great Presidents, left office amid no loud hosannas. Other Presidents began to run downhill after spectacular initial successes, notably Woodrow Wilson with his New Freedom legislation and Franklin Roosevelt with the first Hundred Days of his New Deal. The number of rabbits that a leader can pull out of his hat is limited, and when the going gets tougher the complaint inevitably rises, "What has he done for us lately?"

Another problem for the historian is the shortness of perspective. Kennedy's Alliance for Progress, with its $20 billion over ten years, was hailed as a dramatic achievement. Johnson's Medicare bill, which Kennedy had put into the pipeline, was hailed as manna from heaven by the old folks. Both schemes have run into difficulties, and we shall have to defer judgment as to their final worth when we come to evaluate the two Administrations.

III

Presidents are known largely by their fruits, and the first question is: What did each man achieve on the home front?

Kennedy came into office with much fanfare for his New Frontier program of social and economic betterment. He had behind him, or presumably behind him, a heavy Democratic majority of 64 to 36 in the Senate and 263 to 174 in the House. But the conservative Democrats joined hands with the conservative Republicans to suffocate in committee or slaughter on the floor a number of his pet proposals. He strove desperately to get the legislation passed, but the results were highly frustrating.

Admittedly Kennedy ran into hard luck, but there are always "special circumstances" with which a President must grapple. At stake was Kennedy's leadership of his own party in Congress and in the country, and, whatever the reasons, he failed to achieve his ends. Woodrow Wilson had a refractory Democratic Congress, but he built up a backfire of public opinion and drove through it an impressive sheaf of New Freedom reforms. We judge Presidents by what they do and not by what they would have done if there had been no obstacles in their path.

Even so, the Kennedy legislative output was not bad. It compares rather favorably with the bundle of noncontroversial bills that pass when Congress is controlled by the opposition party. But the record looks unimpressive because it disappointed high hopes. A number of key measures were blocked, and much of what passed came through the grinder with extreme difficulty.

IV

Wheeler-dealer Lyndon Johnson took exactly the same Congress, and with a furious display of coaxing, cajoling, compromising, and plain arm-twisting, finally rang up a remarkable record. He jammed through the legislative mill

the controversial tax cut and the new civil-rights bill—
Kennedy's two top priorities. Vice-President Johnson had
suffered much frustration while playing second fiddle to
President Kennedy, and perhaps his frantic pace was partly
inspired by a determination to show up his predecessor and
discomfit the remaining Kennedys, who were not his most
ardent admirers. Some of these bills, already in the congressional hopper, no doubt would have passed if Kennedy
had lived. And the shock of his death probably helped to
stir Congress into motion, even though hardboiled politicians are not unduly given to sentiment. Yet Johnson
must be credited with having delivered the goods, whereas
Kennedy had done so in only a limited sense.

After his landslide victory in 1964, Johnson really
swung into action. He railroaded through his "hip pocket"
Congress a batch of bills that in some respects eclipsed
Franklin Roosevelt's Hundred Days, hitherto regarded as
the all-time high. Johnson even did the impossible by
threshing out a compromise-aid measure for both public
and parochial schools. It not only enlisted the support of
Protestants and Catholics but of constitutionalists as well.
Kennedy, sensitive about his Catholicism, had leaned over
backward in insisting upon a rigid separation of church
and state as presumably envisaged by the First Amendment.

Kennedy had also failed to come to grips with the
Negro revolution. He was aware of the mounting pressures
but he evidently underestimated them. Throwing sops here
and there to the Negroes, he kept civil rights on the back
burner, fearful of further alienating those Southern Democrats whose votes he so urgently needed for the New Frontier. The blowup was triggered in 1962 when James Meredith entered the University of Mississippi, followed by
bloodshed and hundreds of Federal marshals and troops.

The long, hot summers of 1962 and 1963 will not soon be forgotten.

President Johnson had his troubles with the continuing Negro revolution, and was widely though unfairly blamed for it. But to his credit he reversed his stand as Senator and pressed vigorously for civil rights. The epochal bill of 1964 stands as a landmark, followed by the voting rights bill of 1965. The backlash reaction to Negro rioting in the cities helped to sidetrack the civil rights bill of 1966, but this setback may have been only temporary.[2]

v

A President is now regarded as the Protector-in-Chief of the economy, and the Kennedy-and-Johnson two thousand days spanned the longest and lushest era of sustained prosperity in our history. The continuing momentum was thought to be largely due to the tax cut, which Kennedy had the courage to propose in the face of a red-inked budget, and which Johnson finally forced through Congress. But perhaps this tax cut, followed by the $4.6 billion cut in excise taxes in 1965, came too soon. Inflationary prosperity is illusory prosperity.

Kennedy, the youngish millionaire, failed to enlist the confidence of the business community, especially after his ruthless and not altogether unjustified crackdown on the steel companies for their collusive increase of prices. His ill-advised remarks about the steel tycoons being s.o.b.'s did nothing to increase his standing with these gentry and their associates.

Johnson, the oldish millionaire, succeeded in enlisting the support of both management and labor to an unusual degree, at least until 1966. But labor is becoming increas-

2 A civil rights bill was passed in 1968.

ingly unhappy over the President's failure to secure his promised repeal of Section 14b of the Taft–Hartley Act, and in truth Johnson evidently has not been straining himself twisting congressional arms in an election year. As 1966 lengthened, the business world became disenchanted with Johnson, especially his management of the price–wage clash, with consequent inflation. Kennedy had brought the steel moguls to heel in 1962, but a year later, when they raised their prices with less evidence of collusion, he permitted the increases to stand. Johnson, the superslick politician, was more devious. He undertook to hold down the price of aluminum by dumping government stockpiles on the market, all the while having Administration spokesmen announce that the disposal of these surpluses had no relation whatever to the price increases. Such shenanigans fooled few political sophisticates, and further contributed to the disquieting "crisis in credibility" then developing on the Potomac.

VI

Great Presidents have made powerful enemies by courageously taking unpopular stands. During his lifetime Kennedy was cordially hated by big business, by many anti-Catholics, and by anti-integrationist Southerners, among others. The thousand-day Johnson made fewer enemies. He sprawled so completely over the middle of the road as to leave only the gutters for the radical right and the radical left. So passionately determined was he to be universally loved that he was a "consensuscrat" rather than a Democrat. His Texas-sized straddle worked fairly well at first, but in the long run a President can neither fool nor please all the people all the time.

Johnson's strength as a superpolitician is also a source of weakness, and may ultimately prove his undoing. With the Vietnam war, which he widened clandestinely, came no clarion call for blood, sweat, tears, and belt-tightening. Johnson would give us both guns and butter, all at the same price. By mid-1966 the pinch demanded a drastic cutback of the Great Society, or a sharp increase in taxes, or both. Many voices are clamoring for a call-up of Reserves rather than youthful draftees who are not rich enough or bright enough or white enough to get deferments. But the congressional elections have been looming up—and Johnson not only loves that immense majority in Congress but the vote of confidence that its retention bestows. So preelection paralysis has set in, inflation has inserted its greedy hand into every pay envelope, and strikes have erupted all over the land.

The costly airlines strike of 1966 handed both the Democratic President and the Democratic Congress a hot potato. They tossed it back and forth gingerly, while millions of Americans suffered financial loss or serious inconvenience or both. A settlement finally came, but only after the striking mechanics had defied both their leaders and the President. The White House blandly announced that the terms were within the 3.2 percent anti-inflationary guideline, only they were not. Credibility took another beating.

VII

Kennedy's record in foreign affairs was a spotty one. He began with the Bay of Pigs disaster, which was incredibly bungled but for which he manfully shouldered full blame. He journeyed to Vienna for a grim conference with Premier Khrushchev, who evidently thought the young man lacked nerve and who shortly thereafter pulled one of his periodic Berlin bluffs. Kennedy reacted—perhaps overreacted—by calling up the Reserves. The Berlin Wall of Shame rose, but Kennedy could do nothing about it, except risk wrapping the world in nuclear flames. His Grand Design for Europe, with America the senior partner, ran headlong into the Napoleonic plans of President de Gaulle. The haughty Frenchman flatly vetoed Britain's admission to the Common Market, spurned the dubious mixed-force nuclear fleet, and further undermined the outdated NATO alliance. De Gaulle probably would have gone his own stiff-necked way in any event, but Kennedy's secret huddle with Prime Minister Macmillan at Nassau in 1962 did nothing to promote camaraderie at the highest levels. Allies who are not trusted reciprocate distrust.

Kennedy must be commended for having abandoned cheap "massive retaliation" in favor of "balanced deterrence" with conventional forces. In a crisis the alternatives would not simply be humiliation or holocaust. His Peace Corps was a noteworthy and relatively inexpensive success. His Alliance for Progress, though a forward-looking concept, has proved to be no alliance and its progress has not always been forward. His Trade Expansion Act of 1962, perhaps the most notable and unexpected of his legislative triumphs, clothed him with unprecedentedly flexible powers to manipulate the tariff in the interests of freer trade.

Kennedy's finest hour came with the Cuban crunch of 1962, although one still wonders what the Administration was doing during the many anxious weeks before we suddenly found ourselves looking down the nuclear gun barrel. Yet Kennedy played the game of nuclear chicken with coolness and skill, thereby largely erasing the black mark of the Bay of Pigs. But his victory rang hollow. Cuba was still in the grip of the Communists, the island was still a Soviet satellite, and the Monroe Doctrine was still being flouted daily.

In the more relaxed atmosphere that followed the Cuban crisis, the partial Nuclear Test Ban Treaty of 1963 was negotiated and approved, but the results were over-ballyhooed. No nuclear weapons were scrapped; testing continued underground; the nonsignatory nations continued to spew radioactivity into the air (France, China); and there was good reason to fear that the exclusive Nuclear Club would soon include more self-invited members.

## VIII

Lyndon Johnson inherited all of his major headaches in foreign affairs from Kennedy, including the Dominican dilemma in its less acute form. The agreement for the neutrality of Laos, approved at Geneva in 1962 under Kennedy, has not brought neutrality, but few expected it would. The gold hemorrhage has continued at an alarming rate, despite dainty rather than drastic efforts to insert stoppers. Disarmament discussions in the U.N. and at Geneva have ground on endlessly and seemingly purposelessly. Beleaguered Berlin and the reunification of the Reich remain explosive problems, with a resurgent West Germany wanting a finger in the nuclear pie, and with an apprehensive Russia waving a warning fist.

The disintegration of NATO continues apace, with de Gaulle forcing American men and installations off French soil, at a cost of a billion or so dollars and a further drain on the gold reserve. (Johnson, with characteristic restraint in such encounters, has refrained from paying his disrespects to the formidable Frenchman, at least in public.) The long-frozen policy regarding Red China—non-recognition and nonadmission to the U.N.—has been perpetuated under Johnson. Too many domestic elections had been won on the anti-Communist issue, and he is not one who wishes to be accused of sidling up to the Reds.

Overshadowing everything else, and affecting almost everything else, is Vietnam. Without it, the Johnson thousand days would unquestionably be crowned with greatness. President Eisenhower had promised American financial aid and military hardware for the Diem regime, but Kennedy, in a fateful move, committed thousands of military "advisers" who would assist in combat operations but not engage in them. Arthur M. Schlesinger, Jr., found Kennedy badly shaken after receiving news of Diem's murder, and concluded that the President regarded his inability to solve the Vietnam puzzle as his "great failure in foreign policy."

By the time of his assassination, a turn-tail withdrawal was obviously impossible, without intolerable loss of face and betrayal of faith. Direct involvement was evidently only a matter of time. The extent of the involvement was up to Johnson, and following the Gulf of Tonkin incident in 1964 and the blank check from Congress, he sharply escalated the conflict. He evidently was misled by over-optimistic assessments of airpower by the Pentagon and by his civilian staff. But one of the primary responsibilities of a President, as Kennedy learned the harsh way at the Bay of Pigs, is to spot poor advisers.

Johnson's rush-order Dominican intervention in April, 1965, looks somewhat better than it did, now that free elections have been held and all the foreign troops have been withdrawn. He was again deceived to some extent by his advisers, but he was determined to avert another

Castroized Cuba. Perhaps he did, but at heavy cost to the laboriously built Good Neighbor policy.

IX

The styles of Kennedy and Johnson differ markedly, but are strikingly similar in certain respects. Both men rate as "strong" Presidents—that is, activists determined to "make things happen." Both may be judged covetous of power, enjoying manipulating its levers and appreciating how it can be used to promote the public welfare. Both qualify as high-grade politicians. Both can be called effective speakers, despite Kennedy's broad Boston "a" and Johnson's Texas twang; but Kennedy made better speeches. A Pulitzer Prize winner in biography, he had the magic gift of style, and he also employed better speech writers.

The telegenic Kennedy, readier of both tongue and smile, was a virtuoso in his televised press conferences. Johnson's awareness of such superiority probably accounts in part for his rather gun-shy approach to this medium. Kennedy, as a former journalist, established a better rapport with the press. Johnson, evidently irked by his inability to put the newsmen in his pocket, in turn annoys them by his frenetic movements, his favoritism with certain correspondents, and his warping, sugar-coating, or falsification of the news. "News management" dates back to George Washington's Administration, but Kennedy seems to have been somewhat more forthright than his successor.

Kennedy was Harvard; Johnson is Southwest State Teachers College. Kennedy was more the man of meditation; Johnson more the man of motion. Kennedy stressed abstract ideas and ideals; Johnson stressed deeds and action. Kennedy, the speed reader, was bookish; Johnson, the talkative Texan, gets much of his information by ear, especially over the telephone—the so-called fourth arm of government. Both men are known for complete dedication to their high office and for laboring long hours; but Kennedy was handicapped by his injured back and other physical disabilities. Johnson works harder, partly because he suffers from a disturbing reluctance to delegate responsibility. His job is his hobby, and he seems to find relaxation in it.

A refreshing sense of humor has been associated with both men—but Kennedy was witty while Johnson is funny. Kennedy could laugh wryly at himself, which is something that Johnson finds more difficult. Both are known for sensitivity to criticism, as all Presidents worth their salt are, but Johnson is supersensitive, as no President should be. This failing accounts in large part for his irritability, his volcanic explosions of temper, his feuding with the press corps, his obsession to be liked, and his passion to win and to win big.

x

Kennedy had class, so much so that he looked good losing. After the incredible Bay of Pigs botch, his popularity shot up to its all-time high. Kennedy had dignity: he was to the manner born. One could not conceive of his pulling up his shirt in front and exposing the scar of a recent gall-bladder operation for the world to see. Johnson's private language is salty and earthy, not to say uncouth; seemingly the manure of the Texas ranch clings to his high-heeled boots. A frantic flesh-presser, he is a throwback to the baby-kissing politician who went out of fashion even before Teddy Roosevelt.

Kennedy had the gift of inspiring personal followership. He gathered about him a dedicated group of intellectuals, heavily Harvard, but they gradually deserted the

Johnson ship. They evidently did so with heavy hearts, for like Franklin Roosevelt's Brain Trust, they had tasted the unaccustomed and heady power that comes from being close to the throne.

Johnson has made an effort to carry on with the cultural and artistic festivals that Kennedy staged with such grace in the White House, but somehow they fall flat. Johnson is not arty, and the banks of the Pedernales are not Paris. The devotion of the Kennedy intellectuals is not transferable to Johnson, and much of the criticism of his Vietnam policy arises from pro-Kennedy Democrats, including the Kennedys. They are waiting impatiently in the wings for 1972, perhaps 1968, for the return from Elba and the repatching of shattered dreams.

The Kennedy record is tragically truncated yet complete, except insofar as it is being and will be warped by idolaters or detractors. Kennedy was the promise of a President, as much as a President, perhaps more noteworthy for the ideals he enunciated than for the deeds he consummated.

The Johnson record is not complete. The events of the next few years may or may not elevate him to greatness, but no one can doubt that he is an immensely able though complex leader who has already left a tremendous impact. On the basis of the actual record, Kennedy can never be bracketed with Washington and Lincoln, but Johnson still has a chance, especially if he serves nearly ten years and manages to get us into a really big war. Three of our greatest Presidents—Lincoln, Wilson, and Franklin Roosevelt—were victorious leaders in our three greatest conflicts.

Historians in future decades will probably rate Kennedy somewhat above and Johnson somewhat below their desserts. History is written by intellectuals, and Kennedy's style, crowned by a mysterious martyrdom, has an irresistible appeal. After all, he was one of them.

༄

*As events turned out, historians will be most unlikely to bracket Johnson with the so-called great Presidents. His chances were badly hurt when the stalemated Vietnam conflict, which he had substantially enlarged in 1965, did not become an all-out, victorious war. He finally saw fit not to risk running for a second elective term, what with the swelling unpopularity of the Vietnam involvement and the deepening distrust of his credibility. The great Presidents, we should remember, have all been triumphantly reelected. The nation was convulsed with various discontents, including a racial revolution, and Johnson was probably wise to bow out when he could do so gracefully, rather than hazard further repudiation at the polls. He evidently decided to run for the verdict of posterity rather than the accolade of the Presidency.*

# WRITINGS
# OF
# THOMAS A. BAILEY

## BOOKS

*The March of the Mormon Battalion from Council Bluffs to California, Taken from the Journal of Henry Standage.* Coedited with Frank Golder and J. Lyman Smith. New York, The Century Co., 1928. 295 pp.

*Theodore Roosevelt and the Japanese-American Crises: An Account of the International Complications Arising from the Race Problem on the Pacific Coast.* Stanford, Calif., Stanford University Press, 1934. 353 pp. Reprinted by Peter Smith, Gloucester, Mass., 1964.

*A Diplomatic History of the American People.* New York, F. S. Crofts and Co., 1940. 806 pp. 2d ed., 1942. 864 pp. 3d ed., 1946. 937 pp. 4th ed., Appleton-Century-Crofts, 1950. 986 pp. 5th ed., 1955. 1,008 pp. 6th ed. (completely reset), 1958. 896 pp. 7th ed., 1964. 973 pp. 8th ed., 1969, in press. 1st ed. awarded Commonwealth Club silver medal for the best book in its class.

*The Policy of the United States Toward the Neutrals, 1917–1918.* Baltimore, The Johns Hopkins Press, 1942. 520 pp. Reprinted by Peter Smith, Gloucester, Mass., 1966.

*America's Foreign Policies: Past and Present.* New York, Headline Book, Foreign Policy Association, 1943. 96 pp. Rev. ed., 1945.

*Woodrow Wilson and the Lost Peace.* New York, The Macmillan Co., 1944. 381 pp. Awarded Commonwealth Club gold medal. Paperback ed., Chicago, Quadrangle Books, 1963. Reprinted by Peter Smith, Gloucester, Mass., 1963.

*Woodrow Wilson and the Great Betrayal.* New York, The Macmillan Co., 1945. 429 pp. Paperback ed., Chicago, Quadrangle Books, 1963. Reprinted by Peter Smith, Gloucester, Mass., 1963. Braille ed., 7 vols., Library of Congress, Washington, D.C., 1966.

*Wilson and the Peacemakers.* New York, The Macmillan Co., 1947. 740 pp. Combining *Woodrow Wilson and the Lost Peace* and *Woodrow Wilson and the Great Betrayal.*

*The Man in the Street: The Impact of American Public Opinion on Foreign Policy.* New York, The Macmillan Co., 1948, 334 pp. Reprinted by Peter Smith, Gloucester, Mass., 1964.

*America Faces Russia: Russian-American Relations from Early Times to Our Day.* Ithaca, N.Y., Cornell University Press, 1950. 375 pp. Reprinted by Peter Smith, Gloucester, Mass., 1964. Awarded Commonwealth Club gold medal.

*The American Pageant: A History of the Republic.* Boston, D. C. Heath and Co., 1956. 1,007 pp. Trade ed., Boston, Little, Brown and Co., 1956. Pirated ed., Taiwan, c. 1957. 2d ed., 1961. 1,037 pp. 2d trade ed., Little, Brown, 1961. 3d ed., 1966. 1,058 pp. Paperback ed., 2 vols., D. C. Heath and Co., 1966.

*The American Pageant Quiz Book.* Boston, D. C. Heath and Co., 1958. 191 pp. 2d ed., 1961. 195 pp. 3d ed., 1966. 200 pp.

*The American Spirit: United States History as Seen by Contemporaries.* Boston, D. C. Heath and Co., 1963. 964 pp. Paperback ed., 2 vols., 1963. 2d ed., 1968. 1,008 pp. 2d paperback ed., 2 vols., 1968.

*The American Pageant Guidebook.* With Hugh Ross. Boston, D. C. Heath and Co., 1964. 194 pp. Rev. ed., 1966. 198 pp.

*Presidential Greatness: The Image and the Man from George Washington to the Present.* New York, Appleton-Century Co., 1966. 368 pp. Paperback ed., New York, Appleton-Century-Crofts, 1966. 303 pp.

*The Art of Diplomacy: The American Experience.* Hardback and paperback eds., New York, Appleton-Century-Crofts, 1968.

*Democrats vs. Republicans: The Continuing Clash.* New York, Meredith Press, 1968. 179 pp.

# ARTICLES

(The articles herein reproduced are starred)

"The California Criminal Syndicalism Law," *University Debaters' Annual, 1923–1924,* ed. Edith M. Phelps. New York, H. W. Wilson Co., 1924. Pp. 65–71, 77–78, 80–81.

Series of feature articles on the Republican National Nominating Convention at Kansas City and the Democratic National Nominating Convention at Houston, published in the Honolulu *Star-Bulletin,* June–July, 1928.

"Congressional Opposition to Pure Food Legislation, 1879–1906," *The American Journal of Sociology,* Vol. XXXVI (July, 1930), pp. 52–64.

"Japan's Protest Against the Annexation of Hawaii," *The Journal of Modern History,* Vol. III (March, 1931), pp. 46–61.

"Party Irregularity in the Senate of the United States, 1869–1901," *The Southwestern Political and Social Science Quarterly,* Vol. XI (March, 1931), pp. 355–76.

* "The United States and Hawaii during the Spanish-American War," *The American Historical Review,* Vol. XXXVI (April, 1931), pp. 552–60.

"California, Japan, and the Alien Land Legislation of 1913," *Pacific Historical Review,* Vol. I (March, 1932), pp. 36–59.

"Guam Under American Rule," *The Mid-Pacific Magazine,* Vol. XLIII (June, 1932), pp. 503–07.

"The World Cruise of the American Battleship Fleet, 1907–1909," *Pacific Historical Review,* Vol. I (December, 1932), pp. 389–423.

"The West and Radical Legislation, 1890–1930," *The American Journal of Sociology,* Vol. XXXVIII (January, 1933), pp. 603–11.

"World War Analogues of the *Trent* Affair," *The American Historical Review,* Vol. XXXVIII (January, 1933), pp. 286–90.

"The Lodge Corollary to the Monroe Doctrine," *Political Science Quarterly,* Vol. XLVIII (June, 1933), pp. 220–39.

"The United States and the Blacklist during the Great War," *The Journal of Modern History,* Vol. VI (March, 1934), pp. 14–35.

* "Why the United States Purchased Alaska," *Pacific Historical Review,* Vol. III (March, 1934), pp. 39–49.

* "The North Pacific Sealing Convention of 1911," *Pacific Historical Review,* Vol. IV (March, 1935), pp. 1–14.

* "The Sinking of the *Lusitania,*" *The American Historical Review,* Vol. XLI (October, 1935), pp. 54–73.

"Interest in a Nicaragua Canal, 1903–1931," *The Hispanic American Historical Review,* Vol. XVI (February, 1936), pp. 2–28.

"German Documents Relating to the *Lusitania,*" *The Journal of Modern History,* Vol. VIII (September, 1936), pp. 320–37.

* "Theodore Roosevelt and the Alaska Boundary Settlement," *The Canadian Historical Review,* Vol. XVIII (June, 1937), pp. 123–30.

* "Was the Presidential Election of 1900 a Mandate on Imperialism?" *The Mississippi Valley Historical Review,* Vol. XXIV (June, 1937), pp. 43–52.

"A Multilateral Monroe Doctrine," *Proceedings of the Institute of World Affairs,* Fifteenth Session, Vol. XV (1938), pp. 73–76.

\* "Dewey and the Germans at Manila Bay," *The American Historical Review*, Vol. XLV (October, 1939), pp. 59–81.

"The Root-Takahira Agreement of 1908," *Pacific Historical Review*, Vol. IX (March, 1940), pp. 19–35.

"Finnish Facts," *Pacific Spectator*, Vol. I (Summer 1947), pp. 336–38.

"The Dilemma of Democracy," *American Perspective*, Vol. II (October, 1948), pp. 211–17.

"The Obligation of the Teacher To Be a Scholar," *Social Education*, Vol. XIII (December, 1949), pp. 355–58.

"The Russian Fleet Myth Re-Examined," *The Mississippi Valley Historical Review*, Vol. XXXVIII (June, 1951), pp. 81–90.

\* "Woodrow Wilson Wouldn't Yield," *American Heritage*, Vol. VIII (June, 1957), pp. 22–25, 105–06.

\* "A Hall of Fame for American Diplomats," *The Virginia Quarterly Review*, Vol. XXXVI (Summer 1960), pp. 390–404.

"Revitalizing American History," *Social Education*, Vol. XXIV (December, 1960), pp. 371–74.

\* "America's Emergence as a World Power: The Myth and the Verity," *Pacific Historical Review*, Vol. XXX (February, 1961), pp. 1–16.

\* "Johnson and Kennedy: The Two Thousand Days," *The New York Times Magazine* (November 6, 1966), pp. 30–31, 134–35, 137, 139–40.

\* "The Mythmakers of American History," *The Journal of American History*, Vol. LV (June, 1968), pp. 5–21.

35707